Council for Standards in Human Service Education (CS...

The Council for Standards in Human Service Education (CSHSE) h... ...Service departments and help students acquire the knowledge, values, and sk... ...idelines reflect the interdisciplinary nature of human services.

STANDARD	CHAPTER
Professional History	
Understanding and Mastery...	
Historical roots of human services	I
Creation of human services profession	I
Historical and current legislation affecting services delivery	
How public and private attitudes influence legislation and the interpretation of policies related to human services	
Differences between systems of governance and economics	
Exposure to a spectrum of political ideologies	
Skills to analyze and interpret historical data application in advocacy and social changes	
Human Systems	
Understanding and Mastery...	
Theories of human development	1–16
How small groups are utilized, theories of group dynamics, and group facilitation skills	12
Changing family structures and roles	13–15
Organizational structures of communities	
An understanding of capacities, limitations, and resiliency of human systems	16
Emphasis on context and the role of diversity in determining and meeting human needs	2–16
Processes to effect social change through advocacy (e.g., community development, community and grassroots organizing, local and global activism)	
Processes to analyze, interpret, and effect policies and laws at local, state, and national levels	
Human Services Delivery Systems	
Understanding and Mastery...	
Range and characteristics of human services delivery systems and organizations	I
Range of populations served and needs addressed by human services	I
Major models used to conceptualize and integrate prevention, maintenance, intervention, rehabilitation, and healthy functioning	
Economic and social class systems including systemic causes of poverty	
Political and ideological aspects of human services	
International and global influences on services delivery	
Skills to effect and influence social policy	

Adapted from the October 2010 Revised CSHSE National Standards

STANDARD	CHAPTER
Information Management	
Understanding and Mastery...	
Obtain information through interviewing, active listening, consultation with others, library or other research, and the observation of clients and systems	2–16
Recording, organizing, and assessing the relevance, adequacy, accuracy, and validity of information provided by others	
Compiling, synthesizing, and categorizing information	
Disseminating routine and critical information to clients, colleagues or other members of the related services system that is provided in written or oral form and in a timely manner	
Maintaining client confidentiality and appropriate use of client data	17
Using technology for word processing, sending email, and locating and evaluating information	
Performing elementary community-needs assessment	
Conducting basic program evaluation	
Utilizing research findings and other information for community education and public relations and using technology to create and manage spreadsheets and databases	
Planning & Evaluating	
Understanding and Mastery...	
Analysis and assessment of the needs of clients or client groups	2–16
Skills to develop goals, and design and implement a plan of action	2–16
Skills to evaluate the outcomes of the plan and the impact on the client or client group	
Program design, implementation, and evaluation	
Interventions & Direct Services	
Understanding and Mastery...	
Theory and knowledge bases of prevention, intervention, and maintenance strategies to achieve maximum autonomy and functioning	2–16
Skills to facilitate appropriate direct services and interventions related to specific client or client group goals	2–16
Knowledge and skill development in: case management, intake interviewing, individual counseling, group facilitation and counseling, location and use of appropriate resources and referrals, use of consultation	2–13
Interpersonal Communication	
Understanding and Mastery...	
Clarifying expectations	
Dealing effectively with conflict	
Establishing rapport with clients	2–16
Developing and sustaining behaviors that are congruent with the values and ethics of the profession	17

Council for Standards in Human Service Education (CSHSE) Standards Covered in this Text

STANDARD	CHAPTER
Administration	
Understanding and Mastery...	
Managing organizations through leadership and strategic planning	
Supervision and human resource management	
Planning and evaluating programs, services, and operational functions	
Developing budgets and monitoring expenditures	
Grant and contract negotiation	
Legal/regulatory issues and risk management	
Managing professional development of staff	
Recruiting and managing volunteers	
Constituency building and other advocacy techniques such as lobbying, grassroots movements, and community development and organizing	
Client-Related Values & Attitudes	
Understanding and Master...	
The least intrusive intervention in the least restrictive environment	
Client self-determination	12, 17
Confidentiality of information	17
The worth and uniqueness of individuals including: ethnicity, culture, gender, sexual orientation, and other expressions of diversity	2–16
Belief that individuals, services systems, and society change	2–16
Interdisciplinary team approaches to problem solving	
Appropriate professional boundaries	17
Integration of the ethical standards outlined by the National Organization for Human Services and Council for Standards in Human Service Education	17
Self-Development	
Understanding and Mastery...	
Conscious use of self	4, 12
Clarification of personal and professional values	17
Awareness of diversity	2–16
Strategies for self-care	
Reflection on professional self (e.g., journaling, development of a portfolio, project demonstrating competency)	

STANDARDS FOR EXCELLENCE SERIES

Designed to help students advance their knowledge, values, and skills, the Standards for Excellence Series assists students in associating the Council for Standards in Human Service Education (CSHSE) National Standards to all levels of human services practice.

FEATURES INCLUDE

- **Standards for Excellence grid**—highlighting chapters where various standards are addressed.
- **Standards for Excellence critical thinking questions**—challenges students to think critically about the standards in relation to chapter content.
- **Multimedia links**—correlates content to multimedia assets throughout the text, including video, additional readings, and more.
- **Self-study quizzes**—found throughout the text, self-study quizzes test student knowledge and comprehension of key chapter topics.
- **Chapter review**—links to a scenario-based chapter review including short-answer discussion questions.

Counseling Theories for Human Services Practitioners

Essential Concepts and Applications

Samuel T. Gladding
Wake Forest University

PEARSON

Boston Columbus Indianapolis New York San Francisco Upper Saddle River
Amsterdam Cape Town Dubai London Madrid Milan Munich Paris Montréal Toronto
Delhi Mexico City São Paulo Sydney Hong Kong Seoul Singapore Taipei Tokyo

Editor in Chief: Ashley Dodge
Editorial Assistant: Amandria Guadalupe
Managing Editor: Denise Forlow
Program Manager: Carly Czech
Project Manager: Doug Bell, PreMediaGlobal
Executive Marketing Manager: Kelly May
Marketing Coordinator: Jessica Warren
Digital Media Director: Brian Hyland
Digital Media Project Manager: Tina Gagliostro

Senior Operations Supervisor: Mary Fisher
Operations Specialist: Eileen Corallo
Creative Art Director: Jayne Conte
Cover Designer: Suzanne Behnke
Interior Design: Joyce Weston Design
Cover Art: Shutterstock/alexcoolok
Full-Service Project Management: Sudip Sinha, PreMediaGlobal
Printer/Binder: STP Courier
Cover Printer: STP Courier

Credits and acknowledgments borrowed from other sources and reproduced, with permission, in this textbook appear on appropriate page within text.

Many of the designations by manufacturers and seller to distinguish their products are claimed as trademarks. Where those designations appear in this book, and the publisher was aware of a trademark claim, the designations have been printed in initial caps or all caps.

Library of Congress Cataloging-in-Publication Data
Gladding, Samuel T.
  Counseling theories for human services practitioners : essential concepts and applications/ Samuel T. Gladding, Wake Forest University. — First Edition.
      pages   cm
  Includes bibliographical references and index.
  ISBN-13: 978-0-205-89921-0
  ISBN-10: 0-205-89921-8
 1. Counseling.   2. Social service.   3. Human services.   I. Title.
  BF636.6.G623 2015
  361'.06—dc23   2013035552

10 9 8 7 6 5 4 3 2 1

ISBN-10: 0-205-89921-8
ISBN-13: 978-0-205-89921-0

Contents

15. Solution-Focused Therapy   151   S

16. Crisis Counseling   160   S

Preface

· ·

*To "Pal," aka Inez Barnes Templeman, my maternal grandmother, a positive
and dynamic influence, who accepted me unconditionally, taught me
by example kindness, civility, generosity, and showed me how to love
others who are "different."*

Theories are like guiding lights. They give us some direction when we are with clients who have come to us in pain with problems or concerns they do not know how to address. Like light, theories can and do change. Some become brighter with time; others shift their focus. Some fade because they either lack a solid foundation or lose their relevance for the populations we serve. Wondrously new theories, like emerging lights, are generated as insightful clinicians and academics craft them out of the context in which people live.

Because this text is about counseling theories that are most prevalent for human services practitioners at the beginning of the 21st century, it should be read in the light of its time. Some of the material covered will shine even brighter in the future whereas other ideas will falter or fade. In addition, some theories explained here may change their emphases. New ways of working with client populations will be created as practitioners discover other ways of helping individuals in mental distress. Thus, the knowledge gained from this text will be finite. To keep growing as a practitioner, you will have to study and read continuously about the latest developments in counseling and therapy circles and how theories intersect with human services practice.

So why should you study these theories at this time? They are the best and most complete ways of working with others that we know. Furthermore, they provide ways of conceptualizing the words and actions of individuals and working constructively with them. These theories, if employed judiciously, will shed light on your work and give you direction of what helping professionals at other various levels and specialties do. Without such a basis for making plans and decisions, you and others who provide human services would have to rely on trial and error or intuition, neither of which is apt to be as efficient or effective.

This text is laid out developmentally so that you can see how various theories of counseling and therapy have emerged: psychoanalysis and psychoanalytic theories, Adlerian therapy, existential therapy, person-centered therapy, Gestalt therapy, choice theory/reality therapy, behavioral therapy, cognitive and cognitive-behavioral therapy, rational emotive behavior therapy, transactional analysis, feminist therapy, Bowen family systems therapy, strategic family therapy, solution-focused therapy, and crisis counseling. These theories are distinct as the branches of a tree. Yet like branches they are connected to the trunk of the tree. Conceptually and literally each influences and gives life to the other.

Each theory chapter presents important essentials without irrelevant details and follows a uniform outline: Major Theorist(s), View of Human Nature/Personality, Role of the Counselor, Goals, Process and Techniques, Multicultural Issues, Evaluation of the

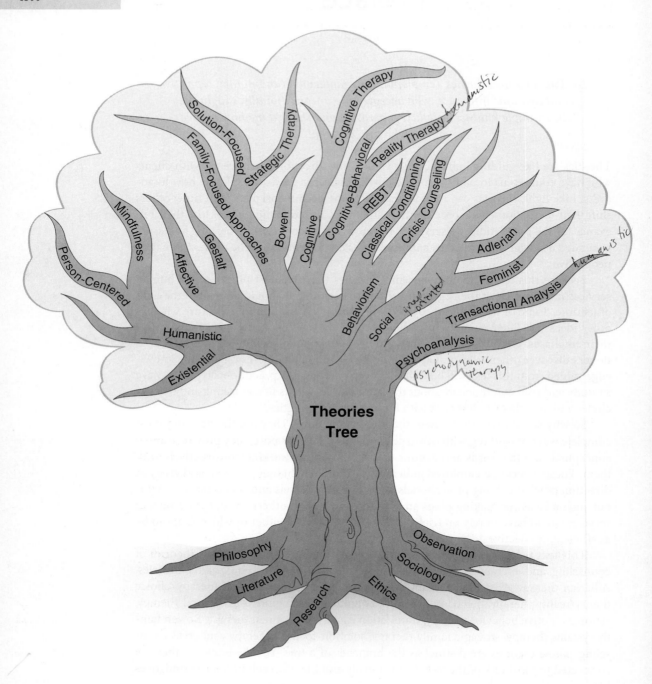

Theory, Treating the Case of Linda with the Theory, and Summary and Conclusion. The final chapter of the book discusses ethical issues related to counseling and human services.

Throughout the text, I routinely use the words *counselor* and *therapist* interchangeably to describe specialists in the helping field. Some individuals prefer other terms. Indeed, there are many specialties in the mental health and helping domains. However, I believe that using just *counselor* and *therapist* makes the text clearer, easier to read, and less distracting in describing the theories covered here.

Features

Many features of this text enhance your experience; by engaging with this text and its resources, you'll gain a variety of skills-based outcomes, including:

- **Connection of Counseling Theories**—providing a focus of how counseling theories work for human services professionals and paraprofessionals
- **Crisis Counseling**—exploring how human services practitioners deal with populations in crisis focusing on theory and therapy bringing forth the importance of treating those with developmental, situational, existential, or ecosystemic crises to prevent growth into a major disorder
- **Ethical and Legal Aspects**—focusing on the principles underlying ethics, how those in human services and counseling make ethical decisions, and what professional and paraprofessional helpers can do to prevent and correct unethical behaviors

Learning Outcomes

Students will be able to achieve a variety of learning outcomes by using this text and its resources, including:

- **Critical Thinking Skills**—Personal Reflections throughout asks readers to apply what they have learned in their life experiences to concepts just covered making the theories more personalized as readers transition into the human services field.
- **CSHSE National Standards**—Students can develop their understanding and mastery of CSHSE National Standards by discussing the Critical Thinking Questions given in the Standards Box.
- **Oral Communication skills**—Students can develop their oral communication skills by engaging with others in and out of class to discuss their comprehension of the theory and the therapeutic process based on the chapter's learning objectives.
- **Research and Professional Development**—Students can enhance their research and professional development by exploring the suggested references and web-based resources for each chapter.
- **Assessment and Writing Skills**—Students can develop their assessment and writing skills in preparation for future certification exams by completing topic-based and chapter review assessments for each chapter.

Acknowledgments

I would like to thank my colleagues both past and present for the many contributions they have made to my understanding of theories and the therapeutic process in human services. My work and interactions with fellow clinicians in mental health, private practice, and academic settings have allowed me to gain firsthand experience as a practicing counselor using major theories. My observations of and collaboration with human services practitioners in the field after natural disasters, in meeting needs in domestic situations, and in providing psychoeducational programs have given me a great appreciation for what those in this specialty do.

I would also like to thank my editors at Pearson Education for their support, encouragement, and hard work on my behalf. Finally, I wish to express my gratitude for the support and love that my family, especially my wife, Claire, has shown me through this writing project. Without a lot of understanding and some rare quiet moments, I could not have completed this project in time.

I hope you will benefit from reading this book. In the writing process, I have grown to appreciate even more the light that theories provide. Such may be the case with you as you reflect on the thoughts of the individuals who have provided the foundation for all that we do in counseling and human services.

Samuel T. Gladding

This text is available in a variety of formats—digital and print.
To learn more about our programs, pricing options, and customization,
visit **http://www.pearsonhighered.com**.

CHAPTER 1

Counseling Theories for Human Services Practitioners

George Dolgikh/Shutterstock

The Osgood family has been shaken to the core. An F2 category tornado has just destroyed their house. They are literally wandering around outside the foundation of the white wooden structure, where they have lived for ten years, as a light rain falls as they begin realizing everything they owned and valued, outside human life, is gone. They are disoriented, shivering, and with different reactions. The mother, Cynthia, is sitting down crying and has noticeable cuts on her face. The father, Harold, is walking around in a daze with a shirt that is almost in shreds. Earl, the 16-year-old son, is scurrying about in a panic trying to find the family's dog that was outside when the tornado hit. Meanwhile, Janet at age 11, is looking through the debris of what was once a two-story dwelling, shaking her head, picking up boards, and repeatedly saying: "Oh no, oh no, oh no!" This is the scene when you and others on your team of human services practitioners arrive.

While the scene from the Osgood crisis is extreme in its intensity and limited in scope, the dynamics that are a part of it are all too real. Both in times of crisis and in calm people from all walks of life need help in multiple ways every day. This is where human services practitioners come in. "The term **human services** refers to activities with the primary goal of enhancing the relationship between people and societal institutions so that people may maximize their potential and alleviate distress" (Monette, Sullivan, & DeJong, 2011, p. 2). Thus, human services practitioners are found in a variety of occupations and organizations, including those that focus primarily on physical and mental health and are government sponsored, such as public health centers and Federal Emergency Management Agency (FEMA), and those that are private and nonprofit, such as the Red Cross and the Salvation Army.

People helped by human services practitioners range from children to geriatrics. They vary from victims of natural disasters, such as earthquakes, floods, and wildfires, to those who suffer from societal ills, such as discrimination, poverty, abuse, and unemployment (Burger, 2011). Human services practitioners focus on everything from meeting the basic needs of people to facilitating environments that promote growth and learning. The professions that compose human services are altruistically based and caring.

Human Services Delivery Systems

Understanding and Mastery: Range of populations served and needs addressed by human services

Critical Thinking Question: What might happen to people in need if human services practitioners were not available to help?

Some of the popular titles for occupations of those who work in human services according to the National Organization for Human Services (http://www.nationalhumanservices.org/what-is-human-services) include: Family Support Worker, Youth Worker, Social Services Liaison, Residential Counselor, Behavioral Management Aide, Alcohol and Drug Abuse Counselor, Adult Day Care Worker, Life Skills Instructor, Client Advocate, Social Services Aide, Social Services Technician, Therapeutic Assistant, Probation Officer, Gerontology Aide, Juvenile Court Liaison, Group Home Worker, Child Abuse Worker, Crisis Intervention Counselor, Mental Health Aide, Community Outreach Worker, Social Work Assistant, Psychological Aide, Halfway House Counselor, and Rehabilitation Case Worker.

Human services practitioners are not professional counselors or therapists and they do not provide counseling or therapy (Neukrug, 2013). Rather they are individuals who hold associate and bachelor's degrees, and in some cases graduates from certificate programs who have been educated as generalists to work alongside professionals with advanced degrees in counseling, social work, and psychology.

Human Services Delivery System

Understanding and Mastery: Range and characteristics of human services delivery systems and organizations

Critical Thinking Question: In what ways would you describe human services practitioners as different from other helping professionals?

Yet, in order to work with professionals educated at this different level, human services practitioners need to know the theories that guide these specialists in their work. Such knowledge gives human services practitioners insight into the practices of helping. It also gives them more awareness of how they can be most supportive when assisting an individual, couple, family, or group.

One of the major questions about human services is how providers who work in this area offer aid, support, and comfort. One way is helping physically such as in disaster relief situations assisting a family whose home has been destroyed, like the Osgoods. The acquiring of temporary, safe shelter as well as food and clothing offers immediate and needed relief. Psychological ways of helping are abundant too, such as setting up crisis and day care services for individuals struggling with personal and interpersonal relationships. In this second way of working, i.e., providing psychological support for those in need, understanding counseling theories is paramount. In entering the field of human services, it is important to examine prominent theories of counseling and the ways in which they work. Theoretical knowledge frees those who work in human services to operate in ethical, legal, and productive ways with those who seek or need their help. It also gives human services practitioners knowledge of how those with more or specialized degrees work and how they may work best with these professionals.

This chapter explores what a theory is, what qualities characterize valid theories, why theories are important, how theoretical points of view have developed, and how human services practitioners use theories singularly, eclectically, and cooperatively in their practices. The emphasis here is not just on theories but on counseling theories that human services practitioners will find both useful to know and essential.

What Is a Theory?

In general terms a **theory** is a group of related laws or relationships that are used to provide explanations within a discipline (Sharf, 2012). In human services, counseling and therapy circles, a theory is thought of as "a set of principles used to explain human thought and behavior, including what causes people to change. In practice, a theory creates the goals of therapy and specifies how to pursue them" (Carlson & Engler-Carlson, 2011, p. viii). Thus, a theory is a model or template that gives a practitioner direction and guidance in working with others.

Most counseling theories have been developed by exceptional practitioners and academicians, who have formulated their ideas about human nature and ways of working productively with people on the basis of collective and evidence-based experiences, research, and observations.

Practitioners employ counseling theories to address problems individuals, groups, and families develop and provide possible solutions to their concerns. Most theories are affective, behavioral, cognitive, or systemic in nature. Based on their educational background, philosophy, and interests, as well as the needs of clients, effective helpers decide which theory or theories to apply to a situation. Not all approaches are appropriate. Indeed, one theory may not be adequate for the same client over an extended period. For example, a client may need to begin thinking rationally before behaving that way. Thus, a clinician might start out focused on correcting cognitive thoughts before changing to a more behavioral-based theory. Therefore, mental health practitioners must not only choose their theoretical positions carefully but also regularly reassess them for effectiveness.

Assess your comprehension of <u>What Is a Theory?</u> by taking this quiz.

Personal Reflection

What formal or informal theory or theories do you hold of others in your environment? For instance do you see people as basically good, somewhat deceptive, or a mixture of many qualities? How do you think most of your friends view those they interact with?

Characteristics of Thorough Theories

Some theoretical models are more thorough and versatile than others. Because of these characteristics these theories are probably used often. According to Hansen, Stevic, and Warner (1986), a **thorough theory** is defined as follows:

1. **Clear, easily understood, and communicable.** It should make sense and be explainable.
2. **Comprehensive.** A good theory encompasses explanations for a wide variety of phenomena in human development.

3. **Explicit and heuristic.** A thorough theory is didactic in laying out its major tenets. It also generates research because of its design, inviting others to explore its uses.

4. **Specific in relating means to desired outcomes.** A well-crafted theory includes a way of achieving a desired end product. It contains guidelines that others can follow to obtain similar results.

5. **Useful to its intended practitioners.** A complete theory is practical and provides strategies its followers may use under certain conditions or with specific populations.

In addition to these five qualities, a thorough theory matches a practitioner's personal philosophy of helping. Shertzer and Stone (1974) suggest that a theory must fit like a suit of clothes. Some theories, like some suits, need tailoring; therefore, effective clinicians realize the importance of alterations. Those who wish to be versatile and effective should learn a wide variety of counseling theories and know how to apply each without violating the theory's internal consistencies (Auvenshine & Noffsinger, 1984). Competent, helping specialists are not to be limited to just a pet theory or two.

Human Services Delivery Systems

Understanding and Mastery: Theories of human development

Critical Thinking Question: What should a human services practitioner do in order to learn a wide variety of theories and find one or more that fit?

· ·

: Assess your comprehension of the <u>Characteristics of Thorough Theories</u> by taking this quiz.

The Pragmatic Value of Theories

The practical value of solidly formulated theories cannot be overstressed (Brammer, Abrego, & Shostrom, 1993). "A theory guides action toward successful outcomes while generating hope in the therapist and the client that recovery is possible" (Carlson & Englar-Carlson, 2011, p. viii). Thus, theories help explain what happens in relationships and assist helpers in predicting, evaluating, and improving results. Furthermore, counseling theories provide a framework for making scientific and accurate observations. Theorizing encourages a coherence of ideas and the production of new ideas (Gladding, 1990). It helps make sense out of observations. As Prochaska and Norcross (2010) put it, "Without a guiding theory . . . clinicians would be vulnerable, directionless creatures bombarded with literally hundreds of impressions and pieces of information in a single session" (p. 4) or extended encounter.

Boy and Pine (1983) elaborate even further on the practical value of theories by suggesting that *theories are the why behind the how of helping*, providing a framework within which helpers can operate. For instance, human services practitioners guided by theories can meet the demands of their roles because they have reasons for what they do with others. Boy and Pine point out six practical functions of theories:

1. Theories help practitioners find unity and relatedness within their diversity of experience.
2. Theories compel helpers to examine relationships they would otherwise overlook.
3. Theories give practitioners operational guidelines by which to work and help them evaluate their development as specialists.
4. Theories assist helpers in focusing on relevant data.
5. Theories enable practitioners to assist clients in making effective behavior modifications when appropriate.
6. Theories assist helpers in evaluating old and constructing new approaches to the processes they are using.

"The ultimate criterion for all . . . theories is how well they provide explanations of what occurs" (Kelly, 1988, pp. 212–213). The value of theories as ways of organizing information "hinges on the degree to which they are grounded in the reality of people's lives" (Young, 1988, p. 336).

Assess your comprehension of **The Pragmatic Value of Theories** by taking this quiz.

The Evolution of Theories

Theories, especially those related to counseling and human services, have evolved over time with a sometime checkered history. In today's world there are those that are antiquated and unproven as well as those that are effective and have evidence-based research.

Antiquated Theories

Even before recorded time there are indications that people had theories about human functioning and mental disorders. Archeological records show that a practice known as **trephining**, essentially the drilling of holes in the skull of the person being treated, occurred in some pre-historic societies. Ancient people believed that individuals who were mentally disturbed were possessed by evil spirits. Thus, the holes were drilled to let the wicked spirits out. In almost all cases, the treatment was worse than the disorder.

In medieval Europe the same physically-based type of theory for treating psychological stress and disorders continued, resulting in the practice of **exorcism**, which was meant to drive out evil spirits and restore mentally deranged individuals to health. Exorcism was initially performed by clergy, mainly in monasteries. It used techniques such as the laying on of hands and insulting the possessing demon(s) with obscene epithets.

As beliefs about the physical nature of evil spirit possession became more fully accepted, additional unpleasant means such as flogging, starving, using chains, immersing in hot water, and even burning were used to drive out demons. The idea behind the treatment was that the possessing spirit(s) would leave a body that was an inhospitable host. Unfortunately, these remedies resulted in the demise of many persons who were mentally disturbed (Butcher, Mineka, & Hooley, 2013).

In Western societies subsequent treatment of people with mental conditions was eventually replaced because the theory of demon possession was discredited but not before tragic events such as the infamous Salem Witch Trials in the American Colonies of the 1600s. Instead of being tortured to death, individuals with psychological troubles or "abnormal/strange behaviors" were locked up in institutions and "cared for." Sometimes they were given humane treatment whereas at other times they were harshly treated. There was almost no treatment besides physical restraint because there was no theoretical construct as to what should be done. Psychiatric patients were sometimes placed on display for public amusement, and chaos reigned inside their facilities. The now-common term **bedlam** (describing madness or chaos) originated from the Bethlem Royal Hospital in London which was the first to specialize in treating the mentally ill. It was renowned for its disarray and turmoil.

Modern Theories

It was not until the 18th century that a new theory of treatment was formulated for working with individuals having emotional problems. That development occurred almost simultaneously in Europe and the American colonies; it was instigated by Benjamin Rust in North America, Phillip Pinel in France, and William Tuke in England. The **humane theory** proposed that those with mental disorder be unchained and receive better treatment, such as time outdoors each day, a more nutritious diet, and communication with others. The idea was that people would get better when they received sunlight, good food, and kind attention (Ziff, 2012).

This reform had varied success and gave rise to **talk therapies**, even before Sigmund Freud. Two early examples were initiated by Paul Dubois (1848–1918), a Swiss physician, and Pierre Janet (1859–1947), a French physician. Both of these practitioners spoke to and with their mentally disturbed patients in a reasonable and logical manner. Those who suffered physical troubles, such as having been in a natural disaster, were not as fortunate in what happened to them unless they lived in a community which was altruistic in nature or had caring neighbors who would assist them.

In more modern times theories of helping have emerged based on a variety of concepts from free will and determinism (Wilks, 2003). For instance, theories such as psychoanalysis and behaviorism, both of which are covered in this text, grew out of biologic/psychic determinism and environmental determinism, respectively. More humanistic theories—such as existential, Adlerian, person-centered, and reality therapy, which are also covered in this book—are grounded in the idea that people have a degree of free will.

Regardless of their base, theories of helping that influence human services practitioners have developed almost exponentially since the 1950s. For instance, in the field of therapy only 36 systems of psychotherapy had been identified in the late 1950s (Harper R. A., 1959). By 1976 M. Parloff had discovered more than 130 therapeutic approaches, some of which were quite questionable. Only three years later, in 1979, *Time* reported that more than 200 therapies had been formulated (Prochaska & Norcross, 2010) and early in the 21st century more than 400 systems of therapeutic interventions have been documented worldwide, ranging from mindfulness to soap opera therapy. Clearly, professional helpers today have a wide variety of theories from which to choose.

Personal Reflection

What comes to your mind when you think of theoretical techniques to helping? Which techniques are you most comfortable (e.g., talking, acting, emoting)? How often do you think therapeutic techniques should be used? How long do you think an ideal counseling/helping process should last?

Human Services Delivery Systems

Understanding and Mastery: Theories of Human Development

Critical Thinking Question: How effective do you think a human services practitioner could be simply using microskills without attaching them to a theory of human development?

Although theory development has not stopped, Okun (1990) states that the **present emphasis**, at least in helping circles, is on connecting counseling theories instead of creating them. This focus rests on the fundamental assumption that "no one theoretical viewpoint can provide all of the answers for the clients we see today" (p. xvi).

Another current trend is helping practitioners adapt techniques and interventions from different theoretical approaches into their work without actually accepting the premises of some theoretical points of view. This flexibility can be seen in the widespread use of **microskills**—atheoretical methods, such as active listening, reflection of feeling and content, immediacy, confrontation, and summarization—that promote relationship formation and exploration of a problem or concern. The **microskills approach**, which is useful in many cases, does not rely on a comprehensive approach of addressing personal difficulties but *assumes that some therapeutic skills transcend theory*. Nonetheless, as helpers consider intrapersonal, interpersonal, and external factors when working with clients, it is theories that generate counseling techniques and blend all these dimensions together in unique, inclusive, and effective ways.

Assess your comprehension of <u>The Evolution of Theories</u> by taking this quiz.

Theories and Eclecticism

Most professional helpers, including those involved in counseling, identify themselves as **eclectic**, that is, "combining theories or techniques from a wide variety of therapeutic approaches" (Sharf, 2004, p. 641). These practitioners use various theories and techniques to match their clients' needs, with "an average of 4.4 theories making up their therapeutic work with clients" (Cheston, 2000, p. 254). As needs change, clinicians may depart from one theory and adopt another—a phenomenon called **style-shifting**.

Counselors make changes related to their clients' developmental levels (Ivey & Goncalves, 1988; Ivey, Ivey, & Zalaquett, 2010). To be effective, practitioners must consider how far their clients have progressed in their development, as described by theorists like Jean Piaget, and what their needs are as outlined by Abraham Maslow (1968). For example, according to Piaget's theory clients who are not developmentally aware of their environments may need a therapeutic approach that focuses on "emotions, the body, and experience in the here and now," whereas clients at a more advanced level of development may respond best to a "consulting-formal operations" approach, in which the emphasis is on thinking about actions (Ivey & Goncalves, 1988, p. 410). Likewise, according to Maslow clients who are lacking basic physical needs should have these addressed before trying to meet their higher needs such as self-esteem. Clinicians and human services professionals must first start with where their clients are and help them develop in a holistic manner.

Even though eclecticism is able to draw on various theories, techniques, and practices to meet client needs, this approach does have its drawbacks. For instance, an eclectic approach can be hazardous if helpers are not thoroughly familiar with all aspects of the theories involved. In such situations helping specialists may become technicians who do not understand why certain approaches work best with specific clients at certain times and in certain ways (Cheston, 2000). In such cases an electric orientation often does more harm than good.

To combat this problem, McBride and Martin (1990) advocate a hierarchy of eclectic practices and discuss the importance of having a sound theoretical base as a guide. They describe the first, or lowest, level of eclecticism as **syncretism**—a sloppy, unsystematic process of putting unrelated clinical concepts together. It is encouraged when students are urged to formulate their own theories without first having experienced how tested models work. The second level of eclecticism is **traditional**. It incorporates "an orderly combination of compatible features from diverse sources [into a] harmonious whole" (English & English, 1956, p. 168). Theories are examined in greater depth and breadth than in syncretism, but no mastery is expected.

The third level of eclecticism is described as theoretical or as **theoretical integrationism** (Lazarus & Beutler, 1993; Simon, 1989). This type of eclecticism requires that helpers master at least two theories before attempting any combinations. This approach assumes a degree of equality between theories, which may not be accurate, and the existence of criteria "to determine what portions or pieces of each theory to preserve or expunge" (Lazarus & Beutler, 1993, p. 382).

The fourth level of eclecticism is called **technical eclecticism** and is exemplified in the works of Arnold Lazarus (1967, 2000, 2009) and the BASIC ID (**behavior, affect, sensation, imagination, cognition, interpersonal, drugs and biology**) acronym. In this approach procedures from different theories are selected and used in treatment "without necessarily subscribing to the theories that spawned them" (Lazarus & Beutler, 1993, p. 384). The idea is that techniques, not theories, are used in treating individuals. Therefore, after properly assessing clients, practitioners can use behavioral methods (such as assertiveness training) with interpersonal techniques (such as confronting persons about the meaning they find in relationships) or other combinations. This approach is in line with what Cavanagh and Levitov (2002) propose as a healthy way to conduct helping. It requires those who offer clinicians in all helping specialties to have

- a sound knowledge and understanding of the theories used,
- a basic integrative philosophy of human behavior that brings disparate parts of differing theories into a meaningful collage, and
- a flexible means of fitting the approach to the client.

The critical variables in being a healthy eclectic helper are a mastery of theory and an acute sensitivity to knowing which approach to use when, where, and how (Harman, 1977).

A final type of eclectic approach is the **transtheoretical model (TTM)** of change (Prochaska & DiClemente, 1992; Prochaska & Norcross, 2010). This model is developmentally based and has been empirically derived over time. It is "an alternative to technical eclectic approaches that tend to be inclusive to the point that various components are 'poorly' held together" (Petrocelli, 2002, p. 23). The model proposes five stages of change—**precontemplation, contemplation, preparation, action,** and **maintenance**. Not everyone is ready to change when help is available. Some are not aware they need to change and are precontemplative. Others are contemplative of making a change but are not prepared to act. They need to get ready. Once action is taken, it needs to be maintained if it is going to make a difference. The transtheoretical levels of change in an entity and progressive model are shown in Figure 1.1.

Personal Reflection

Think of when you have made a change in your life. When and how did you realize you needed to change? What behaviors (described above) did you experience?

"Counseling from a TTM perspective allows for a more **macroscopic approach** (involving a broad and comprehensive theoretical framework) and **personal adaptation** (involving an increase in critical, logical, accurate, and scientific-like thinking) rather than simple personal adjustment" (Petrocelli, 2002, p. 25). Its main drawbacks are its comprehensiveness and complexity and the fact that TTM has been tested only among limited groups, such as addictions populations.

Assess your comprehension of <u>Theories and Eclecticism</u> by taking this quiz.

FIGURE 1.1
Progressive
Model Showing
Transtheoretical Levels
of Change

Theories and Application: The Case of Linda

The major theories discussed in subsequent chapters have significant differences in their approaches to psychological helping: **counseling**. To highlight those differences and show the ways in which therapists would operate from each of the theoretical perspectives, each theory is applied to a common case—that of a young woman named Linda. She is the person seeking help and in therapeutic terms is called a **client**. Comparing different theories at work with the same person should reveal those theories in action and permit an informed decision about their use, either singly or in combination.

Linda is a recently divorced, 32-year-old Caucasian woman who is seeking help because of relationship problems. Linda was married for seven years but recently ended her marriage with her husband because she no longer found him exciting and thought he was being verbally abusive—for example, he often criticized her looks, weight, and dress. During her married life Linda had an abortion because her husband insisted and the fact that she did not feel she was ready to be a responsible parent yet. However, she states that her former husband's insistence on remaining childless was the primary reason for the abortion. That event took place about two years earlier, and Linda still has mixed emotions about it. When discussing it, her mood is both sad and angry.

Linda grew up in a lower-class neighborhood in a midsize western city. Her father, Ralph, was a construction worker with a seventh-grade education. He drank heavily on weekends but otherwise seemed to have a good work ethic and a positive attitude toward his work. Ralph had definite conservative opinions about politics, religion, and the place of women in society; and he never hesitated to voice his views, sometimes quite loudly. Linda kept her distance from him. Linda's mother, Marian, did not work outside the home. Instead, she took care of Linda and her siblings: Ted, two years older than Linda; Claudia, 13 months younger; and Patricia, three years younger. A high school graduate, Marian took in sewing to earn extra income for the family. She was a rather quiet and introverted woman, and although Linda felt close to her in many ways, she never really identified with her mother. In fact, Linda reports that she is not emotionally close to her family at all.

As a teenager Linda was mildly rebellious. She occasionally skipped school and church services and engaged once in petty theft at a local department store. She dated older boys, most of whom were friends of her brother. Linda was flirtatious but never really acted out sexually. She states that her brother was her protector; she was grateful for his presence in her adolescent life. Otherwise, she thinks she would have probably gotten into trouble and may even have gotten married before finishing high school.

All of Linda's siblings graduated from high school but, like their parents, married young and got jobs either in a trade or in retail. Linda made good enough grades to be admitted to a regular four-year college. However, she did not feel confident enough to apply because it would have gone against family norms. She states that her father discouraged her thoughts of further education. As a compromise, Linda enrolled in a local community college, where she completed a course in business administration. Since graduation she has drifted from job to job as an administrative assistant or a secretary, never challenged in any of her jobs. She admits to having a temper and says that she gets fed up with the treatment she receives from her bosses, who are sexist she thinks. She also gets tired of the routine work, especially the filing, which she has to do.

Linda likes to read romance novels, watch the home-and-garden television channel, and go to action movies where there are car chase scenes. All of these activities make her feel better; they take her away from her mundane existence. Since her divorce, she has felt aimless, anxious, and depressed. She has not found a peer group of singles or divorcees to associate with, and most of her former friends and acquaintances have either married or moved away. Both of her younger sisters are still in town, as are her parents, but Linda does not feel close to any of them. She finds them boring; they do not "stretch their minds." Thus, she sees them only once a week, for Sunday lunch, and leaves as soon as possible.

Linda reveals that she has had thoughts about ending her life by stepping out in front of a truck. However, she doubts if she would ever do such a thing. She has recently contemplated finding a new job and has given two weeks' notice to her current employer. She does not want life to pass her by, but she is beginning to think it is doing just that. Her voice sounds almost desperate as she asks for help.

Summary and Conclusion

The helping professions, especially human services associated with counseling, are evolving. Current ways of working with people who have concerns or problems are based on theories that have been researched and tested for effectiveness with client populations. Such was not always the case. The first theories for the treatment of people in mental pain were degrading, based on superstition, and potentially deadly. Clients were thought to be possessed by evil spirits that had to be driven out. This viewpoint eventually gave way to more humane approaches, and theories of treatment, initially slow to evolve, exploded in number during the last half of the 20th century.

Recall what you learned in this chapter by reviewing and completing the Chapter Review.

Today, the creation and development of theories have slowed; movement is toward the combination of approaches and eclecticism. Most counselors and human services practitioners use multiple theories, and some focus more on techniques than theories. Nonetheless, the value of theories remains. They provide the foundation for the most effective counseling approaches.

CHAPTER 2

Psychoanalysis and Psychoanalytic Theories

Blaj Gabriel/Shutterstock.com

Psychoanalysis is important for human services practitioners to know about. It was the first theory to gain public recognition and acceptance, especially in Europe and the Americas, for example, in Austria and in the United States. It was the genius of Sigmund Freud that created psychoanalysis. From his ideas sprang all other psychoanalytic theories—those of Anna Freud, Erik Erikson, Harry Stack Sullivan, Karen Horney, and Heinz Kohut. In addition, many prominent therapists in the history of practitioner helping who did not become psychoanalysts—for example, Alfred Adler, Carl Jung, Albert Ellis, Rollo May, and Fritz Perls—were directly influenced by Freud's concepts, either through association with Freud himself or through instruction in his ideas. Other theorists—including Carl Rogers, B. F. Skinner, and Otto Rank—developed theories in direct opposition to Freud's principles. Sigmund Freud and concepts of psychoanalysis permeate human services literature. To be uninformed about psychoanalysis is to be undereducated as a helping specialist even though few individuals in human services practice this theory and it is usually not appropriate for most of clients seen in human services settings.

Major Theorist: Sigmund Freud

The life of Sigmund Freud (1856–1939) has been the focus of many books, such as Irving Stone's *The Passions of the Mind*. His official biographer, Ernest Jones, wrote a definitive three-volume work (1953, 1955, 1957) on Freud's life and the development of his ideas.

Chapter Outline

Sigmund Freud was born in Freiburg, Austria, the first son of Jacob Freud's second marriage. Sigmund's mother, Amalia, gave him special privileges because she had higher hopes for Sigmund than for her five daughters and two sons born later. In 1860 Freud's father moved the family to Vienna, and there Freud spent most of the remainder of his life.

An excellent student, Freud was limited in his occupational choices because of finances and the discrimination in Europe at the time against Jews entering certain lines of work. Thus, Freud enrolled at the University of Vienna in 1873 with the idea of pursuing medicine since this was a career open to Jews. He received his medical degree in 1881, having mastered research methods as well as the normal course work. He married Martha Bernays in 1886 and fathered six children, the youngest of whom, Anna, became famous in her own right as a child psychoanalyst.

Freud supported his family through his private practice in psychiatry, working primarily with individuals with hysteria. Initially, he used hypnosis as his main form of treatment, a technique he had mastered in France under the tutelage of neurologist Jean Charcot. Though Freud was not a good hypnotist, he soon discovered that this deficit was beneficial. Indeed, much of his success depended on the relationship he developed during the treatment process rather than on the hypnosis. This revelation led Freud to explore how he might use his clinical relationship with a client in combination with the client's concentration to bring about change (Freud, 1925/1959).

During medical school Freud had been impressed with Josef Breuer's **cathartic method** of treating people with hysteria. Breuer had his patients relive painful experiences and work through emotional events suppressed for years. Breuer's method also used hypnosis. Freud modified that approach by dropping the hypnosis and sitting behind his patients as they lay on couches. From this position he would press his hand on their foreheads whenever they began to block out memories, assuring them that they could remember long-forgotten important events and thoughts. Freud called this method **free association** and used it to explore the unconscious minds of his patients. The material uncovered in the process became the stuff of interpretation and analysis, and thus, psychoanalysis was born. Freud's work with others, as well as years of self-analysis, gave him new insight into the nature of persons, and he began to stress the importance of the unconscious in understanding personality (Monte, 1991).

Many of Freud's colleagues, and later the general public, were outraged by his emphasis on the importance of sexuality and aggression in the etiology of personality. Nevertheless, his ideas attracted a number of followers, and in 1902 he formally organized in his home the **Wednesday Psychological Society**, which met to discuss personality theory. This group, which at times included Carl Jung and Alfred Adler, became known in 1908 as the **Viennese Psychoanalytic Society**. It acquired international prominence when Freud and some of his followers accepted an invitation in 1908 to lecture at Clark University in the United States. Even though Freud suffered a number of personal and practitioner setbacks, his theory of psychoanalysis continued to grow and develop. Practitioner journals and international congresses devoted to the theory, as well as Freud's prolific and heuristic writings, assured the historical prominence of psychoanalysis. Freud died in London, a refugee from the Nazi occupation of Austria.

Freud's theory of psychoanalysis evolved throughout his lifetime. Many of its main tenets were set down in his books *The Interpretation of Dreams* (1900/1955), *New Introductory Lectures on Psychoanalysis* (1923/1933), and *The Ego and the Id* (1923/1947).

The **Freudian view of human nature** is dynamic; that is, Freud believed in the transformation and exchange of energy within the personality (Hall, 1954). Much of what he described, however, is metaphorical because a majority of the hypotheses he proposed could not be proven scientifically at the time (Olson & Hergenhahn, 2011). Nevertheless, Freud hoped that his theory would eventually be empirically verified, and he developed techniques for working with his patients that were based on that hope. He focused particularly on levels of consciousness, the formation of personality, psychosexual development, and defense mechanisms.

Levels of Consciousness

For Freud, human nature can be explained in terms of a conscious mind, a preconscious mind, and an unconscious mind. The **conscious mind** is attuned to events in the present, to an awareness of the outside world. The **preconscious mind** is an area between the conscious and unconscious minds and contains aspects of both. Within the preconscious are hidden memories or forgotten experiences that can be remembered with the proper cues. For example, after a long separation a person may recall another person's name if enough reminders are generated. Finally, beneath the preconscious mind is the **unconscious mind**, the most powerful and least understood part of the personality. The instinctual, repressed, and powerful forces of the personality exist in the unconscious.

Formation of Personality

Freud hypothesized that the **personality** is formed from the interaction of three developing parts—the id, the ego, and the superego—which are imbedded in the various conscious states. The id and the superego are confined to the unconscious, whereas the ego operates primarily in the conscious but also in the preconscious and the unconscious.

The **id** comprises the basic inherited givens of the personality and is present from birth. It is amoral, impulsive, and irrational and works according to the **pleasure principle;** that is, it pursues what it wants because it cannot tolerate tension. The id operates through drives, instincts, and images (e.g., dreaming, hallucinating, and fantasizing), a thought process known as **primary process**. Although primary process thinking may bring temporary relief, it is ultimately unsatisfying. Consequently, the id discharges energy to the ego, which is another way of obtaining what it wants.

If empowered and left on its own, the id would probably destroy a person or at least cause trouble by acting on its primitive, aggressive, and sexual drives. Those who let their ids guide their action lack insight into the consequences of what they are doing. The id contains basic life energy, collectively known as **eros**, and basic death instincts, known as **thanatos**. At first Freud associated eros with sexuality but later modified this idea, describing all life-preserving instincts as eros and the psychic energy that accompanies them as libido. The idea that each person has some sort of death wish was the result of Freud's observation of the destructiveness of World War I and his belief that humans, composed of inorganic matter, ultimately have a desire to return to this state of being. The premise of thanatos was never fully developed, but Freud saw it in acts of aggression, as well as in foolishly dangerous behaviors such as taking unnecessary risks.

To keep the person from being either too self-indulgent or too morally restrained, the ego moderates the wishes and desires of the id and the superego.

The **ego**, the second system to develop, keeps the id from getting out of control and is, thus, often called "the executive of the mind." When the ego is fully developed, it functions to keep the desires of the id and the superego in check while realistically helping the person interact with the outside world. The ego works according to the **reality principle**, with reality being what exists (Hall, Lindzey, & Campbell, 1998). The ego devises ways to achieve appropriate goals, obtain energy for activities from the id, and keep the person in harmony with the environment. The ego's way of thinking is known as the **secondary process**, which is nothing more than rationally thinking through situations. A strong ego is essential to healthy functioning.

The **superego**, in contrast to the id, is the moral branch of the mind, operating according to what is ideal. The superego arises from the moral teachings of a child's parents and is said to function according to the **moral principle**. Through a mechanism known as the **ego ideal**, it strives for perfection and rewards actions that follow parental and societal dictates. For example, children who have been taught that neatness is a virtue feel good when they keep a room neat. On the other hand, those who act against what they have been taught are punished through the part of the superego called the **conscience**, which induces guilt. The superego locks a person into rather rigid moral patterns if given free reign. Because its goal is perfection, the superego sometimes forces people into restrained action or no action when they face a dilemma.

Personal Reflection

Reflect on your life and when you have engaged in behaviors that were foolish or admirable. What messages did you give yourself that influenced your actions? How does this information affect your acceptance of Freud's idea of personality and consciousness?

Psychosexual and Psychosocial Stages of Development

In addition to levels of consciousness and Freud's concept of personality, psychoanalysis is built on what he referred to as **psychosexual developmental stages**. Each of four main stages focuses on a zone of pleasure that is dominant at a particular time. In the first stage, the **oral stage**, the mouth is the chief pleasure zone. Children under the age of 1 are in this stage and obtain basic gratification from sucking and biting. In the second stage, the **anal stage**, children between the ages of 1 and 2 delight in either withholding or eliminating feces. This stage involves the first really significant conflict between a child's internal instincts and external demands, such as toilet training.

In the third stage, the **phallic stage**, children from 3 to 5 attempt to resolve their sexual identities. The chief zones of pleasure are the sex organs, and children of both genders must work through their sexual desires in a conflict of feelings known as the **Oedipus complex**. Freud thought that the conflict was clearer and more completely resolved in boys than in girls. Initially, both boys and girls are attracted to the mother because she is the source of great pleasure. Both genders see the father as a rival for the mother's love and attention. However, feelings about the mother change as boys and girls discover their own sexual identities.

For a boy, there is a desire to possess his mother sexually. Yet there is a fear that if he makes his wishes known, his father, who is bigger and stronger, will become angry and castrate him. A boy assumes that his penis is the source of conflict between his father and himself and girls, because they lack a penis, have been castrated. Although the boy may feel hostile toward his father, he represses his desire for his mother and eventually comes to identify with his father, thereby gaining vicarious satisfaction through father–mother interactions.

The Oedipus complex for a girl, sometimes called the **Electra complex**, is less clearly resolved. A young girl comes to notice that she does not have a penis and that boys do. Freud says she blames her mother for the lack of this valued organ and envies her father for possessing one (i.e., penis envy). Thus, she has both negative and positive feelings toward each parent and is sexually ambivalent at the end of this stage. She takes some consolation from learning that she has the ability to have babies and boys cannot have. Therefore, she identifies with her mother and, according to Freud, hopes to receive later gratification by having children, especially boys.

The wishes of young boys and girls are not manifested directly during the **phallic stage**. Rather they are disguised in dreams, fantasy, and play. Nevertheless, the wishes are real and, if not resolved, will lead to future intra- and interpersonal difficulties. Freud thought that the basic ingredients of the adult personality had formed by the end of the phallic stage.

After the phallic stage, between the ages of 6 and 12, comes a period known as **latency**, at which time there is little manifest interest in sexuality. Instead, energy is focused on peer activities and personal mastery of cognitive learning and physical skills. Around puberty the last of the psychosexual phases occurs, the **genital stage**. If all has gone well previously, each gender takes more interest in the other, and normal heterosexual patterns of interaction appear. If there were unresolved difficulties in any of the first three stages, collectively known as the **pregenital stages**, the person may have difficulty adjusting to the adult responsibilities that begin in the genital stage. Freud believed that two difficulties could arise in the pregenital stages—**excessive frustration** or **overindulgence**—causing a person to become fixated or arrested at that level of development and overly dependent on the use of defense mechanisms.

Human Systems

Understanding and Mastery: Theories of human development

Critical Thinking Question: How do Freud's ideas about psychosexual stages of development match up with what you have observed about human development?

Freud's psychosexual stages of development are the aspects of his theory that have been modified most by others who have stayed in the psychoanalytic tradition. Psychoanalyst Heinz Kohut (1971, 1984) proposed a much less sexually based view of childhood development. His psychodynamic approach is known as **object-relations theory**. An **object** is anything that satisfies a need, whether it is a person or a thing. It is used interchangeably with the term "other" to refer to an important person to whom the child and later the adult become attached. Others are perceived by an infant as **not-me objects** for gratifying basic and instinctive needs, rather than as individuals with separate identities.

Kohut's theory proposes that children introject what they perceive from others as good and both reject and project what they perceive as bad. In this way, children form an identity with others through interactions, both real and imagined. The challenge for children "is to learn to negotiate with this outside world without trading away satisfaction of such fundamental needs as love, security, and esteem for individual autonomy and a sense of self" (Bankart, 1997, p. 179). Mature individuals are both independent and attached to others, and they are able to integrate all aspects of themselves and avoid **splitting**, a defense mechanism that keeps incompatible feelings separate from oneself.

Table 2.1		Erikson's Stages of Development
Stage	**Age in Years**	**Tasks**
Trust vs. mistrust	Birth to 1	Emphasis on satisfying basic physical and emotional needs
Autonomy vs. shame/doubt	2 to 3	Emphasis on exploration and developing self-reliance
Initiative vs. guilt	4 to 5	Emphasis on achieving a sense of competence and initiative
Industry vs. inferiority	6 to 12	Emphasis on setting and attaining personal goals
Identity vs. role confusion	12 to 18	Emphasis on testing limits, achieving a self-identity
Intimacy vs. isolation	18 to 35	Emphasis on achieving intimate interpersonal relationships
Generativity vs. stagnation	35 to 65	Emphasis on helping next generation, being productive
Integrity vs. despair	65 +	Emphasis on integration of life activities, feeling worthwhile

Note: From *Counseling: A Comprehensive Profession* (4th ed., p. 190) by Samuel T. Gladding. Copyright 2000. Reprinted by permission of Pearson Education, Inc., Upper Saddle River, NJ.

Erik Erikson (1963, 1982) went even further than Kohut in modifying Freud's psychosexual theory of development. For Erikson, development extends over the life span, and **psychosocial development** is most important. Thus, Erikson's theory extends Freud's development emphasis from birth to death and focuses on the achievement of specific life-enhancing tasks. Like a number of other modifiers of Freud's theory, Erikson emphasizes the *central role of the ego* in life tasks rather than the interplay between the id, the ego, and the superego. Because of this emphasis, he and other theorists like him are sometimes known as **ego psychodynamic theorists**. Erikson's stages of development and the accompanying ages and tasks are presented in Table 2.1.

Assess your comprehension of <u>Psychosexual and Psychosocial Stages of Development</u> by completing this quiz.

Personal Reflection

Most people prefer Erickson's psychosocial stages of development as a way of explaining human growth and behavior. Nonetheless, what truths might there be in Freud's psychosexual stages of development?

Defense Mechanisms

Defense mechanisms are the last crucial part of Freud's theory as they relate to human nature and personality. Basically, **defense mechanisms** protect a person from being overwhelmed by anxiety, through adapting to situations or distorting or denying events. Such mechanisms are normal and operate on an unconscious level. Anna Freud (1936) and other ego psychodynamic theorists elaborated on Freud's original ideas. Among the main defense mechanisms are the following:

• **Repression.** Repression is the most basic defense mechanism, the one on which others are built. Using this mechanism, the ego involuntarily excludes from consciousness any unwanted or painful thoughts, feelings, memories, or impulses. The ego must use energy to keep excluded areas from consciousness, but sometimes the repressed thoughts slip out in dreams or verbal expressions. Repression is considered the cornerstone, or foundation stone, of psychoanalysis (Nye, 2000).

- **Projection.** Persons using projection attribute an unwanted emotion or characteristic to someone else in an effort to deny that the emotion or characteristic is part of themselves. For example, a woman may say that her boss is angry at her instead of saying that she is angry at her boss.

- **Reaction formation.** With this mechanism, anxiety-producing thoughts, feelings, or impulses are repressed and their opposites are expressed. For example, a host at a party may shower a disliked guest with attention. A reaction formation is often detected by the intensity with which the opposite emotion is expressed.

- **Displacement.** Displacement channels energy away from one object to an alternative, that is, to a safe target. For instance, a person who has had a hard day at the office may come home and yell at the dog. A positive form of displacement is known as **sublimation**, in which a drive that cannot be expressed directly is channeled into constructive activities. For example, those who are unable to express themselves sexually may take care of children. Freud thought sublimation was a major means of building civilization.

- **Regression.** In regression a person returns to an earlier stage of development. For example, after suffering a trauma during early adolescence, a child may begin to wet the bed. Virtually all people regress if placed under enough pressure or stress.

- **Rationalization.** Rationalization allows a person to find reasonable explanations for unreasonable or unacceptable behaviors in order to make them sound logical and acceptable. An individual might say, "I did it because everyone else was doing it," or "I really didn't think it was going to be worth the time I'd have to spend, so I didn't do it."

- **Denial.** A person in denial does not consciously acknowledge an unpleasant or traumatic event or situation. Denial protects people from having to face painful experiences. For instance, a couple may deny that they are having marital problems even though both are aware that the relationship is deteriorating. Denial may initially help a person cope with certain situations, such as war, but if perpetuated, it ultimately becomes destructive and can result in acute or posttraumatic stress disorders.

- **Identification.** In identification a person incorporates the qualities of another, thereby removing any fear that person might have of the other and giving him or her new behavioral skills. For example, a child might identify with a feared parent. Identification, like sublimation, differs from other defense mechanisms in that it can help a person realistically solve problems.

Freud's view of human nature stresses conflict between conscious and unconscious forces (Luborksy, O'Reilly-Landry, & Arlow, 2011; Monte, 1991). The theory is **deterministic**, holding that a person's adult personality is formed by resolving the gender-specific stages of childhood. If a person has a traumatic childhood and fails to resolve a psychosexual stage, that person will need to work through this unresolved stage later in life.

Planning and Evaluating

Understanding and Mastery: Analysis and assessment of the needs of clients or client groups

Critical Thinking Question: How can a knowledge of defense mechanisms give human services practitioners insight into the needs of clients?

FIGURE 2.1
Client–Analyst
Positioning During
Therapy.

Role of the Counselor

Practitioners of psychoanalysis play the role of **experts**. They encourage their clients to talk about whatever comes to mind, especially childhood experiences. To create an atmosphere in which clients feel free to express difficult thoughts, psychoanalysts, after a few face-to-face sessions, often have clients lie down on a couch while the analyst remains out of view, usually seated behind the client's head (see Figure 2.1).

The expert's role is to let clients gain insight by reliving and working through unresolved past experiences that come into focus during therapy sessions. To help clients deal realistically with unconscious material, therapists encourage them to project onto the therapists' emotions associated with others in the clients' lives. Unlike some other approaches, psychoanalysis encourages clinicians to interpret for their clients.

Overall, psychoanalytic therapists employ both active and passive techniques. Psychological assessment instruments are sometimes employed, especially perceptual tests such as the Rorschach Ink Blots (Exner, 2003). Practitioners of psychoanalysis almost always use diagnostic labels to classify clients and from those labels develop treatment plans. Psychoanalysts rely on the latest edition of the American Psychiatric Association's *Diagnostic and Statistical Manual (DSM),* the standard reference for diagnoses.

Goals

The goals of psychoanalysis vary according to the clients being treated. However, clinicians of this persuasion focus mainly on **personal adjustment**, usually inducing a reorganization of internal forces within the persons they see. In most cases, a primary goal is to help clients become more aware of the unconscious aspects of their personalities, including repressed memories and wishes too painful or threatening to have been dealt with initially. Repression does not stop thoughts from having influence; it just makes identifying them more difficult. Psychoanalysis strives to help clients gain insight into themselves.

A second major goal, often tied to the first, is to help clients work through **developmental stages** not previously resolved. If accomplished, clients become unstuck and are able to live more productively. However, working through unresolved developmental stages may require a major reconstruction of the personality. As a consequence, classical psychoanalysis, as practiced by Freud, is often a long, intense, and expensive process (Nye, 2000).

A final goal of psychoanalysis is helping clients cope with the demands of the society in which they live. According to this theory, unhappy people are not in tune with themselves or society. Thus, psychoanalysis stresses **environmental adjustment**, especially in the areas of work and intimacy. The focus is on strengthening the ego so that perceptions and plans become more realistic.

Assess your comprehension of Goals by completing this quiz.

Process and Techniques

Traditional psychoanalysis is a time-consuming process. Clients are usually seen a minimum of three times a week for a number of months or even years. Psychoanalytic techniques are most often applied within a specific setting, such as a therapist's office or the interview room of a hospital. Among the most prominent techniques are *free association, dream analysis, analysis of transference, analysis of resistance*, and *interpretation*. Although each technique is examined separately here, in practice they are integrated into the process of therapy.

Free Association

Repressed material in the unconscious is always seeking release. On a daily basis this material may be expressed in the form of sexual or aggressive jokes or through **Freudian slips**, errors of speech such as "I loathe you" instead of "I love you." In psychoanalysis, clients are encouraged to relax and freely recall early childhood memories or emotional experiences. During free association clients abandon the normal way of censoring thoughts by consciously repressing them and instead say whatever comes to mind, even if the thoughts seem silly, irrational, suggestive, or painful. In this way the id is requested to speak, and the ego remains silent (Freud, 1936). Unconscious material thus enters the conscious mind, and there clinicians interpret it.

At times, clients resist free association by blocking their thoughts, denying their importance, or both. Often, such resistance is concerned with significant earlier unresolved relationships. Nonetheless, therapists attempt to help clients work through their resistance, assuring them that even seemingly trivial thoughts or feelings are important. Many times such assurance is enough to overcome the resistance.

Dream Analysis

Clients report dreams to their therapists on a regular basis. Freud believed that **dreams** were "the royal road to the unconscious," an attempt to fulfill a childhood wish or express unacknowledged sexual desires. He insisted on getting at the nature of dreams by breaking them down into parts and treating them in as much detail as possible (Capuzzi & Black, 1986).

In **dream analysis**, clients are encouraged to dream and remember dreams, even though not everything in a dream is considered important. Clinicians are especially sensitive to two aspects—the **manifest content** (obvious meaning) and the **latent content** (hidden but true

Information Management

Understanding and Mastery: Obtain information through interviewing, active listening, consultation with others, library or other research, and the observation of clients and systems

Critical Thinking Question: How do you think free association and dreams might be used by human services practitioners to help those they work with?

meaning) (Jones, 1979)—and help to interpret both. Some dream symbols are obvious, such as hostility expressed as death or an accident (Nye, 2000). Other symbols are vague and difficult to interpret. Freud's method of dream analysis is considered the first scientific approach to the study of dreams.

Analysis of Transference

Transference is the term that denotes a client's response to a clinician as if the clinician were some significant figure in the client's past, usually a parent figure. Analysts encourage transference and interpret the positive or negative feelings expressed. The release of feelings is therapeutic, providing an emotional catharsis, but the real value lies in clients' increased self-knowledge, which comes through therapists' analysis of the transference. Clients who experience transference and learn from it are then freed to move on to another developmental stage (Singer, 1970). It should be stressed that "working through" transference is a continual process that consists of repetition, elaboration, and amplification (Luborksy, O'Reilly-Landry, & Arlow, 2011). Understanding and insight grow with each analysis of the transference experience.

Analysis of Resistance

Sometimes clients make initial progress while undergoing psychoanalysis and then slow down or stop. Their **resistance** to the therapeutic process may take many forms, such as missing or being late for appointments, not paying fees, persisting in transference, blocking thoughts during free association, or refusing to recall dreams or early memories. When resistance occurs in any form, clinicians must deal with it immediately. Analysis of resistance can help clients gain insight into it as well as other behaviors. But if resistance is not dealt with, the therapeutic process will probably come to a halt.

Interpretation

Interpretation is part of the other techniques already examined and complementary to them. Through interpretation therapists help clients understand the meaning of past and present personal events. The technique also encompasses explanations and analysis of clients' thoughts, feelings, and actions. However, human services practitioners who are clinicians must carefully time the use of interpretation. If it comes too soon in a relationship, it can drive a client away. On the other hand, if it is not employed at all or is used infrequently, a client may fail to develop insight. Only when clients are ready can interpretation make a significant impact on their growth and development.

Assess your comprehension of Process and Techniques by completing this quiz.

Personal Reflection

A number of Freudian techniques are discussed frequently in public. Which ones have you heard most often? How useful and effective do you think these techniques are?

Multicultural Issues

Multiculturalism deals with culture, gender, disability, sexual orientation, socioeconomic disadvantage, and the world of military service. Sigmund Freud and his theory of psychoanalysis were influenced by the times in which they emerged: the late Victorian Era and the beginning of the 20th century. Consequently, many of the concepts and ideas that developed in psychoanalysis are not considered relevant in the 21st century. Because Freud worked with upper-class Viennese women, almost all of whom suffered from hysteria, some clinicians and human services practitioners today dismiss psychoanalysis as an irrelevant theory.

Nonetheless, a good deal of psychoanalysis has transcended cultural barriers and has much to contribute. A specific aspect of psychoanalysis that is relevant for culture is its emphasis on **intraindividual diversity** (i.e., diverse components of being that exist within the individual) (Hansen, 2010). In addition to this inside focus, psychoanalysis is also multicultural in regard to where it is practiced. Outside the United States, the greatest number of psychoanalytic practitioners live in Brazil, a very diverse society. In addition, the work of Anna Freud and Erik Erikson in studying the development of children and child-rearing practices with an emphasis on the ego has helped to make psychoanalysis more palatable and useful than originally set forth. Furthermore, concepts ranging from transference to defense mechanisms seem to have relevance for people in different parts of society throughout the world.

Gender-sensitive issues were initially another story. While Freud's concept of the Electra complex and penis envy are largely discredited now (Horney, 1967), these concepts caused many women to avoid psychoanalysis and its offshoots because of what they considered a bias in the theory, which saw women inferior to men. However, now a variety of disciplines and theoretical orientations combine feminism with psychoanalytic and postmodern theories to celebrate diversity in gender and sexual experience (Glassgold & Iasenza, 2004).

Self-Development

Understanding and Mastery: Awareness of diversity

Critical Skills Question: How do you think intraindividual diversity complements cultural diversity?

Evaluation of the Theory

Strengths and Contributions

As developed by Freud and modified by others, psychoanalysis has several unique emphases. First, psychoanalysis emphasizes *the importance of sexuality and the unconscious in human behavior.* Before this theory came into being, sexuality (especially childhood sexuality) was denied, and little attention was paid to unconscious forces. Now, many theories acknowledge both the importance of the person as a sexual being and the power of the unconscious mind.

Another positive aspect of this theory is that it lends itself to *empirical studies*; it is **heuristic**. Since the early 1900s, Freud's proposals have generated a tremendous amount of research. Much of the research supporting the theory has been reported in the form of case histories and reactions in journals such as the *American Psychoanalytic Association Journal*, the *International Journal of Psychoanalysis*, and *Psychoanalytic Review*. A good deal of the research attacking the theory has been reported as empirical studies in other reputable journals. The theory itself challenges researchers to develop sophisticated methods of inquiry so that studies can be comparable.

Third interesting aspect of psychoanalysis is that it provides a *theoretical base of support for a number of diagnostic instruments*. Some psychological tests, such as the Thematic Apperception Test and the Rorschach Ink Blots, are rooted in psychoanalytic theory. Many other tests used by human services practitioners who are therapists are outgrowths of this theory or reactions to it.

Another strength of the psychoanalytic approach is that it reflects the *complexity of human nature*. Human services practitioners who are clinicians can gain a greater appreciation of human development and various associated problems connected with development by understanding psychoanalysis (Monte, 1991).

A fifth strength of psychoanalysis is that it has become more *diverse* through the years. While there are over 10,000 classical psychoanalysts in the United States, there are also many clinicians who engage in a modified form of psychoanalysis. Two of these modified forms of psychoanalysis are **ego psychology** (which focuses on the ego's normal and pathological development) and **object-relations theory** (which postulates that relationships, beginning with the mother-infant dyad, are primary, and that intrapsychic, interpersonal, and group experiences lay the foundation for the development of individual identity). Psychoanalysis continues to evolve and most recently has emphasized adaptive processes, social relations, and brief forms of treatment.

Another contribution of psychoanalysis is that it appears to be effective for those who suffer from a wide variety of disorders, including hysteria, narcissism, obsessive-compulsive reactions, character disorders, anxiety, phobias, and sexual difficulties (Luborksy, O'Reilly-Landry, & Arlow, 2011).

The final strength of psychoanalysis is that it *stresses the importance of developmental growth stages*. This emphasis on growth is very important for human services practitioners since much of the focus in the profession is on development. A significant amount of investigation since Freud's time, especially the work of Erikson (1963) and Levinson et al. (1978), has stressed developmental aspects of people. Such knowledge of human development is invaluable to human services practitioners when proposing plans for those with whom they work.

Limitations and Criticisms

Despite the unique emphases of psychoanalysis, most human services practitioners who are clinicians do not use this approach. The reasons are numerous. First of all, psychoanalysis is time-consuming and expensive. A person undergoing psychoanalysis is usually seen three to five times a week for a period of years (Bankart, 1997; Nye, 2000). Although psychoanalytically oriented psychotherapy, an alternative to psychoanalysis, is a briefer form of treatment, its effectiveness is debatable.

Another drawback is that psychoanalysis does not seem to lend itself to working with older clients. Thus, many psychoanalysts will not see clients over the age of 50.

A third limitation of psychoanalysis is that it has been claimed almost exclusively by psychiatry, despite the wishes of Freud (Vandenbos, Cummings, & Deleon, 1992). Therapists who are human services practitioner without medical degrees have had a difficult time getting extensive training in psychoanalysis (Turkington, 1985). In a 1988 settlement, the American Psychoanalytic Association, the most prestigious psychoanalytic society in the United States, "agreed that roughly 40 percent of its training slots [would] be filled by psychologists and other non-medically trained mental health practitioners" (Bule, 1988, p. 15). Still, psychoanalysis tends to be a rather restricted profession. Most nonmedical mental health practitioners are members of the American Academy of Psychoanalysis and the National Psychological Association for Psychoanalysis, organizations that are less prestigious than the American Psychoanalytic Association.

A fourth limitation of psychoanalysis is that many of its concepts are not easily communicated or understood. For instance, the id, the ego, and the superego might be represented in more easily understood ways. Psychoanalytical terminology seems at times to be overly complicated.

Another criticism of the psychoanalytic approach, especially the theory created by Freud, is that it is **deterministic**. For example, Freud attributed certain limitations in women to their gender. This controversial aspect of his theory has subsided because of the influence of ego psychology and women scholars' interpretation of Freud (Winkler, 1986), yet the appropriateness of psychoanalysis for women continues to be questioned.

Still another limiting aspect of the psychoanalytic approach is the fact that psychoanalysis does not lend itself to the needs of most individuals. The psychoanalytic model has become associated with people who have major adjustment difficulties or who want or need to explore the unconscious. However, most individuals who seek out human services have less disruptive developmental or situational problems.

> Assess your comprehension of <u>Evaluation of the Theory</u> by completing this quiz.

Treating Linda with Psychoanalytic Therapies

Conceptualization

From a psychoanalytic perspective you notice several problems in Linda's life. She states that she never felt close to her mother and is not close to her father either. You therefore hypothesize that she has never really resolved the phallic/electra stage of childhood. If that is true, then it is little wonder that she has not been able to sustain a marriage and that she continues to have trouble with her bosses at work. Linda's psychosexual development is a major theme that you identify immediately.

You also note, not surprisingly, that Linda is dependent on a number of defense mechanisms, one of which is repression of her hostile thoughts about the way she has been and is being treated in her life. Instead of dealing with these thoughts and feelings constructively and in a straightforward manner, Linda uses escape literature, movies, and television to help her feel better. Overall, Linda has a stronger-than-average death wish and a weak ego. She has not found satisfaction in either love or work, and she is most likely diagnosable under one of the DSM categories dealing with depression or personality disorder.

Treatment Process

As a human services practitioner steeped in psychoanalysis you are the expert who directs the course of treatment. You are particularly interested in Linda's past and in any early childhood memories. You hope that Linda can gain insight into her situation by reliving past experiences and thereby resolving them. In order to help Linda, you employ a number of procedures to bring out repressed and unconscious material. For example, you encourage Linda to engage in free association and dream analysis. Your ultimate goal is to enable her to adjust to society and to be intimate with others as she chooses.

You begin your work with Linda in one of two ways. If you wish to help her using the classical psychoanalysis method you see Linda four times a week for 1 hour at a time, stressing to her that treatment is likely to take years. In order to be unobtrusive and yet facilitate Linda's therapy, you have her lie down on a couch while you sit behind her head. In addition to free association and dream analysis, you try other standardized psychoanalytic techniques, including analysis of transference, analysis of resistance, and interpretation. If you use a more modified psychoanalysis model with Linda, your focus with her is on strengthening her ego and relationship skills. You see her weekly and the main agenda in your sessions is on consciously assisting Linda in becoming more competent in her interpersonal relationships by becoming more competent as a person.

In either of these procedures, conscious and unconscious material that Linda has repressed come into greater awareness. Often the process is a struggle, and Linda is surprised at what she says. For example, she blurts out that she loathed (instead of loved) her father. The interpretation of the latent content of her dreams, too, astonishes her. And with you she works through her transference of feelings related to her father and her former husband.

Through the process of psychoanalysis, Linda gains insight into her defense mechanisms and comes to understand why she has been depressed and has become obsessed with escape materials. When she ends treatment, she has made considerable progress, manifest in a less passive and more productive role within her family, especially with her mother. She has also begun to date and is feeling optimistic that her next relationship will be healthy.

Summary and Conclusion

Psychoanalysis is considered by many clinicians to be the grandparent of most modern theories of helping. Although Freud's ideas are controversial, his thoughts about human nature and the helping process are comprehensive. Since his death his ideas have been elaborated on and refined by his daughter, Anna Freud, who elaborated on defense mechanisms and childhood problems, and by many of his followers, such as Heinz Kohut, who concentrated on interpersonal relationships, and Erik Erikson, who focused on lifespan development. Psychoanalysis, along with modifications to the approach, is still widely practiced in human services professions, especially in psychiatry.

Overall, psychoanalysis is biologically based and stresses biological causality, psychosexual development, the dynamics of the mind, and defense mechanisms. This approach makes use of the psychological diagnoses. However, psychoanalysis is not used by many human services practitioners because it is costly, can be time-consuming, and is usually not one they are educated in. In addition, this approach is also not applicable for the client populations that most human services practitioners serve. It needs to provide the public and clinicians in the helping fields with more empirical evidence of its effectiveness.

Recall what you learned in this chapter by reviewing and completing the Chapter Review.

CHAPTER 3

Adlerian Therapy

Monkey Business Images/Shutterstock

Adlerian counseling is an internationally popular form of helping that some human services practitioners use. It is based on the common sense thinking of Alfred Adler, who was a contemporary of Sigmund Freud and proposed his ideas in the early days of psychotherapy. Adler had a keen interest in people and their motivations for behavior. He noted the inherent social interest of individuals and based his ideas around this concept. From the Adlerian point of view, the **essence of normality** is having a feeling of concern for others (Corsini, 1988; Sweeney, 2009). Such an emphasis is manifested in activities that center on social development, cooperation, and education.

In addition to his emphasis on social interests, Adler focused his theory on the influence of early memories on a person's life. The impact of one's family of origin was another focus of Adler's theory, especially the ordinal position of children in families. Adler based his therapeutic approach on including such concepts as **lifestyle**, **beliefs** (which he referred to as **fictions**), **psychological environment**, and the importance of **striving for completeness and wholeness** (Carlson, Watts, & Maniacci, 2006).

Major Theorist: Alfred Adler

Alfred Adler (1870–1937) was born in Penzig, Austria, a suburb of Vienna. He was the second of six children in a middle-class Jewish family. Adler shared a close relationship with his mother until his younger brother was born. Then, feeling abandoned, he sought the support of his father. Adler was also close to his older brother, Sigmund.

Adler was a sickly child and was injured often. He was run over in the street, suffered from rickets, and almost died of pneumonia at age 5. At age 3 he had witnessed the death of a younger brother. It is little wonder that he was later attracted to the profession of medicine.

To make up for his physical limitations, Adler spent a great deal of his childhood outside playing with other children and went out of his way to cultivate their friendship. Initially, he was not a good student; he did so poorly in mathematics at the secondary level that his teacher suggested his father take him out of school and apprentice him to a shoemaker. Adler reportedly overheard the conversation and studied to overcome this deficiency. Eventually, he became skilled in math.

In 1895 Adler received a degree in medicine from the University of Vienna. In his first practice he worked as an ophthalmologist, but his interests turned to neurology and finally to psychiatry. As a practicing psychiatrist, Adler was invited in 1902 to join Freud's Vienna Psychoanalytic Society, where he quickly gained prominence. Adler always thought of himself as a colleague rather than a disciple of Freud and disagreed early on with much of Freud's theoretical approach, especially Freud's emphasis on biology and sexuality. Adler developed a theoretical orientation that was less deterministic and more practical and hopeful. Unlike Freud, Adler stressed the importance of subjective feelings rather than biological drives as the primary motivating force of life (Datler & Gstach, 2001).

Because of his differences with Freud, Adler resigned as president of the Vienna Psychoanalytic Society in 1910 and also gave up his co-editorship of the *Journal of Psychoanalysis*, a periodical he had cofounded with Freud. Adler then established the rival Society of Individual Psychology.

During World War I Adler served as a physician in the Austrian army. After the war, in 1922, he was instrumental in setting up child guidance clinics in the Vienna schools and eventually in other parts of Europe. All the while, Adler worked to refine his theory and spoke widely in Europe and the United States. Adler fled from Austria following Hitler's rise to power and in 1932 was appointed to a position in medical psychology at the Long Island College of Medicine in New York. He died of a heart attack in 1937 while on a lecture tour in Aberdeen, Scotland. He was survived by his wife, two daughters, and a son.

Although Adler was a popular speaker and the author of more than 300 published papers and books, he has not generally received credit for many of the concepts he formulated. Such terms as *inferiority complex*, *social interest*, *empathy*, and *lifestyle* originated with Adler and were quickly absorbed by other scholars and the public. His theory waned in popularity during the 1940s and 1950s, was revitalized during the 1960s and 1970s, and has been widely used since that time. An excellent introduction to Adlerian theory is *The Practice and Theory of Individual Psychology* (Adler, 1969).

View of Human Nature/Personality

Adler thought that people were primarily motivated by **social interest**, a "feeling of being part of the social whole" and having an interest in others as well as a "need and willingness to contribute to the general social good" (Corsini & Wedding, 2000, p. 469). Thus, social interest is "not only an interest in others but an interest in the interests of others" (Ansbacher, 1977, p. 57).

In addition, Adler's theory holds that conscious aspects of behavior, rather than the unconscious, are central to the development of personality. A major Adlerian tenet is that individuals strive to become successful, that is, the best they can be. Therefore, their behavior is goal-directed and purposeful. Underlying this paramount belief is Adler's conviction that each person strives for growth and has a need for wholeness. Adler gave his theory the name **Individual Psychology** to emphasize the holistic perspective, with the term *individual* deriving from the Latin *individuum*, meaning "indivisible" (Mosak & Maniacci, 2011).

The tendency of people to try to fulfill their own unique potential is a process Adler called striving for perfection or completeness (Adler, 1964). Another tendency for each person to feel initially inferior to others, if not overcome, leads to an **inferiority complex** and can become the basis for defining one's personality. A person who overcompensates for feelings of inferiority develops a **superiority complex** (Ansbacher & Ansbacher, 1964), which Adler described as a neurotic fiction that is unproductive.

Adler believed that people are as influenced by future goals as by past causes. His theory places considerable emphasis on birth order (Eckstein & Kaufman, 2012). He thought those who share ordinal birth positions (e.g., firstborns) may have more in common with one another than with siblings from the same family (Dreikurs, 1950). Five ordinal positions are emphasized in Adlerian literature on the family constellation: *firstborns, secondborns, middle children, youngest children,* and *only children* (Dreikurs, 1967; Dreikurs & Soltz, 1964; Sweeney, 2009).

Planning and Evaluation

Understanding and Mastery: Analysis and assessment of the needs of clients or client groups

Critical Thinking Question: How do you think a knowledge of Adler's view of human nature, that is, that people have social issues and strive to be the best they can be, helps human services practitioners analyze and assess the needs of clients or client groups?

- **Firstborns.** Firstborns are initially the *reigning monarchs* of a family because they receive undivided attention from parents. They are socialized to conform, achieve, behave, and please. They take responsibility when parents are absent and often act as parent substitutes in large families. All firstborns experience the loss of their unique position in the family when a second child is born. The experience of being *dethroned* may cause them to become resentful or help them better understand the significance of power and authority.
- **Secondborns.** The position of secondborn is an enviable one, according to Adler, but does have drawbacks. Secondborns never have to worry about issues of power and authority because they are born into a family atmosphere in which they will never be dethroned. Usually, these individuals are more outgoing, carefree, and creative and less concerned with rules than firstborns. They frequently pursue roles not taken by firstborns and are likely to be just the opposite of their older siblings.
- **Middle children.** Children born in the middle positions of a family often feel squeezed in and treated unfairly. They do not develop the close, personal types of alliances that an oldest or a youngest child may form; but because of their position, middle children learn a great deal about family politics and the art of negotiation. These skills can prove useful in manipulating events to get what they want and choosing areas where they can be successful.
- **Youngest children.** Youngest children in the family have difficulties and opportunities that are different from those of their older siblings. Youngest children receive a great deal of attention from others, who are likely to cater to their needs. These children may become charmers but may also have difficulty breaking out of the role of baby or family pet. They face the danger of becoming spoiled but at the same time may make great strides in achievement because of role models provided by older siblings.

• **Only children.** Any child born seven or more years apart from siblings is psychologically an only child. These children, as a group, are never dethroned and are at an advantage, like oldest children, in receiving a great deal of attention. They may mature early and become high achievers. They may also develop rich imaginations because of the amount of time they spend alone. Major disadvantages are that only children may become pampered and selfish and may not be well socialized.

Personal Reflection

How do you think your ordinal position in your family of origin has influenced you? Think of your siblings or cousins and what influence you think their ordinal position has had on their development.

In addition to birth order, the family environment is important to a person's development, particularly in the first five years of life. Adlerian theory stresses that by age 5 each person creates a **lifestyle**, or style of life, which is one's characteristic way of living and pursuing long-term goals. This lifestyle is gained primarily through interacting with other family members. A **negative family atmosphere** might be authoritarian, rejecting, suppressive, materialistic, overprotective, or pitying (Dreikurs & Soltz, 1964), whereas a **positive family atmosphere** might be democratic, accepting, open, and social. Nevertheless, perception of the family atmosphere, rather than any events themselves, is crucial to the development of a lifestyle (Adler, 1964).

Individuals are also guided by their **fictions**, that is, their subjective evaluations of themselves and their environments. Five basic mistakes are caused by fictions (Mosak & Maniacci, 2011):

1. **Overgeneralizing**—viewing everything as the same, for example, believing that all African-Americans think similarly
2. **False or impossible goals of security**—trying to please everyone, for example, being aggressive or passive to please certain individuals
3. **Misperceptions of life and life's demands**—believing that one never gets any breaks
4. **Minimization or denial of one's worth**—thinking that one will never amount to anything
5. **Faulty values**—believing in the necessity of being first no matter what needs to be done to achieve that goal

In contrast, a **healthy style of life** focuses on three main areas—*society, work*, and *sexuality*. Adlerian theory places strong emphasis on contributing to society. It also holds that work is essential for human survival and that we must learn to be interdependent. Furthermore, individuals must define their sexuality, in regard to self and others, in a spirit of cooperation rather than competition. Adler mentions two **challenges of life**, although he does not fully develop them—*spirituality* and *coping with self* (Dreikurs & Mosak, 1966). Adlerian theory emphasizes that every life task requires **courage**, a willingness to take risks without knowing what the consequences may be.

Assess your comprehension of <u>View of Human Nature/Personality</u> by completing this quiz.

Role of the Counselor

Counselors who are Adlerian function primarily as diagnosticians, teachers, and models in the egalitarian relationships they establish with their clients. Adlerian clinicians try to assess why clients are oriented to a certain way of thinking and behaving. They are active in making an assessment by gathering information on the family constellation and clients' earliest memories. They then share interpretations, impressions, opinions, and feelings with their clients and concentrate on promoting the therapeutic relationship. Those that they work with, in turn, are encouraged to examine and change a faulty lifestyle by developing social interests (Adler, 1927, 1931). Adlerian practitioners frequently share hunches or guesses with clients and are often directive when assigning clients homework—for example, suggesting that they act as if they were the persons they want to be.

Adlerians employ a variety of techniques, some of which are borrowed from other approaches. Adler was not specific in detailing how those who help others should operate when using his theory. As a general rule, Adlerian specialists make little use of assessment tools, such as psychological tests, but usually employ life-history questionnaires to gather data. They generally avoid the types of diagnoses found in formal assessment texts, such as the *Diagnostic and Statistical Manual*, but use their own language (e.g., "discouraged") to describe the dynamics they encounter within clients.

Interventions and Direct Services

Understanding and Mastery: Skills to facilitate appropriate direct services and interventions related to specific client or client group goals

Critical Thinking Question: How might the use of homework, as advocated by Adler, help human services practitioners assist clients in reaching their goals? What are the drawbacks to assigning homework?

Goals

The goals of Adlerian practitioners revolve around *helping persons develop healthy, holistic lifestyles* (Carlson et al., 2006). This focus may mean educating or reeducating clients about what such lifestyles are, as well as helping them overcome feelings of inferiority.

One of the major goals of Adlerian specialists is to *encourage clients to cultivate social interest* (Adler, 1931). According to Adler, social interest is an innate potentiality "that must be consciously developed or trained" (Watts, 1996, p. 169). A **faulty style of life** is self-centered and based on mistaken goals and incorrect assumptions associated with feelings of inferiority. These feelings might stem from being born with a physical or mental defect, being pampered by parents, or being neglected. In order to correct the feelings and stop inappropriate forms of behavior, practitioners must assume the roles of teachers and interpreters of events. In short, Adlerians deal with the whole person, and clients must ultimately decide whether to pursue social or self-interests (Kern & Watts, 1993).

Interventions and Direct Services

Understanding and Mastery: Theory and knowledge bases of prevention, intervention, and maintenance strategies to achieve maximum autonomy and functioning

Critical Thinking Question: What are the advantages and disadvantages of human services practitioners assuming the roles of teachers and interpreters when working with clients?

Assess your comprehension of <u>Goals</u> by completing this quiz.

Process and Techniques

Adlerian techniques are practiced in conjunction with the four different phases of treatment that are part of the Adlerian therapeutic process (Nystul, 2011). These phases are identified as *establishing a relationship, performing analysis and assessment, promoting insight,* and *reorienting* (Dreikurs, 1967; Kottman & Warlick, 1990; Mosak & Maniacci, 2011).

Establishing a Relationship

Establishing a relationship is crucial if the goals of Adlerians are to be achieved, and certain techniques enhance this process. Counselors who practice Adlerian theory try to develop a warm, supportive, empathic, friendly, and egalitarian relationship with clients.

They are encouraging and try to win the respect of their clients. Adlerian helping is seen as a **collaborative effort** (Adler, 1956), with encouragement and hope a part of the process. Clinicians actively listen and respond in reflective and probing ways (James & Gilliland, 2003), trying to *help their clients define specific goals and discover what prevents the achievement of these goals.* Adlerians may focus on clients' strengths but may confront at times, pointing out clients' inconsistencies. The primary objectives are to maintain a flexible interaction process that stresses clients' responsibilities and abilities (Dinkmeyer & Sperry, 2000).

Performing Analysis and Assessment

After a relationship has been established, Adlerian counselors concentrate on *analyzing their clients' lifestyles, examining family constellations, early memories, dreams, priorities, and ways of responding.* As previously noted, the family constellation and the atmosphere in which children grow greatly influence both self-perception and perceptions of others. Clients are encouraged to recall early memories, especially events before the age of 10. Adler (1931) contended that people remember childhood events that are consistent with their present view of self, others, and the world in general. Adlerian counselors look both for *themes* and for *specific details* within these early recollections (Slavik, 1991; Statton & Wilborn, 1991; Watkins, 1985). Figures from the past are treated as **prototypes** rather than specific individuals; they may represent clients' attitudes toward power, weakness, men, women, or almost anything else. Recent and past dreams are also a part of lifestyle analysis. Adlerian theory holds that **dreams** are a possible rehearsal for future courses of action, making recurrent dreams especially important.

A look at client priorities is also helpful in understanding style of life and ways of responding. Unless challenged, a client may persist in one predominant lifestyle that is filled with basic mistakes (Mosak & Maniacci, 2011). These faulty or irrational views of life, or fictions, have already been elaborated on. In this second phase of counseling, lifestyle priorities and ways of responding are challenged.

Promoting Insight

Counselors next try to help clients develop insight, especially by asking open-ended questions and offering interpretations. **Open-ended questions**, that is, those that invite a thoughtful response of more than a few words, allow clients to explore patterns in their lives that may have gone unnoticed. **Interpretation**, from an Adlerian perspective, often takes the form of intuitive guesses, sometimes based on counselors' general knowledge of ordinal positions and family constellations. However, true to the egalitarian spirit of the process, a client is never forced to accept a human services practitioner's point of view. **Empathy**, the ability to feel what it is like to be the client, is especially important in this process.

REORIENTING To accomplish behavioral change and put insight into action, counselors use specific techniques.

> **Confrontation:** In this process counselors challenge clients to consider their own private logic. When clients examine their logic, they often realize they can change both it and their behavior.
>
> **Asking the question:** In this procedure counselors ask, "What would be different if you were well?" Clients are often asked this question during the initial interview, but it is appropriate at any time.
>
> **Encouragement:** Encouragement implies faith in a person (Dinkmeyer & Losoncy, 1996; Dreikurs & Soltz, 1964). Counselors encourage their clients by stating their belief that behavior change is possible. Encouragement is the key to making productive lifestyle choices.
>
> **Acting "as if":** Clients are instructed to act as if they are the persons they want to be, for instance, the ideal persons they see in their dreams (Gold, 1979). Adler originally got this idea from Hans Vaihinger (1911), who wrote that people create the worlds they live in by making assumptions about the world.
>
> **Spitting in the client's soup:** In this technique, counselors point out certain behaviors to clients thereby ruining the payoff for the behaviors. For example, a mother who always shows up her daughter in order to feel superior may continue to do so after the behavior has been pointed out but will no longer reap the reward of feeling superior.
>
> **Catching oneself:** Clients learn to become aware of self-destructive behaviors or thoughts. At first, counselors may help in the process, but eventually clients take over this responsibility.
>
> **Task setting:** Clients initially set short-range, attainable goals and eventually work up to long-term, realistic objectives.
>
> **Push button:** Clients are encouraged to realize that they have choices about the stimuli to which they will pay attention. They are taught to create the feelings they want by concentrating on their thoughts. The technique is like pushing a button because clients can choose to remember negative or positive experiences (Mosak & Maniacci, 2000).

In the process of using these techniques, counselors must avoid the **tar baby**, that is, "the perceptions on life that the client carries into counseling and attempts to fit into the counselor. Anger, discouragement, seductiveness, martyrdom, and a host of other traps are set for the unwary counselor as the client resists change" (James & Gilliland, 2003, p. 121).

Assess your comprehension of <u>Process and Techniques</u> by completing this quiz.

Personal Reflection

On the surface the four-step process of Adlerian counseling seems straight forward. What parts of the process do you think are most difficult? Why?

age?

Multicultural Issues

Multiculturalism deals with culture, gender, disability, sexual orientation, socioeconomic disadvantage, and the world of military service. Because of its emphasis on social interest, Adlerian counseling is well suited for use in multicultural areas (Sharf, 2012). For example, many minority cultures in the United States—such as American Natives, Asian-Americans, and Latinos—value social interaction and social groups. The Adlerian approach emphasizes that healthy individuals need to extend themselves beyond themselves and their families, regardless of the cultural groups to which they belong. Such a concept often requires learning about and understanding different cultural groups. In that process individuals learn much about themselves and may also realize that certain Adlerian concepts may need to be modified within a cultural context.

Likewise, the Adlerian approach is sensitive to equality issues between the genders (Ansbacher & Ansbacher, 1978). Adler believed that both men and women want to be **superior**, perfect (that is their best), and never inferior. He referred to this attitude in women as the **masculine protest**, since men in his era held superior roles to those of women. Because Adler's concern for women's rights and equality is still a part of Adlerian theory and practice, both women and men find Adlerian counseling appropriate.

> ### Client-Related Values and Attitudes
>
> *Understanding and Mastery: The worth and uniqueness of individuals including ethnicity, culture, gender, sexual orientation, and other expressions of diversity*
>
> Critical Thinking Question: Why do you think Adler's emphasis on equality of the genders makes this theory attractive to men as well as women?

Evaluation of the Theory

Strengths and Contributions

Adlerian therapy has a number of unique emphases that make it an important theory. The Adlerian approach fosters an egalitarian atmosphere through positive counseling techniques. Rapport and commitment are enhanced, thereby increasing the chances for change. Adlerian counselors offer encouragement and support and approach their clients with an educational orientation and an optimistic outlook on life.

Adlerian therapy is also versatile over the life span. "Adlerian theorists have developed counseling models for working with children, adolescents, parents, entire families, teacher groups, and other segments of society" (Purkey & Schmidt, 1987, p. 115). **Play therapy** for children of ages 4 to 9 seems to be especially effective, allowing children to communicate through the language of play and then verbally talk about their feelings (Kottman & Warlick, 1990). An approach that emphasizes verbal and behavioral consequences is recommended for adolescents, particularly those dealing with the faulty goals typical of this age group (Kelly & Sweeney, 1979; Sweeney, 2009). Parents may benefit from Adlerian theory through educational support groups that help them understand their children better and plan effective intervention strategies (Dinkmeyer, 1982a, 1982b; Dinkmeyer, McKay, & Dinkmeyer, Jr., 1997; Dinkmeyer, McKay, McKay, & Dinkmeyer, Jr., 1998). The Adlerian approach has been successfully applied to complex family interactions, too (Lowe, 1982; Walsh & McGraw, 1996).

In addition, the Adlerian approach is useful in the treatment of a variety of DSM disorders—conduct disorders, antisocial disorders, anxiety disorders of childhood and adolescence, some affective disorders, and personality disorders (Seligman & Reichenberg, 2010).

Another valued aspect is the Adlerian contribution to other helping theories and to the public's knowledge and understanding of human interactions. Adlerian concepts such as freedom, phenomenology, interpretation of events, life scripts, growth, and personal responsibility are found in existential, Gestalt, rational emotive behavior, person-centered, and reality-based counseling and therapy. Adlerian terms such as inferiority complex have also become part of the public's vocabulary.

A final strength of Adlerian therapy is that it can be employed selectively in different cultural contexts (Brown, 1997). For instance, the concept of encouragement is appropriately emphasized in working with Hispanic and Asian-American groups, which have traditionally emphasized collaboration, whereas the concept of sibling rivalry may be highlighted with traditional Americans of European descent, who stress competition.

Limitations and Criticisms

The Adlerian approach, like any theory, has limitations and weaknesses. First of all, the therapy lacks a firm, supportive research base. Relatively few empirical studies clearly outline the effectiveness of Adlerian counseling (Wallace, 1986). More investigations are needed if the theory is to develop systematically. Journals devoted to the Adlerian viewpoint, such as the *Journal of Individual Psychology*, may rectify this situation.

In addition, the Adlerian approach is vague in regard to some of its terms and concepts. Corey (2013) notes that Adler emphasized practice and teaching rather than theoretical definitions and organization. Although a number of prominent educators—such as Dreikurs, Mosak, Dinkmeyer, and Sweeney—have attempted to clarify the Adlerian approach, some of its ideas remain unclear. Adler was especially nebulous about how to work with clients.

A third factor that may be considered a drawback is that this therapy may be too optimistic about human nature. Adler, who called his theory "individual psychology," stressed social cooperation and interest. Some critics consider his view neglectful of other life dimensions, such as the power and place of the unconscious (Prochaska, 1984).

Yet a fourth possible limitation of the Adlerian approach centers on some of its basic principles. For instance, a concept like democratic family structure may not fit well with clients whose cultural contexts stress a lineal social relationship, such as that of traditional Arab Americans (Brown, 1997). If all basic principles of Adlerian counseling cannot be followed, then the impact of the theory may be lessened.

Finally, the Adlerian approach relies heavily on verbal erudition, logic, and insight and may thus be limited in its applicability to clients who are not intellectually bright (James & Gilliland, 2003). This limitation applies to many theories and is not singularly targeted to Adlerian work in human services settings.

Assess your comprehension of Evaluation of the Theory by completing this quiz.

Personal Reflection

Do you think the strengths of the Adlerian approach outweigh its limitations? If not, why not? If so, how do you think you would work around its limitations?

Treating Linda with Adlerian Therapy

Conceptualization

From an Adlerian viewpoint, Linda is a person who is discouraged; she has tried to be successful but has failed. Yet she is goal-directed and wants more in her life than escape mechanisms. Linda is also seeking to connect socially. Her family life and her former husband were both less than ideal. In addition, Linda has an inferiority complex that has kept her from reaching her potential vocationally and interpersonally. As the second-born child in her family and the first girl, Linda is in an enviable position. However, her negative perception of her family and its authoritarian, suppressing, and rejecting attitude has handicapped her.

Linda has bought into a couple of Adlerian fictions that hinder her, too. She has overgeneralized, believing that she will never get a break. And she has minimized her worth as a person; hence, she thinks about suicide. In essence, Linda's style of life—especially as it relates to work, society, and sexuality—has been unhealthy and needs to be rectified.

Treatment Process

As an Adlerian human services practitioner you recognize first that Linda is discouraged. To promote a positive relationship with Linda, you are warm, supportive, empathic, encouraging, and collaborative in working with her. You actively listen and give her feedback. In addition, you ask Linda about early childhood memories; they center around staying clean, being neat, being proper, and doing what she was told. These are not pleasant recollections, and you share your impressions of what it must have been like as you continue to develop your relationship with Linda. You note that Linda has developed a faulty lifestyle that has made her overly dependent on the opinions of others. Therefore, in the therapeutic session you take the role of being an interpreter and teacher.

As your work progresses, you as well as Linda begin to concentrate on her strengths. You ask her what her dreams are and how she would like to respond to situations around her. To give Linda practice in being the person she wishes to be, you invite her to act as if she were that person. In addition, you ask Linda open-ended questions and allow her to explore her life more closely, especially in regard to how she wants it to be.

As your time with Linda moves toward a conclusion, you help Linda become reoriented to a new life by confronting her and challenging her private logic, which tells her that she is not capable of being more than she is now. You also ask her the question about how her life would look if she were well. You encourage her to live a more productive lifestyle and to catch herself when she begins to have destructive or negative thoughts. You also urge Linda to set short-term goals, such as taking a course at a nearby college, hoping that the achievement of these short-term goals will lead to long-term goals. Overall, you help Linda strive toward her own perfection, or completeness, and resist getting trapped into her former unproductive lifestyle.

Summary and Conclusion

Alfred Adler, a contemporary of Sigmund Freud, developed a theory of individual psychology, based on the premise that people have a specific concern and need for social interest. The theory has been clarified and expanded since his death, especially by

Rudolph Dreikurs and Don Dinkmeyer, making the approach more understandable and popular, particularly in North America. Adlerian theory is a social-based, interpersonal, and subjective (i.e., phenomenological) approach to counseling. It emphasizes the future, holism, collaboration, and choice and focuses on the importance of childhood (i.e., working through real or perceived unresolved situations) and behavioral goals. Ordinal family positions, lifestyle, and the importance of socialization and encouragement are a few concepts that have made strong contributions to the helping professions.

The Adlerian approach stresses definable stages and techniques and is widely practiced in educational and institutional settings. Its popularity can be attributed to its hopefulness and its useful application in multiple settings, such as in groups and families. Even as more research needs to be conducted on its practice, this approach remains a popular way of working with people of all stages and backgrounds.

Recall what you learned in this chapter by reviewing and completing the **Chapter Review**.

CHAPTER 4

Existential Therapy

Chris Rout/Alamy

Chapter Outline

The basis for **existentialism** comes from the 19th-century theologian and philosopher Soren Kierkegaard. He was the first to develop a philosophy focused on the pursuit of becoming an individual, "formulating truth as a guidepost, and emphasizing the necessity of commitment." His approach was named "existentialism" by German and French theorists Martin Heidegger and Jean Paul Sartre. The approach was later formulated into a therapeutic process by Swiss psychiatrist Ludwig Binswanger (Austin, 1999, p. 53).

The essence of existentialism as a therapeutic approach is represented in the writings of several prominent American theorists—including Sidney Jourard, Abraham Maslow, Irvin Yalom, Rollo May, Clemmont Vontress, James Bugental, and Clark Moustakas—even though its philosophical roots are European. Other notable contributors to existentialism include Fyodor Dostoyevski, Albert Camus, Edmund Husserl, Friedrich Nietzsche, Martin Buber, and Viktor Frankl. In recent years the most prominent practitioners of existential psychotherapy in the United States and Europe have been Rollo May, Viktor Frankl, Irvin Yalom, and Clemmont Vontress. Of these, May (1961) and Frankl (1962) are probably the best-known theorists.

As a group, existentialists differ widely in their emphases. For example, Dostoyevski stressed the importance of consciousness, Kierkegaard concentrated on human anxiety and dread, and Buber (1970) focused on the treatment of persons in "it" or "thou" relationships, that is, treating others as inanimate objects or as unique individuals. However, despite their diversity, existentialists hold some beliefs in common:

- The importance of anxiety, values, freedom, and responsibility in human life
- An emphasis on finding meaning in one's actions

Major Theorists: Rollo May and Viktor Frankl

Rollo May (1909–1994) was born in Ada, Ohio. Like Alfred Adler, May was the second of six children; but unlike Adler, May was the oldest son in his family. The relationship between May's parents was discordant, leading May to describe his boyhood home life as unhappy. Consequently, he became a loner and a rebel during his adolescence (Rabinowitz, Good, & Cozad, 1989).

In 1930, May graduated with a degree in English from Oberlin College and accepted a position teaching English at Anatolia College in Greece. During two of his summer vacations there, he traveled to Vienna and enrolled in seminars conducted by Alfred Adler, which sparked his interest in psychoanalysis. However, during his years in Greece, he was also extremely lonely and began working incessantly, which resulted in a breakdown. As he reflected years later, "I had learned enough psychology at college to know that these symptoms meant that something was wrong with my whole way of life. I had to find some new goals and purposes for my living and to relinquish my moralistic, somewhat rigid way of existence" (May, 1985, p. 8).

In 1933, May returned to the United States to enter Union Theological Seminary, where he was strongly influenced by Paul Tillich, an existential theologian. After a brief career as a Congregationalist Minister, May decided to pursue a degree in clinical psychology at Columbia University, but tuberculosis interrupted his studies. He struggled with the illness for almost two years during which time he was strongly impressed with the writings of the Danish existentialist Soren Kierkegaard. After his recovery, May completed his doctorate at Columbia in 1949 and joined the faculty of the William Allanson White Institute in New York City.

May's most influential book, *The Meaning of Anxiety*, was published a year later. May believed that anxiety could work for the good as well as the detriment of people. He lectured on this subject at some of the most distinguished universities in the United States, including Yale and Harvard, while continuing to practice psychotherapy and serve "as an adjunct faculty member at the New School of Social Research and New York University" (Rabinowitz et al., 1989, p. 437). May was a cofounder of the Association for Humanistic Psychology in the 1960s and later wrote two other well-known books, *Love and Will* (1969) and *The Courage to Create* (1975). In the 1980s he retired to the San Francisco area, where he concentrated on writing about the meaning of myths for modern society and continued to promote a humanistic approach to psychology until his death at the age of 85.

Viktor Frankl (1905–1997) was born in Vienna, Austria. He received a medical degree in 1930 and a Ph.D. in 1949 from the University of Vienna. Frankl established the Youth Advisement Centers in Vienna and directed them from 1928 to 1938. He also held several hospital appointments in the city between 1930 and 1942.

Although Frankl was a contemporary of Freud and Adler and had interactions with both, he became interested in existentialism in the 1930s while reading the works of philosophers such as Heidegger, Scheler, and Legan. He began formulating his ideas about an existential approach to counseling, using the term **logotherapy** as early as 1938. The Greek word *logo* implies a search for meaning.

During World War II, Frankl was imprisoned from 1942 to 1945 in Nazi concentration camps at Auschwitz and Dachau, where his parents, a brother, and his wife died. The impact of the concentration camps crystallized his thoughts about the meaning of life and suffering, and it was partly his determination to share those beliefs that kept him alive.

In 1947, Frankl joined the faculty of the University of Vienna and later became associated with the United States International University in San Diego, lecturing widely at many prestigious universities throughout the world. He wrote extensively also; his best-known books are *Man's Search for Meaning* (1962), which has been translated into 24 languages, and *The Will to Meaning* (1969b). According to Frankl, "the will to meaning is the central drive of human existence" (Dollarhide, 1997, p. 181), but meaning is attained as a by-product of discovery rather than through direct pursuit.

Frankl is sometimes referred to as the founder of the third school of Viennese psychotherapy (i.e., logotherapy), with Freud's psychoanalytic theory being first and Adler's individual psychology second. At the age of 92, Frankl died of heart failure in Vienna and is buried there.

View of Human Nature/Personality

As a group, existentialists believe that people form their lives by the choices they make. Even the worst situations, such as the Nazi death camps, provide an opportunity to make important life-and-death decisions, such as whether to struggle to stay alive (Frankl, 1969b). Existentialists focus on this freedom of choice and the action that goes with it, viewing people as the authors of their lives. Existentialists contend that people are responsible for any choices they make and that some choices are healthier and more meaningful than others. For example, individuals who prize creativity, services to others, friendship, and self-growth within a community or family environment may, as Abraham Maslow describes, have **peak experiences**, in which they feel truly integrated and connected with the universe in a very emotional way (Hoffman, 1990). Such persons are characterized as having "a holistic perspective of the world, [having] a natural tendency toward synergy [cooperative action], [being] intrapsychic, interpersonal, intercultural and international, [being] more consciously and deliberately metamotivated" (Chandler, Holden, & Kolander, 1992, p. 168).

Personal Reflection

What healthy choices have you made in your life? How have they helped shape the person you are today?

On the other hand, individuals who are self-indulgent may feel a sense of normlessness and valuelessness. They may experience what Frankl (1959) calls an **existential vacuum**, a sense that life has lost all meaning. Carried to an extreme, these individuals would develop a disorder Frankl calls **noogenic neurosis**, characterized by a feeling that one has nothing to live for (Das, 1998).

According to Frankl (1962), the "meaning of life always changes but it never ceases to be" (p. 113). **Meaning** goes beyond self-actualization and exists at three levels: (a) *ultimate* *meaning* (e.g., an order to the universe); (b) *meaning of the moment*; and (c) *common, day-to-day meaning* (Das, 1998). Frankl believes we can discover life's meaning in three ways:

- **by doing a deed**—that is, by achieving or accomplishing something
- **by experiencing a value**—such as, a work of nature, culture, or love
- **by suffering**—that is, by finding a proper attitude toward unalterable fate

Existentialists believe that **psychopathology** is a failure to make meaningful choices and maximize one's potential (McIllroy, 1979). Choices may be avoided and potentials unrealized because of the anxiety involved in action. Anxiety is often associated with paralysis, but May (1977) argues that normal anxiety can be healthy and motivational and can help people change. Clients may leave existential counseling more anxious than they began, but in such cases they are consciously aware of their anxiety and can therefore channel it toward constructive use (May, 1967). Thus, existentialism, unlike other theories, focuses on the meaning of anxiety in human life, emphasizing the inner person and the ways in which authentic individuals search for value in life. By being aware of feelings and the finite nature of human existence, people come to make healthy, life-enhancing choices.

Planning and Evaluation

Understanding and Mastery: Skills to develop goals, and design and implement a plan of action

Critical Thinking Question: How could human services practitioners use Frankl's three ways of discovering life's meaning to help clients who are anxious and failing to make meaningful choices?

Assess your comprehension of <u>View of Human Nature/Personality</u> by completing this quiz.

Role of the Counselor

There are no uniform roles that existentialists adopt; indeed, the **existential approach** to counseling is unique in its diversity. Nor is there agreement among existentialists about how to systematically formulate their ideas into a uniform way of helping others. Part of the reason for this variety among practitioners is that existentialists believe every client is distinctive, regardless of similar concerns, heritages, or backgrounds. Therefore, existentialists are sensitive to the discrete aspects of their clients' characteristics, "such as voice, posture, facial expression, even dress and apparently accidental movements of the body" (May, 1939, p. 101). Basically, existentialists concentrate on being authentic with their clients and entering into deep and personal relationships with them.

In the therapeutic process it is not unusual for helpers to share personal experiences with their clients to deepen the relationship and help clients realize a shared humanness and struggle. Buhler and Allen (1972) suggest that existentialists focus on **person-to-person relationships** that emphasize mutuality, wholeness, and growth. Existentialists who practice from a Frankl perspective are Socratic in engaging their clients in dialogue (Das, 1998). However, all existentialists serve as a model of how to achieve individual potential and make decisions. They concentrate on helping clients experience subjective feelings, gain clearer self-understanding, and move toward a new way of being in the world. The focus is on living productively in the present, not recovering a personal past. They also focus on ultimate human concerns (death, freedom, isolation, and meaninglessness) (Yalom & Josselson, 2011).

Intervention and Direct Services

Understanding and Mastery: Skills to facilitate appropriate direct services and interventions related to specific client or client group goals

Critical Thinking Question: How do you think focusing on ultimate human concerns, such as death, freedom, isolation, and meaninglessness, can be helpful to clients in formulating and carrying out their goals individually or in a group?

Existentialists do not use psychological tests, nor do they make diagnoses in accordance with the latest Diagnostic and Statistical Manual of Mental Disorders (DSM). Both of these procedures would be antithetical to the thrust of the approach that stresses the uniqueness of each client. It is interesting to note, however, that some psychological instruments, such as the *Purpose of Life Test*, are based on existential premises and that the DSM deals with anxiety on several levels. In addition, existentialists do assess how meaningfully and purposefully individuals they are working with see life.

Goals

The goals of existential helping include assisting clients realize the importance of meaning, responsibility, awareness, freedom, and potential. Existentialists hope that during the course of the helping relationship, clients will take more responsibility for their lives: "The aim of therapy is that the patient experience his existence as real" (May, Angel, & Ellenberger, 1958, p. 85). If all works well, clients are freed from being observers of events and become shapers of meaningful personal activity.

Clients become more responsible through the relationships they build with their existential helper because in relationship they develop a greater awareness of personal freedom. Thus, a major **goal** is for clients to shift from an outward to an inward frame of reference, no longer depending on the judgment of others but evaluating their own activities first. Further goals include

Assess your comprehension of Goals by completing this quiz.

- making clients sensitive to their existence
- calling attention to clients' unique traits and characteristics
- helping clients improve their encounters with others
- assisting clients in establishing a will to meaning
- encouraging clients to make a decision about both present and future directions in life (Cunningham & Peters, 1973; Das, 1998; May, 1975; Reeves, 1977)

Personal Reflection

What unique traits and characteristics do you have? How do you use them? How might you use them more?

Process and Techniques

Because the existential approach is not a clearly defined process for most of its practitioners, specific techniques are rarely used repeatedly. In fact, the existential approach claims fewer techniques than almost any other major model of helping. "Approaching human beings merely in terms of techniques necessarily implies manipulating them," and manipulation is opposed to what existentialists espouse (Frankl, 1967, p. 139).

This apparent weakness is paradoxically a strength because it allows existentialists to concentrate on building deep and meaningful relationships with their clients, thereby helping them become more aware of themselves and others. It also allows these practitioners to borrow ideas from other areas and to use a wide range of skills in a highly personal manner. Thus, they are free to use techniques as widely diverse as desensitization and free association or to disassociate themselves from these practices entirely (Corey, 2013).

Clients usually benefit from existentialists who are able to address client needs in a multidimensional and highly customized way. For example, depressed persons tend to adopt emotion-focused strategies for dealing with their pain, whereas nondepressed individuals use multiple and vying strategies (Stevens, Pfost, & Wessels, 1987). Thus assessing whether a person is depressed or not gives an existentialist an idea of what approach to use. Existentialists can offer a variety of approaches—some that may be cognitively or even behaviorally based, as well as some that may be emotionally oriented—to help depressed individuals and assist them in seeing options. Of uppermost importance is the existential view that working with clients is open and inquiring. As such, they accept the truth unique to each individual (Kemp, 1976).

In addition, developing some vision of the true, the good, and the beautiful is essential from an existential perspective. Such a vision gives meaning to individuals' personal lives and humanizes society as well (Partenheimer, 1990). However, sometimes the process of finding personal truth requires a willingness to work through ambiguity. In such cases existentialists have a most effective and powerful tool to aid in exploration—their relationships with clients. Ideally, existentialists transcend their own needs and focus on their clients during this phase of therapy (Wallace, 1986), remaining open and self-revealing in an attempt to help their clients become more in touch with personal feelings and experiences. The emphasis is on authenticity, honesty, and spontaneity.

Existentialists also make use of confrontation; clients are confronted with the idea that everyone is responsible for his or her life. For this purpose existentialists borrow some techniques from other models, such as imagery exercises, awareness exercises, and goal-setting activities. For example, existentialists may lead clients through a typical day in their lives five years in the future. Through this process clients are able to see more clearly the meaning in life by recognizing the choices they are making now that will shape their futures.

Interpersonal Communication

Understanding and Mastery: Establishing rapport with clients

Critical Thinking Question: Do you think confrontation could be used by human services practitioners to establish rapport with clients? Why or why not?

Assess your comprehension of <u>Process and Techniques</u> by completing this quiz.

Multicultural Issues

Multiculturalism deals with culture, gender, disability, sexual orientation, socioeconomic disadvantage, and the world of military service. Because existentialists concentrate on human conditions that are universal in all walks of life and all circumstances, this approach to helping is probably as multicultural as any. A leading proponent of the existentialist approach in the United States, Clemmont Vontress, is African-American and has proposed existential theory as a base for multicultural counseling (Moodley & Walcott, 2010; Vontress, 1979; Vontress, Johnson, & Epp, 1999). In addition, Viktor Frankl's form of existentialism, logotherapy, is particularly adaptable to multicultural counseling, having grown out of the cultural oppression of the Jews during the Holocaust (Ivey, D'Andrea, & Ivey, 2012).

Gender issues are deemphasized in the existential approach. Both men and women have feelings of meaninglessness, isolation, and anxiety with which they must deal. Even though ways

Client-Related Values and Attitudes

Understanding and Mastery: The worth and uniqueness of individuals including ethnicity, culture, gender, sexual orientation, and other expressions of diversity

---

Critical Thinking Question: Do you think the fact that gender issues are deemphasized in the existential approach means that the uniqueness and worth of men and women are devalued?

of addressing these feelings and other conditions in life may vary with the genders, a common emphasis remains within existentialism on working with men and women in unique ways that help them transcend common human difficulties such as disabilities or socioeconomic circumstance.

Evaluation of the Theory

Strengths and Contributions

A strength of existentialism is its *emphasis on the uniqueness of each individual*. It is a very humanistic way of working with others (Yalom, 1980). It also stresses continued human growth and development, offering hope to clients through directed readings and therapeutic encounters with the counselor. The life of Viktor Frankl is a good illustration of this strength. Furthermore, existential therapy recognizes that anxiety is not necessarily a negative condition. Anxiety is a part of human life and can motivate some individuals to make healthy and productive decisions.

Another contribution of existentialsim is its *effectiveness in multicultural situations*. Because of its global view of human existence, existentialism allows clinicians to focus on the person of the client in an "I-thou" manner without regard to ethnic, social, or sexual background (Epp, 1998; Jackson, 1987; Miars, 2002). In addition, an existential approach gives practitioners access to a tremendous amount of philosophy and literature that is both informative and enlightening about human nature. This philosophical base has the potential to support a systematic counseling theory. Existential theory also helps connect individuals to universal problems faced by humankind, difficulties such as the search for peace, the absence of caring, or finding employment (Baldwin, 1989; Schultze & Miller, 2004). In the latter situation, the existential themes of death, freedom/responsibility, aloneness, and meaninglessness may serve as a process-oriented framework that the existential counselor uses to support a person in entering or reconnecting with a turbulent and unpredictable job marketplace (Maglio, Butterfield, & Borgen, 2005).

Finally, an existential approach is valuable to helping relationships because it can be combined with other perspectives and methods, such as those based on learning principles and behaviorism, to treat extremely difficult problems, for example, addiction. In these cases a major focus is on the existential value of facing "life problems and feelings through honest expression" (Wilbur, Roberts-Wilbur, & Morris, 1990, p. 157).

Limitations and Criticisms

Despite its strengths and contributions the existential approach has not produced a fully developed model of counseling. Practitioners who stress developmental stages of growth are particularly vehement in this criticism. Existential therapy also lacks educational and training programs; the uniqueness of each practitioner prohibits the systematic teaching of theory. As a result, some wonder whether the existential approach will last as a counseling approach.

A related limitation is that existential counseling is difficult to implement beyond an individual level because of its subjective nature. Existentialism lacks the type of methodology and validation processes prevalent in most other therapeutic approaches and the uniformity and systematic outline that beginning helpers readily understand.

Another shortcoming of the existential approach, according to some critics, is that existentialists as a group do not diagnose or test their clients. Critics claim that the failure to evaluate and diagnose may be irresponsible; therapists may miss opportunities to assess their clients more thoroughly and subsequently gear their practices more specifically to clients' needs.

Finally, critics charge that existential theory and therapy are closer to existential philosophy than to other counseling theories and therapies. This distinction and separation limit the usefulness of existentialism.

Assess your comprehension of Evaluation of the Theory by completing this quiz.

Personal Reflection

How useful do you think you could be to people in need if you were an existentialist? What makes you think so?

Treating Linda with Existential Therapy

Conceptualization

From an existential perspective Linda seems to be living a meaningless life, just drifting. She has contemplated suicide and is anxious about her ability to succeed at work and in relationships. Thus, her life is characterized by a feeling that she has nothing to live for. Although Linda has made a number of bad choices, you, as an existentialist, believe she is capable of making healthy choices and maximizing her potential.

Treatment Process

As an existential you focus on the uniqueness of Linda and her distinctiveness. You attempt to be authentic with her and to enter into a deep relationship. You self-disclose and share with Linda some of your own struggles as she reveals hers. You try to serve as a role model for her and help her focus on living a productive life in the present.

Your hope in working with Linda is that she will take more responsibility for her life. You want her to shift from an outer to an inner frame of reference, from which she can evaluate situations first. You want her to be more sensitive to herself. In order to help her in envision the good and the beautiful, you borrow several techniques from guided imagery and use them with her. You also confront Linda with the fact that she alone is responsible for her life. Because Linda likes to read, you assign her books on the lives of Viktor Frankl and Rollo May as well as some of the existential writings of Irvin Yalom including some of his popular fiction such as *Love's Executioner* and *Momma and the Meaning of Life*. When she returns for her appointments, you discuss the books with her and talk about how each of these and other individuals have had to overcome obstacles to find meaning in life.

Linda leaves therapy with a new sense of herself and others. She begins to engage in social activities within the community and to explore opportunities for personal and professional growth. She maintains a relationship with you even after treatment has officially ended.

Summary and Conclusion

Existentialism is both a philosophy and a philosophical approach to counseling. It has European roots but has been adopted and adapted by a number of prominent American clinicians. The approach is centered on the premise that human beings have universal feelings and experience universal conditions, such as anxiety, loneliness, death, and the search for meaning in existence. Leading existentialists of the 20th century include Rollo May and Viktor Frankl. Notable therapists today include Irvin Yalom and Clemmont Vontress.

There is no uniform existentialist approach, although one form of existentialism, Frankl's logotherapy, is more systematic than any other. Nonetheless, the focus in all forms of existentialism is on the relationship between the helper and client, and on that relationship a dialogue about issues relevant to the client is built. In the process, existentialists confront and share personal experiences. Most borrow techniques from other approaches and concentrate on working with clients in the moment, using whatever techniques further insight and movement within clients to address their concerns.

Recall what you learned in this chapter by reviewing and completing the Chapter Review.

In recent years, some have argued that existential psychotherapy is a positive psychology because it focuses on both possibilities and limitations and recognizes human potential without succumbing to an unrealistic optimism (Bretherton & Orner, 2003). Existential counseling remains an effective approach for working in multicultural and gender-sensitive venues.

CHAPTER 5

Person-Centered Therapy

light poet/Shutterstock

Person-centered counseling was created by Carl Rogers in the early 1940s. It was considered a radical approach when it began because it differed greatly from the primary theories in use. At that time, the predominant theories of counseling were counselor centered (e.g., the work of E. G. Williamson), symptom focused (e.g., behaviorism), or oriented to personality change (e.g., psychoanalysis). Rogers altered the counseling landscape with his initial emphasis on being nondirective and letting clients take the lead in directing change.

Rogers's approach to helping was revolutionary. He emphasized caring, empathy, understanding, and acceptance in ways that had never been tried before. He trusted that his clients would grow if the right conditions were established. His journey as a clinician, his development as a person, and the growth of his theory were all achieved despite resistance and, at times, adversity. The validity of the person-centered approach to counseling may seem obvious to people in the 21st century, but its therapeutic process and procedures were considered anything but routine when it emerged.

Major Theorist: Carl Rogers

Carl Rogers (1902–1987), the individual most identified with person-centered counseling, was born in Oak Park, Illinois, a suburb of Chicago. He was the fourth of six children. As fundamentalist Christians, his parents discouraged Rogers from forming friendships outside the family because of the bad influence others might have on him. Thus, Rogers (1980) describes his childhood as solitary, with "no close friend and only superficial personal contact" (p. 29). When he was 12, his family moved to a farm outside Chicago, where he developed a strong interest in science and reading. Among his early scientific experiments was one investigating a species of moth.

As a teenager Rogers read everything he could, including encyclopedias and dictionaries. However, his academic interests and abilities did not help him socially, and Rogers (1967a) describes himself as being generally inept in his interpersonal relations during his high school years. A major turning point occurred when Rogers enrolled at the University of Wisconsin in 1919 to study agriculture. There he became involved with a YMCA group and began to develop friendships. He also started dating and began to trust others. A life-changing event for him was a six-month trip in 1922 as one of 10 American students attending the World Student Christian Federation conference in Peking (*Beijing* now), China. The trip exposed him to people of other cultures, religions, and ways of thinking (Kirschenbaum, 2007).

After his return, Rogers broke away from the domination of his parents and changed his major to history, intending to become a minister. After graduation in 1924, he enrolled in New York's Union Theological Seminary but became discouraged two years later about the prospect of entering the ministry. Thus, he transferred to Teachers College, Columbia University, "a hotbed of radical behavioristic thinking in the 1920s" (Bankart, 1997, p. 293). At Columbia University he studied clinical and educational psychology, receiving an M.A. degree in 1928 and a Ph.D. in 1931. As a graduate student Rogers studied briefly with Alfred Adler, who was a visiting instructor at the Institute for Child Guidance in New York City, where Rogers was an intern (Watts, 1996).

After completing his studies, Rogers took a position with a child guidance agency in Rochester, New York. His 12-year tenure there was productive and significantly influenced his later theory of counseling. He found that the psychoanalytic approach, which was dominant in this work setting, was time consuming and often ineffective. However, clients with whom Rogers formed an open and permissive relationship seemed to improve. During this time, Rogers was reinforced in his clinical beliefs by the works of Otto Rank and his followers (Raskin, Rogers, & Witty, 2011).

Rogers left Rochester in 1940 to accept a professorship at Ohio State University. Two years later he published his ideas on counseling in his first book on theory, *Counseling and Psychotherapy* (1942). He refined and revised those ideas during extensive research in the 1950s and 1960s at the University of Chicago and the University of Wisconsin. At Wisconsin, Rogers first examined the effectiveness of his approach in a hospital setting with persons diagnosed as schizophrenic. In 1964, he became a resident fellow at the Western Behavioral Sciences Institute, and in 1968 he helped establish the Center for the Study of Persons in La Jolla, California.

A prolific writer, Rogers published more than 200 articles and 15 books (Heppner, Rogers, & Lee, 1990). Among his most noteworthy books are *Counseling and Psychotherapy* (1942), which laid the foundation for person-centered counseling; *Client-Centered Therapy* (1951), which thrust him and his theory into national prominence; and *On Becoming a Person* (1961), which "solidified his reputation in his chosen profession" (Whiteley, 1987, p. 8) and with the public at large.

Rogers wrote five books after the age of 65, including *Freedom to Learn* (1969), *Carl Rogers on Encounter Groups* (1970), and *A Way of Being* (1980). He considered his theory to be constantly evolving, becoming relevant in groups, marriages, families, and international relations, especially the peace movement of the 1980s (Goodyear, 1987; Rogers, 1987). He died unexpectedly at the age of 85 on February 4, 1987, from complications following hip surgery.

View of Human Nature/Personality

Implicit in **person-centered counseling** is the view that people are essentially good (Rogers, 1961). Humans are characteristically "positive, forward-moving, constructive, realistic, and trustworthy" (Rogers, 1957, p. 199). From infancy on, each person is aware, inner-directed, and moving toward self-actualization.

- Whatever an infant perceives is that infant's reality. An infant's perception is an internal process of which no one else can be aware.
- All infants are born with a self-actualizing tendency that is satisfied through goal-directed behavior.
- An infant's interaction with the environment is an organized whole, and everything an infant does is interrelated.
- The experiences of an infant may be seen as positive or negative according to whether they enhance the actualization tendency.
- Infants maintain experiences that are actualizing and avoid those that are not. (Rogers, 1959)

According to Rogers, **self-actualization** is the most common and motivating drive of existence; it encompasses actions that influence the total person. "The organism has one basic tendency and striving, to actualize, maintain, and enhance the experiencing organism" (Rogers, 1951, p. 487). Person-centered theorists believe that each person is capable of finding a personal meaning and purpose in life.

Rogers views the individual from a **phenomenological perspective**: What is important is a person's perception of reality rather than an event itself (Rogers, 1955). This view is similar to Adler's, as is the concept of self. But for Rogers the concept is so central to his theory that his ideas are often referred to as **self theory**. The self is an outgrowth of what people experience, and an awareness of self helps individuals differentiate themselves from others (Nye, 2000).

For a healthy self to emerge, people need **positive regard**—love, warmth, care, respect, and acceptance. But in childhood, as well as in later life, individuals often receive conditional regard from parents and others. **Conditional acceptance** teaches persons to feel valued only when they conform to others' wishes. Thus, those persons may have to deny or distort a perception when others on whom they depend for approval see a situation differently. Individuals who are caught in such a dilemma become aware of incongruities between their self-perceptions and their experiences. If they conform, they open up a gap between the **ideal self** (what they are striving to become) and the **real self** (what they are). The further the ideal self is from the real self, the more alienated and maladjusted persons become.

> ### Human Systems
>
> *Understanding and Mastery: Theories of human development*
>
> Critical Thinking Question: What evidence do you see in life that the most common and motivating drive of existence is self-actualization?

Personal Reflection

How do you picture your ideal self? How are you striving to achieve it?

Assess your comprehension of the <u>View of Human Nature/Personality</u> by taking this quiz.

Role of the Counselor

Person-centered counselors take on a holistic role in their work. They set up and promote a climate in which clients are free and encouraged to explore all aspects of their lives (Rogers, 1951, 1980). This atmosphere focuses on the **counselor-client relationship**, which Rogers describes as having a special *I-Thou* personal quality. Person-centered counselors are aware of the verbal and nonverbal language of their clients, and they reflect back what they hear or observe (Braaten, 1986). Neither clients nor counselors know what direction sessions will take or what goals will emerge in the process. Yet counselors trust clients to develop the agenda; counselors work as *facilitators* rather than as directors. In the person-centered approach counselors are process experts and expert learners. Patience is essential (Miller, 1996).

Person-centered counselors make limited use of psychological tests. Testing is usually done only at the request of clients and only after clients have had an opportunity to be reflective about their past decisions. If testing does take place, counselors focus on the meaning of the test for clients rather than on test scores. One innovative test occasionally used in evaluating clients is the **Q Sort Technique** (Olson & Hergenhahn, 2011). First, the client is given 100 cards, each of which contains a self-descriptive sentence, such as "I am intelligent" or "I despise myself." Next, the client is asked to place the cards in nine piles, from most-like-me to least-like-me. Then the client sorts the cards again according to how he or she would like them to be. The final step of the process is correlating the degree of similarity between the two sortings—before, during, and after counseling.

Interpersonal Communication

Understanding and Mastery: Establishing rapport with clients

Critical Thinking Question: Do you think displaying unconditional positive regard is enough to establish rapport with a client?

The use of diagnosis, at least on a formal level, is eschewed in person-centered counseling because diagnosis is philosophically incompatible with the objectives of the approach. Diagnosis categorizes people, implying that each person is not unique. It also puts the counselor in charge because, once a diagnosis is made, a treatment plan follows. Thus, the Diagnostic and Statistical Manual of Mental Disorders (DSM) is not used by person-centered counselors. However, clinicians who are person centered are aware of the degree to which individuals they work with are functioning and at least on an informal level assess their growth and development over time.

Goals

The goals of person-centered counseling are geared to clients as people, not to their problems. Rogers (1977) emphasizes that people need to be assisted in learning how to cope with situations so that they become fully functioning persons with no need to apply defense mechanisms to everyday experiences. Such individuals are increasingly willing to change and grow; they are more open to experience, more trusting of self-perception, and more engaged in self-exploration and evaluation (Rogers, 1961). Fully functioning persons develop a greater acceptance of themselves and others and become better decision makers.

Ultimately, person-centered counseling helps clients identify, use, and integrate their own resources and potential (Boy & Pine, 1982; Miller, 1996). Rogers (1961) holds that clients should become more realistic in their self-perceptions; more confident and self-directing; more positively valued by themselves; less likely to repress aspects of their experiences; more mature, socialized, and adaptive in their behavior; less upset by stress and quicker to recover from it; and more like the healthy, integrated well-functioning person in their personality structures. (p. 375) Thus, a major goal of person-centered counseling is to bring about a harmony "between the client's real self-concept and his or her perceived self-concept" (Benjamin & Looby, 1998, p. 92).

Assess your comprehension of the Goals by taking this quiz.

Process and Techniques

Person-centered processes and techniques have evolved over the years. Hart (1970) identifies the following three periods of evolution, each of which is distinctively different in its emphasis:

- **Nondirective period** (1940–1950). During this period person-centered counselors emphasized forming a relationship with clients by creating a permissive atmosphere of nonintervention. Their main techniques were acceptance and clarification.
- **Reflective period** (1950–1957). This seven-year span was characterized by an emphasis on the creation of nonthreatening relationships. Techniques included responding to clients' feelings and reflecting underlying affect back to clients. During this period Rogers changed his terminology from nondirective to client-centered to deemphasize techniques and focus on the therapeutic relationship.
- **Experiential period** (1957–1980). This period began when Rogers (1957) issued his statement on the necessary and sufficient, or core, conditions of counseling: *empathy; positive regard or acceptance;* and *congruence or genuineness* (Gelso & Carter, 1985; Watts, 1996). **Empathy** is the ability to feel with clients and convey this understanding back to them. It is an attempt to think with, rather than for or about, them (Brammer, Abrego, & Shostrom, 1993). Rogers (1975) notes, "The research keeps piling up and it points strongly to the conclusion that a high degree of empathy in a relationship is possibly the most potent and certainly one of the most potent factors in bringing about change and learning" (p. 3). **Positive regard**, also known as acceptance, is a deep and genuine caring for clients as persons; that is, prizing people just for being (Rogers, 1961, 1980). **Congruence** is the condition of being transparent in the therapeutic relationship by giving up roles and facades (Rogers, 1980). This period helped make person-centered counseling more active and well defined.

Since 1980, person-centered counselors have tried a number of other procedures for working with clients, such as limited self-disclosure of counselors' feelings, thoughts, and values. However, because clients grow by experiencing themselves and others in relationships (Cormier & Cormier, 1998), Rogers (1967b) holds that "significant positive personality change" cannot occur except in relationships (p. 73). He lists six necessary and sufficient conditions for a counseling relationship:

1. Two persons are in psychological contact.
2. The first person, the client, is in a state of incongruence and is vulnerable or anxious.
3. The second person, the counselor, is congruent, or integrated, in the relationship.

4. The counselor experiences unconditional positive regard for the client.
5. The counselor experiences an empathic understanding of the client's internal frame of reference and attempts to communicate his or her experience to the client.
6. There is at least a minimal degree of communication to the client of the counselor's understanding and unconditional positive regard.

Interventions and Direct Services

Understanding and Mastery: Skills to facilitate appropriate direct services and interventions related to specific client or client group goals

Critical Thinking Question: What other skills and methods besides those listed in the chapter, for example, active and passive listening and open-ended leads, do you think would help promote a client relationship?

According to Rogers (1959) these six conditions exist on a continuum and, except for the first condition, are not on an all-or-nothing basis.

Methods that help promote the counselor-client relationship include, but are not limited to, the following: active and passive listening, accurate reflection of thoughts and feelings, clarification, summarization, confrontation, and general or open-ended leads (Poppen & Thompson, 1974). All of these techniques have been incorporated into other helping approaches and systematic human-relations training courses.

Overall, the person-centered approach places minimal emphasis on formal techniques and maximal focus on creating a therapeutic relationship. A classic example of this emphasis can be seen in an interview of Rogers (1965) with a client named Gloria, in which he focuses on her acceptance of herself and their relationship rather than on Gloria's problem.

Personal Reflection

When have you been totally accepted by someone? How did it feel? How did you respond?

Assess your comprehension of the <u>Process and Techniques</u> by taking this quiz.

Multicultural Issues

Multiculturalism deals with culture, gender, disability, sexual orientation, socioeconomic disadvantage, and the world of military service. Person-centered counseling receives mixed reviews regarding its appropriateness in multicultural contexts. On the positive side, this approach to human relationships has been used in a number of countries to promote cross-cultural communication and understanding. Rogers himself conducted many such workshops in countries as diverse as Japan, Mexico, China, Northern Ireland, and the former Soviet Union. That work continues, and as Spangenberg (2003) points out, the person-centered approach provides an excellent cross-cultural approach in South Africa, where there is a relationship between person-centered counseling and traditional African healing practices. In addition, person-centered theory has some similarities to Eastern philosophies and psychologies in which there is an openness to the development of people and the self is seen as a process rather than a fixed being (Sharf, 2012). There is a deep appreciation in the person-centered approach of the many ways clients can benefit from therapy (Cooper & Mcleod, 2011).

However, Rogers's beliefs about the necessary and sufficient conditions for therapy are not necessarily universal. Also, in some cultures help from others is valued if it is direct and comes from an authority—just the opposite of the person-centered approach.

Gender issues receive a mixed report as well. On the one hand, Rogers appears to be effective with Gloria, a young divorced woman in the film demonstrating his approach. A number of other incidents are documented in which person-centered therapy conducted by Rogers seems to be successful with both women and men, in groups and other settings. Gender-related concerns arise primarily because Rogers did not address them in his lifetime and some question whether people of one gender can truly empathize with and relate to the others of another gender or those without disabilities can empathetically relate to individuals who have them.

Evaluation of the Theory

Strengths and Contributions

Person-centered therapy revolutionized the counseling and human service professions by demystifying the helping process. Rogers provided actual transcripts of counseling sessions (Goodyear, 1987). Basically, Rogers "turned the field of counseling upside down" (Rogers, 1974, p. 115). Furthermore, he made the person-centered approach applicable to a wide range of human problems, including institutional changes, labor-management relationships, leadership development, career decision making, and international diplomacy. He summed up his view of the approach in this way: "I am no longer talking about psychotherapy, but about a point of view, a philosophy, an approach to life, a way of being, which fits any situation in which growth, of a person, a group, or a community is part of the goal" (Rogers, 1980, p. ix).

Besides transforming the therapeutic community, the person-centered approach has contributed to the profession by generating a great deal of research (Kirschenbaum, 2004, 2007). Initially, it set the standard for doing research on counseling variables, especially those that Rogers (1957) deemed necessary and sufficient to bring about therapeutic change. In addition, Rogers was the first clinician to make audiotape recordings of counseling sessions and insisted that the person-centered approach be compared only to theories that were as empirically verified (Rogers, 1986). "Above all, Rogers was the quintessential scientist practitioner. He continually put his formulations to the test of research. In fact, no model of therapy is more extensively researched than his own" (Goodyear, 1987, p. 523).

A third contribution of person-centered counseling is its focus on the *open relationships*. More than most, Rogers's theory emphasizes the importance of an accepting counselor-client relationship. Specific dimensions of that relationship have been examined for their impact on the total helping process (Carkhuff, 1969a, 1969b).

Another strength of the person-centered approach is its *effectiveness*. It helps improve psychological adjustment, learning, and frustration tolerance and helps decrease defensiveness (Grummon, 1972). In addition, it is appropriate in treating mild to moderate anxiety states, depression, self-esteem issues, adjustment disorders, relationship concerns, and conditions not attributable to mental disorders, such as uncomplicated bereavement or interpersonal relations (Seligman & Reichenberg, 2010; Neukrug, 2011).

A further strength of person-centered counseling is that the basics of the approach take a relatively short time to learn, although a lifetime to master. With its emphasis on relationship and listening skills, the person-centered approach has become a foundation for training many practitioners to work in varied settings, including the wide range of careers in human services (Glauser & Bozarth, 2001).

Yet another beneficial aspect of person-centered therapy is its *positive view of human nature* (Heppner et al., 1990; Kirschenbaum, 2004), which is different from the more pessimistic and deterministic views that some theories hold. One of the strongest reasons that people change is the belief that they can change, and person-centered helpers are strong believers in the change process.

Finally, the person-centered approach has generated a number of relatively new therapeutic ways of conducting counseling that either claim to be person-centered or based on Rogers's theory. These treatment methods include child-centered play therapy, person-centered expressive therapy, focusing-oriented psychotherapy, and process-experiential/emotion-focused therapy (Kirschenbaum, 2012). In addition, Rogers's daughter, Natalie, claims the person-centered approach of her father as the theoretical underpinnings of her person-centered expressive arts therapy (Rogers, Tudor, Tudor, & Keemar, 2012).

Limitations and Criticisms

One initial drawback to person-centered therapy is that it provides few instructions for counselors on how to establish relationships with clients and bring about change. The work of Carkhuff (1969a, 1969b) and Gazda (1973) have helped rectify this deficiency; however, person-centered theory is still sometimes viewed as an approach without clearly defined terms or techniques (Nye, 2000).

Another limitation of the person-centered approach is that it depends on bright, insightful, hard-working clients for best results. Thus, this theory of helping has limited applicability and is seldom employed with the severely handicapped or with young children (Henderson & Thompson, 2011).

A third criticism of being person-centered is that practitioners of this theory ignore diagnosis, the unconscious, and innately generated sexual and aggressive drives. Many critics think that it is overly optimistic. Even though Rogers compiled a great deal of data supporting his point of view, much of that research has been attacked as being simplistic and based on self-reports (Olson & Hergenhahn, 2011).

Assess your comprehension of the Evaluation of the Theory by taking this quiz.

A fourth limitation of person-centered counseling is that the process is directed by clients and may thus deal only with surface issues. Believing that only deep change is lasting, critics charge that clinicians who are person-centered oriented do not challenge their clients to explore those deeper areas. Because the person-centered approach is relatively brief in nature and is not directed by an expert practitioner, critics claim that it cannot have a permanent impact on clients.

Personal Reflection

What changes have you made that were not directed by others? Do you think Rogers is right about human beings being self-directed? Why?

Treating Linda with Person-Centered Therapy

Conceptualization

From a person-centered perspective what is important is that Linda has been accepted conditionally throughout her life. She has been valued as a daughter and a wife only when she has performed these roles as others have defined them. Linda's relationship with her ex-husband lasted only as long as she conformed to his wishes that she look and act in a certain way. Now she is searching to be accepted for herself unconditionally, and so far she has not found people that value her just for herself. She does not get close to her family members because they, too, judge her.

As Linda looks at life, she sees a rather hostile environment. Men are mean or sexist. Families do not offer support or comfort. Thus, it is little wonder that she has retreated to books, television, and movies as ways to escape and feel safe. On the other hand, Linda knows that she is more capable than she has been allowed to be.

Treatment Process

As a person-centered therapist you immediately set up a therapeutic environment in which Linda is accepted and encouraged. You use yourself and the relationship you establish with her to help her see herself. You actively listen and reflect back to her what you hear her saying. You empathize, clarify, confront, and show her unconditional positive regard. You convey to her that you trust her to make observations, insights, and decisions. You are genuine in your statements and try to create an atmosphere in which Linda can be herself. In the process she begins to feel like a person capable of finding her own direction in life.

As Linda begins to disclose, she initially ventilates anger toward her father, her former husband, and individuals in her work environments. You self-disclose and reveal that you would be angry, too, if you had been through her experiences. After a while Linda shifts away from her anger and begins to concentrate on who she can be and how she can be. Her thoughts and feelings move into the present, and she recognizes that she has a quick mind and is capable of going back to school or finding a higher level job. She also realizes that all men are not like her father or her ex-husband and that she might be able to be in a relationship in which she is valued for herself.

With these ideas in mind, Linda begins to make plans that will expand her environment and her opportunities, such as taking a yoga class at the YMCA and joining a reading club at the library. After a few more sessions, Linda reveals that she is ready to trust herself to make other plans and arrangements. Thus, she leaves therapy with an optimistic sense of hope and a new perspective on herself.

Summary and Conclusion

The person-centered approach to counseling created a great deal of excitement and controversy when it was introduced to the therapeutic community in 1942 by Carl Rogers. It emphasized that clients could and would make important and needed changes in their lives if a proper relationship was set up and someone listened to them. The emphasis on being nondirective was just the opposite of prominent theories of the time that put therapists in charge of change. Yet this approach has prevailed because of research supporting its underlying tenets.

Even though the person-centered approach has undergone a number of changes since its introduction, it still places priority on creating a therapeutic relationship and fostering the conditions necessary and sufficient for change to take place. It continues to be one of the most popular theories of helping and has been used both domestically and internationally in a number of venues, ranging from group work to peace talks.

Recall what you learned in this chapter by reviewing and completing the Chapter Review.

CHAPTER 6

Gestalt Therapy

Jaqui Farrow/Bubbles Photolibrary/Alamy

Gestalt therapy is associated with Gestalt psychology, a school of thought that stresses the perception of completeness and wholeness. In fact, the translation of the term *gestalt* means "whole figure." Gestalt therapy arose as a reaction to the reductionist emphasis in other schools of counseling and psychotherapy, such as psychoanalysis and behaviorism, which tried to break down the personality or client behaviors into explainable parts. In contrast, Gestalt theory emphasizes how people function in their totality—a major emphasis of counseling and human services (Levine, 2012).

Gestalt therapy was popularized in the 1960s by Fritz Perls, who focused on helping individuals become more aware of the many aspects of their personhood. Laura Posner Perls, Fritz's wife, and Paul Goodman, a colleague, helped Perls write, enlarge, and refine his original ideas (Masquelie, 2006). Later theorists, particularly Joen Fagan and Irma Lee Shepherd (1970), developed the model still further. However, since Fritz Perls is the best known of Gestalt theorists, he is highlighted here.

Major Theorist: Fritz Perls

Frederick Salomon Perls (1893–1970) was born into a middle-class Jewish family in Berlin. He had a younger and an older sister. Even though his parents fought bitterly and Perls disliked his older sister, he remembered his childhood as happy. Initially, he loved to read and was a top student in his grade school. However, in secondary school Perls encountered difficulty because of a conservative learning environment and his own rebellious spirit. He had trouble obeying authorities and failed the seventh grade twice. Nevertheless, he completed his secondary education once placed in a more permissive environment and was later awarded a medical degree from Frederich Wilhelm University in 1920. His schooling was interrupted by World War I where he serviced as a medic in the German army.

Perls trained as a psychoanalyst in both Vienna and Berlin. Psychoanalysts Wilhelm Reich and Karen Horney each participated in Perls's analysis as part of his training. Subsequently he took a position in Frankfurt at the Institute for Brain Injured Soldiers. There Perls became associated with Kurt Goldstein, from whom he learned to view humans as complete, or holistic, entities rather than as individuals made of separate parts.

In 1933, Perls fled Nazi Germany, first to Holland and then to Johannesburg, South Africa, where he and his wife, Laura, built a strong psychoanalytic practice, just as they had previously done in Germany. In 1936, Perls sailed his private yacht 4,000 miles from South Africa to Germany to attend an international psychoanalytic congress in Czechoslovakia. There he arranged an audience with Freud, which left Perls feeling humiliated because of Freud's comments to him. Having been frequently demeaned by his father, Perls dedicated himself to proving Freud and psychoanalysis wrong as a revenge for the incident.

Perls immigrated to the United States in 1946. Although his ideas were not readily accepted, he gained prominence through the publication of *Gestalt Therapy* (1951), which he coauthored with Hefferline and Goodman. Perls also established the Institute for Gestalt Therapy in New York City in 1952 and offered lectures and workshops around North America. In 1960, he moved to the Esalen Institute in Big Sur, California.

Perls was an actor at heart and loved to parade his ideas before the public at Esalen. Laura, long separated from Fritz, continued to be supportive of her husband until his death in British Columbia at the Gestalt kibbutz, a commune he had founded (Bankart, 1997). Perls recounted many of the more personal moments of his life in his autobiography, *In and Out of the Garbage Pail*, published posthumously in 1972.

View of Human Nature/Personality

Gestaltists believe that human beings work for wholeness and completeness in their lives. Each person has a self-actualizing tendency that emerges through the beginning of self-awareness and personal interaction with the environment. Self-actualization is centered in the present; it "is the process of being what one is and not a process of striving to become" (Kempler, 1973, p. 262). The Gestalt view of human nature places trust in the inner wisdom of people, much as person-centered counseling does. Each person seeks to live integratively and productively, striving to coordinate the various parts of his or her personhood into a healthy, unified whole. From a Gestalt perspective, persons are more than a sum of their parts (Perls, 1969).

The Gestalt view is **antideterministic**: Each person is able to change and become responsible (Hatcher & Himelsteint, 1997). Thus, individuals are actors in the events around them, not just reactors to actions. Overall, the Gestalt point of view is **existential, experiential,** and **phenomenological**: The *now* is what really matters. People discover different aspects of themselves through experience rather than talk, and individuals' own assessment and interpretation of their lives at any given moment are what matter most.

Human Systems

Understanding and Mastery: Theories of human development

Critical Thinking Question: How do you think Gestalt therapy is like person-centered and Adlerian theory? What makes it distinct?

According to Gestalt therapy, many troubled persons have an overdependence on intellectual experience (Simkin, 1975). Such an emphasis diminishes the importance of emotions and the senses, limiting people's abilities to respond to various situations. Another frequent problem is the inability to identify and resolve unfinished business; that is, earlier thoughts, feelings, and reactions that still affect personal functioning and interfere with living life in the present. The most common unfinished business is the failure to forgive parents for their mistakes. Gestaltists do not attribute either of these difficulties to any unconscious force within persons but rather to a lack of awareness, "the ability of the client to be in full mental and sensory" contact and to be "experiencing the now" (Gilliland & James, 2003, p. 142).

Every person operates on some conscious level, ranging from very aware to very unaware. Healthy individuals are those who are most aware. Such people realize that body signs, such as headaches or stomach pains, may indicate a need to change behaviors. They are also conscious of personal limitations. For instance, in conflicts with others they may be able to resolve the situation or they may have to dismiss it. Healthy people avoid complicating such situations, refusing to embellish them with fantasy. Instead, they focus sharply on one need (*the figure*) at a time while relegating other needs to the background (*the ground*). When the need is met—or the Gestalt is closed or completed—it is relegated to the background and a new need comes into focus (becomes the figure) (Henderson & Thompson, 2011). Such functioning requires that persons recognize internal needs and learn how to manipulate those needs and the environment (Perls, 1976).

Personal Reflection

How do you recognize needs in your life? What do you do once you recognize needs?

According to Gestaltists, persons experience difficulties in several ways:

1. They may lose contact with the environment and the resources in it.
2. People may become overinvolved with the environment and thus grow out of touch with themselves.
3. Individuals may fail to put aside unfinished business.
4. They may become fragmented or scattered in many directions.
5. Persons may experience conflict between the **top dog** (what they think they should do) and the **underdog** (what they want to do).
6. People may have difficulty handling the dichotomies of life, such as love/hate, masculinity/femininity, and pleasure/pain (Assagioli, 1965).

Individuals who become neurotic try to attend to too many needs at one time and therefore do not take care of any one need fully. They also depend on others for care instead of caring for themselves, as they are capable of doing.

Planning and Evaluating

Understanding and Mastery: Analysis and assessment of the needs of clients and client groups

Critical Thinking Question: How can the Gestalt view of "neurotic individuals" help you and human services practitioners in analyzing what is going on in their lives?

Assess your comprehension of the <u>View of Human Nature/Personality</u> by taking this quiz.

Role of the Counselor

The role of the Gestalt clinician is to create an atmosphere that encourages clients to explore what they need to grow. Practitioners provide such a climate by being intensely and personally involved with clients, by being honest, and being non-judgmental (Miller, 2008). They must be exciting, energetic, and humane as well (Polster & Polster, 1973). Involvement occurs in the now, which is a continuing process (Perls,1969) in which practitioners help clients learn to redirect energy in positive and adaptive ways (Zinker, 1978). The now also entails helping clients recognize patterns in their lives (Fagan, 1970).

Gestalt therapists follow several rules in helping clients become more aware of the now (Levitsky & Perls, 1970):

- They follow the principle of **now**—always using the present tense
- An **"I-and-thou relationship"**—always addressing someone directly instead of talking about him or her
- The use of *I*—substituting the word *I* for *it*, especially when talking about one's body
- The use of an **awareness continuum**—focusing on how and what rather than why
- The **conversion of questions**—asking clients to convert questions into statements

Gestaltists do not use standardized assessment instruments, such as psychological tests. Furthermore, they do not diagnose their clients according to Diagnostic and Statistical Manual of Mental Disorders (DSM) classification standards. However, they do assess individuals they work with on their willingness to engage in activities that help them act and become more mature.

Goals

The goals of Gestalt therapy are well defined. They include an **emphasis** on the here and now and a recognition of the immediacy of experience (Bankart, 1997). The importance of these first two goals can be seen in the fact that the term *contact* is used to refer to the sensory and motor immediacy that can be experienced when the environment is met directly (Perls et al., 1951). Further goals include a focus on both nonverbal and verbal expression and on the concept that life involves making choices (Fagan & Shepherd, 1970).

The Gestalt approach concentrates on helping clients become integrated by resolving the past, completing the process of growing up mentally, and becoming mature (Perls, 1969). It emphasizes the coalescence of the emotional, cognitive, and behavioral aspects of a person. A primary focus is the acceptance of polarities within the person (Gelso & Carter, 1985).

As a group, Gestalt therapists stress **action**, pushing their clients to experience feelings and behaviors. They also emphasize the meaning of the word "**now**." Perls (1970) developed a formula that expresses the word's essence: "**Now = experience = awareness = reality**. The past is no more and the future not yet. Only the now exists" (p. 14).

To be mature in the now, a person must often shed neurotic tendencies. Perls (1970) identifies the following five layers of neurosis that interfere with being authentically in touch with oneself:

- **The phony layer** consists of pretending to be something that one is not, often involving game playing and fantasy enactment. When persons become more aware of the games they are playing, they can be more honest, open, and in touch with unpleasantness and pain.

- **The phobic layer** is an attempt to avoid recognizing aspects of oneself that an individual would prefer to deny. People at this layer of awareness are afraid that they will be rejected if they acknowledge who they are and present that to others.
- **The impasse layer** has no sense of direction. Individuals wonder how they are going to make it in the environment and are adrift in a sea of helplessness and dread.
- **The implosive and explosive layers** are often grouped together; people at these layers frequently feel vulnerable to feelings. As they peel back the layers of defensiveness built up over the years (the implosive layer), they may explode in intense feelings of joy, sorrow, or pain (the explosive layer). When persons reach this point, they can become authentic with themselves and others.

Assess your comprehension of the Goals by taking this quiz.

Personal Reflection

The Gestalt approach emphasizes action and resolution of the past while living in the present. What actions do you think people can take that will help them resolve matters in their lives? What is an advantage of doing as opposed to thinking?

Process and Techniques

Some of the most innovative counseling techniques ever developed are found in Gestalt therapy (Harman, 1997). These techniques take two forms—*exercises* and *experiments*. **Exercises** are ready-made techniques, such as the enactment of fantasies, role-playing, and psychodrama (Covin, 1977). They are employed to evoke a certain response from clients, such as anger or exploration. **Experiments**, on the other hand, are activities that grow out of the interaction between counselors and clients. They are not planned, and what is learned is often a surprise to both participants. Even though many of the techniques of Gestalt therapy do take the form of unplanned experiments (Zinker, 1978), the concentration here is on exercise-oriented techniques.

Intervention and Direct Services

Understanding and Mastery: Skills to facilitate appropriate direct services and interventions related to specific client or client group goals

Critical Thinking Question: What are the strengths and drawbacks to using experiments?

One common exercise is **dream work**. Perls describes dreams as messages that represent a person's place at a certain time (Bernard, 1986). Unlike psychoanalysts, however, Gestalt counselors do not interpret; instead, clients present dreams and are then directed to experience what it is like to be in each part of the dream—a type of dramatized free association. In this way clients get more in touch with the multiple aspects of themselves. Individuals with repetitive dreams are encouraged to realize that unfinished business is being brought into their awareness and that they need to take care of the message being delivered.

FIGURE 6.1
The Empty Chair.

Another effective technique is the **empty chair** (see Figure 6.1). In this procedure clients focus on an empty chair and talk to the various parts of their personality, such as the part that is dominant and the part that is passive. Clients may use the chair as a representative of the self or may use different chairs to represent different parts of themselves. In this dialogue both rational and irrational parts of the client come into focus, and the client becomes able to deal with the inner dichotomies. Overall, the empty chair technique is a three-stage model: *opposition, merging,* and *integration.* It works well with many clients, such as those who may be in a pre-divorce situation (Mackay, 2002), but it is not recommended for the severely emotionally disturbed (Bernard, 1986).

One of the most powerful Gestalt exercises is confrontation. In **confrontation,** counselors point out to clients incongruent behaviors and feelings, such as smiling when nervous. Confrontation involves asking clients what and how questions. Why questions are avoided because they lead to intellectualization. Therapists may purposely frustrate their clients to help them move beyond present states of denial (Harman, 1975), hoping that clients will make valuable interpretations when confronted. Techniques that center on working in the here and now help clients focus on breaking out of old habits and becoming more in touch with themselves.

Other powerful Gestalt exercises that are oriented to individuals are often used in groups (Harman, 1997):

- **Making the rounds.** Counselors use this exercise when a particular theme or feeling should be faced by every person in the group. For instance, one client may say, "I can't stand anyone," and is then instructed to repeat this sentence to each person in the group, adding some remarks about each group member. The exercise is flexible and may include nonverbal as well as positive feelings. It helps clients become more aware of inner feelings.
- **I take responsibility.** In this exercise clients make statements about perceptions and close each statement with the phrase "and I take responsibility for it." The exercise helps clients integrate and own their perceptions and behaviors.

- **Exaggeration.** Clients accentuate their own unwitting movements or gestures and in the process make the inner meaning of these behaviors more apparent.
- **May I feed you a sentence?** Aware of implicit attitudes or messages in what a client is saying, the counselor asks whether the client will repeat a certain sentence that makes the client's thoughts explicit. If the counselor is correct about the underlying message, the client will gain insight as the sentence is repeated.

Personal Reflection

Which of the exercises just described appeals the most to you? Ask yourself what it is about the exercise that you think would be most effective in bringing about change in someone.
● ●

Assess your comprehension of the <u>Process and Techniques</u> by taking this quiz.

Multicultural Issues

Multiculturalism deals with culture, gender, disability, sexual orientation, socioeconomic disadvantage, and the world of military service. Gestalt therapy is widely used throughout the world, for example, in a recent survey of European psychotherapy training, Gestalt therapy was one of only four modalities practiced in the majority of the 32 countries polled (Zerbetto & Tantam, 2001). One reason for this popularity may be that Gestalt experiments can be used "to help individuals deal with and perceive their own culture" (Sharf, 2012, p. 272). Gestalt experiments may also help clients recognize polarities between cultures in which they live, such as a minority culture within a majority culture.

> ### Self-Development
>
> *Understanding and Mastery: Awareness of diversity*
>
> Critical Thinking Question: How can helping individuals deal with and perceive their own culture contribute to their self-development?

However, because Gestalt therapy is very individualistic, it contrasts sharply with cultures that are more oriented to group values and traditions. Thus, for Gestalt therapy to be practiced effectively and ethically in such communities, it needs to focus more attention on the importance of human interconnectedness (Ivey, D'Andrea, & Ivey, 2012).

Gestalt therapy is probably as open to sensitive gender issues as any other counseling modality. At its conception and during its formative years, the approach was influenced strongly by women, such as Laura Perls, Joen Fagan, and Irma Lee Shepherd.

Evaluation of the Theory

Strengths and Contributions

A strength of Gestalt therapy is its emphasis on helping people incorporate and accept all aspects of their lives. An individual cannot be understood outside the context of the whole person, who is choosing to act on the environment in the present (Levine, 2012; Passons, 1975). The Gestalt approach also helps lients focus on resolving areas of unfinished business so that their lives can be lived productively.

A third contribution of Gestalt therapy is that it places primary emphasis on doing rather than talking. Activity helps individuals experience what the process of change is about and thus make more rapid progress. In addition, the change is likely to be enduring (Melnick, 2003).

Furthermore, the Gestalt approach is flexible and is not limited to a few techniques (Mann, 2010; Yontef & Jacobs, 2011). Any activity that helps clients become more integrative can be employed in Gestalt therapy. Such activities are readily available in the *Gestalt Journal*, "the literary organ that disseminates research, theory, and innovative techniques of the approach" (Gilliland & James, 2003, p. 137).

A final strength of Gestalt therapy is its appropriateness for certain affective disorders, anxiety states, somatoform disorders, adjustment disorders, occupational problems and interpersonal problems (Glinnwater, 2000). In short, Gestalt therapy is versatile.

Limitations and Criticisms

Gestalt therapy lacks a strong theoretical base. In fact, some critics view Gestalt counseling as all experience and technique—that is, too gimmicky (Corey, 2013). They maintain that it is antitheoretical and often cite a line from Fritz Perls: "Lose your mind and come to your senses."

A second limitation of Gestalt therapy is that it deals strictly with the now and how of experience (Perls, 1969). Thus, it does not allow for passive insight and internal change, which some clients are more likely to use.

Still another criticism of Gestalt therapy is that it eschews diagnosis and testing in formal ways, such as using the DSM or standardized tests. However, Gestalt clinicians do assess. For example, they screen individuals before exposing them to their intense methods of promoting therapeutic change.

Assess your comprehension of the Evaluation of the Theory by taking this quiz.

Finally, Gestalt therapy is too concerned with individual development and a self-centered approach to helping; it focuses primarily on feelings and personal discovery. Although many other counseling theories are also centered on individual development, Gestalt therapy is considered extreme by some. An example of its self-centeredness is seen in the Gestalt prayer which centers around being yourself, not living up to anyone's expectations, and letting relationships happen (Perls, 1969).

Treating Linda with Gestalt Therapy

Conceptualization

From the perspective of Gestalt therapy, Linda is having relationship problems but her difficulties are as much internal as they are external. Linda is not aware of how fragmented she is as a person and how much unfinished business she has in regard to her family of origin and her former husband. Although Linda did some mild acting out as a teenager, she was mostly submissive, as her father insisted. Instead of breaking away from family constraints by going to college, she denied herself that opportunity and instead earned a two-year degree locally in an area in which she was not even interested. As a result, Linda has hopped from one glorified secretarial position to another because of boredom. Externally she blames the situation on her bosses, but internally she blames herself.

In addition to her resentment about the past, Linda is angry about her present situation. She is lonely and does not have a support system. Consequently, she reads fantasy novels and watches exciting movies and instructional television programs. All of this activity is an attempt to escape rather than construct a productive life.

Treatment Process

As a Gestaltist you establish rapport with Linda and then begin to challenge her in regard to what she is aware of and what she is doing now. At first Linda wants to guide you back into the past and discuss what has been, but you insist on staying in the present, even if it involves dealing with unfinished business. You direct Linda to be an actor as opposed to a reactor. You are also adamant that she use *I* messages to promote responsibility and that she focus on how rather than why questions. You notice that Linda sometimes smiles when she talks about being abused by her husband or put down by her father. To get her to be more aware, you call her on this action, saying that she is playing games and being phony. Linda becomes angry with you in the process but continues in therapy.

In order to help Linda become more congruent and real, you ask her to engage in some anger exercises with you. In one of these she shows you, by hitting a pillow with her hand, how angry certain events, people, or situations make her. As Linda completes this exercise, she starts growling spontaneously each time she hits the pillow. You then move her into a chair and have her talk as the more active person she is now to the inactive, passive side of herself. She switches chairs as she switches from active to passive. This empty chair technique helps her to integrate her life. As homework you ask her to keep a diary of her dreams and to bring it with her each time so that she can reenact and understand the messages that her unconscious is sending her.

As Linda continues to be active in therapy, she begins to gain insight into what she is doing and feels more empowered. She realizes she cannot dwell on what has been but can live in the now. She decides to complete a four-year degree, join a women's support group, and participate in several community clubs that engage in interesting activities, such as biking and cooking. She lets her family know what she is doing and talks with them about how she is changing. She resists their attempts to pull her back and continues to develop greater self-awareness as she begins to accomplish new tasks.

Summary and Conclusion

Gestalt therapy has been a force in the field of counseling and therapy since the 1950s. It was initially associated primarily with Fritz Perls; but since Perls's death in 1970, a number of other proponents—including Dave Mann, Gary Yontef, Talia Bar-Yoseph Levine, Philip Brownell, and Phil and Charlotte Sills—have been its main developers as well as its strong advocates.

As a therapeutic modality Gestalt therapy is action oriented. It stresses acting in the present, that is, the now. Basically, changes in thoughts and feelings follow changes in behaviors. Gestalt therapy uses both structured exercises and spontaneous experiments. Exercises are planned, whereas experiments grow out of client/counselor relationships. Both may lead clients to greater awareness of themselves and others, which is a primary goal.

Although the Gestalt approach does help individuals and groups act differently, it has been criticized for not having a stronger theoretical base and for dealing too much with the here and now, eschewing formal diagnosis and standardized tests, while being too self-centered, that is, focused on the individual. Nevertheless, Gestalt therapy is quite flexible and holistic, helps clients resolve unfinished business, and is appropriate for certain affective disorders.

Recall what you learned in this chapter by reviewing and completing the Chapter Review.

CHAPTER 7

Choice Theory/ Reality Therapy

Blue Jean Images/Alamy

Choice Theory, originally referred to as **reality therapy**, was formulated by William Glasser in the early 1960s. It began as a major theoretical approach in 1965 with the publication of Glasser's book *Reality Therapy* (1965). This approach emphasizes choices that people can make to change their lives and focuses on two general concepts: the environment necessary for conducting counseling and the procedures leading to change (Wubbolding, 1998, 2011). It is usually essential to establish a safe environment before change can occur.

Reality therapy is a flexible, friendly, and firm approach to working with clients. It is also action oriented. Overall, it emphasizes the fulfillment of psychological needs, the resolution of personal difficulties, and the prevention of future problems.

Major Theorist: William Glasser

William Glasser (1925–2013) was born in Cleveland, Ohio, the third and youngest child in a close-knit family. He describes his childhood as happy and uneventful, but like his theory he does not emphasize the past. In school he played in the band and developed a strong interest in sports. After graduating at the age of 19 from the Case Institute of Technology with a degree in chemical engineering, he began graduate work in clinical psychology. He finished work for a master's degree in 1948, but his doctoral dissertation was rejected. He then entered medical school at Western Reserve University, graduating with a medical degree in 1953.

Glasser moved to California with his wife, Naomi Judith Silver, for a psychiatric residency at UCLA, which he completed in 1957. Although he hoped to establish a private psychiatric practice, he found that referrals were slow in coming because of his open resistance to traditional psychoanalytic treatment. Therefore, he took a position as head psychiatrist at the Ventura School for Girls, a state-operated facility for juvenile delinquents.

At Ventura in the 1960s, Glasser began to formalize his approach to counseling. As a resident his doubts about the effectiveness of classical psychoanalysis had been supported by one of his faculty supervisors, G. L. Harrington. Harrington helped Glasser develop some of the basic tenets of reality therapy and even assisted Glasser in verifying these primary concepts. Glasser's first book, *Mental Health or Mental Illness?* (1961), contained many of the ideas that were later more formally expressed in *Reality Therapy: A New Approach to Psychiatry* (1965). Glasser developed reality therapy because he thought "conventional psychiatry wastes too much time arguing over how many diagnoses can dance at the end of a case history" (1965, p. 49). He wanted an approach that was practical and more easily understood by both clinicians and the public. By using the basic principles of reality therapy, he was able to cut recidivism at the Ventura School to only 20 percent.

Shortly after the publication of *Reality Therapy*, Glasser founded the Institute of Reality Therapy in Canoga Park, California, where he did some of his most creative work. He applied reality therapy to school settings in *Schools without Failure* (1969) and to areas of identity in *The Identity Society* (1972). In *Positive Addiction* (1976) he asserted that individuals can become stronger instead of weaker from so-called addictive habits; for example, both jogging and meditation may improve physical and mental health.

In 1981 Glasser linked his original ideas with **control theory**, which argues that all behavior is generated internally. Thus, the only thing that people obtain from the outside world is information (Glasser, 1988). Two of Glasser's books, *Stations of the Mind* (1981) and *Control Theory: A New Explanation of How We Control Our Lives* (1984), reflect this theoretical stance and emphasize how the brain influences inner perceptions. However, Glasser abandoned control theory as a part of his approach in 1996 and incorporated **choice theory** in its place, asserting that people choose to be the way they are. This tenet is reflected in Glasser's most recent books.

View of Human Nature/Personality

Reality therapy does not include a comprehensive explanation of human development, as Freud's system does. Instead, it offers practitioners a focused view of some important aspects of human life and human nature. One major tenet of reality therapy is its focus on consciousness: Human beings operate on a conscious level and are not driven by unconscious forces or instincts (Glasser, 1965, 1988).

A second belief about human nature is that a health/growth force exists within everyone (Glasser & Wubbolding, 1995). This force is manifested on two levels—the physical and the psychological. Physically, there is the need to obtain and use life-sustaining necessities such as food, water, and shelter. According to Glasser, human behavior was once controlled by the physical need for survival. He associates behaviors such as breathing, digesting, and sweating with physical, or old-brain, needs because they are

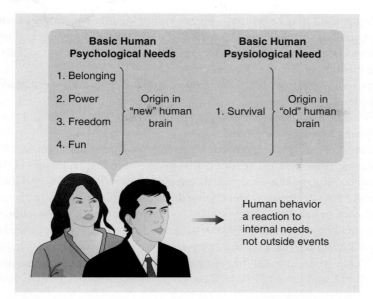

FIGURE 7.1
Basic Needs According to Reality Therapy.
Source: From Samuel T. Gladding *Group Work: A Counseling Specialty* (4th ed., p. 402). Copyright 2003. Reprinted by permission of Pearson Education, Inc., Upper Saddle River, NJ.

automatically controlled by the body. In modern times, most important behavior is associated with psychological, or new-brain, needs. The four primary psychological needs include the following:

- **Belonging**—the need for friends, family, and love
- **Power**—the need for self-esteem, recognition, and competition
- **Freedom**—the need to make choices and decisions
- **Fun**—the need for play, laughter, learning, and recreation (see Figure 7.1)

Personal Reflection

What do you do for fun? Think of at least three things.

Associated with these psychological needs is the need for **identity**, that is, a psychologically healthy sense of self. Identity needs are met when a person is accepted by others. Especially important in this process is the experience of love and worth. When these needs are met, people achieve a **success identity**; those whose needs are not met establish a **failure identity**, a maladjusted personality characterized by a lack of confidence and a tendency to give up easily. Because "almost everyone is personally engaged in a search for acceptance as a person rather than as a performer of a task," personal identity precedes performance (Glasser, 1972, p. 10).

In regard to identity, Glasser thinks there are two critical periods in children's lives. First, between the ages of 2 and 5, children learn *early socialization skills*—such as, how to relate to their parents, siblings, and friends—and they begin to deal with frustrations and disappointments. During this period, children especially need the love, acceptance, guidance, and involvement of their parents. If these are not

Human Systems

Understanding and Mastery: Theories of human development

Critical Thinking Question: Do you think performance could ever precede personal identity, and if so, what might that mean for someone achieving a success identity?

forthcoming, a child may begin to establish a failure identity. Second, between the ages of 5 and 10, children are *involved with school, where they gain knowledge and self concept.* Many children establish a failure identity during this period because of socialization difficulties or learning problems (Glasser, 1969).

Reality therapy proposes that *human learning is a lifelong process based on choice.* If individuals do not learn something early in life, such as how to relate to others, they can choose to learn it later. In the process they may change their identity and the way they behave (Glasser & Wubbolding, 1995).

A final tenet of reality therapy is a new psychology of personal freedom called choice theory (Glasser, 1998, 2000). The idea is that people have mental images of their needs and behave accordingly; thus, individuals are ultimately *self determining* (Glasser, 1984; Wubbolding, 1994). Individuals can choose to be miserable or mentally disturbed; they may also choose to behave in positive ways and give up trying to control others. People who are mentally healthy are in noncontrolling relationships with significant others, such as a parent, a child, a spouse, or an employee/employer. They choose to "care, listen, support, negotiate, encourage, love, befriend, trust, accept, welcome, and esteem" rather than "coerce, force, compel, punish, reward, manipulate, boss, motivate, criticize, blame, complain, nag, badger, rank, rate, and withdraw" (Glasser, 1998, p. 21).

Assess your comprehension of the View of Human Nature/Personality by taking this quiz.

Role of the Counselor

Practitioners who use reality therapy serve primarily as teachers and models, accepting their clients in a warm, involved way and creating an environment in which choice and change can take place. They immediately seek to build relationships with clients by developing trust through friendliness, firmness, and fairness (Wubbolding, 1998, 2000). They also use -*ing* verbs, such as angering or bullying, to describe clients' thoughts and actions. Thus, there is an emphasis on choice, on what clients choose to do. Counselor-client interactions focus on behaviors that clients would like to change and ways to go about achieving these desires. Positive, constructive actions are emphasized (Glasser, 1988), with special attention paid to metaphors and themes that clients verbalize.

There is little attempt by those who use reality therapy to test, diagnose, interpret, or otherwise analyze clients' actions, except to ask questions such as, *"What are you doing now?" "Is it working?"* and *"What are the consequences?"* Reality therapists do not concentrate on early childhood experiences, clients' insights, aspects of the unconscious, mental illness, blame, or stimulus-response perception of interaction. They emphasize aspects of the clients' lives that can be controlled and give little consideration to the latest editions of diagnostic manuals.

Planning and Evaluation

Understanding and Mastery: Analysis and assessment of the needs of clients or client groups

Critical Thinking Question: Can clients and client groups be functional if they do not always have choices and concentrate on what they can control?

Goals

The primary goal of reality therapy is to help clients become psychologically strong and rational and realize that they have choices in how they treat themselves and others. If this goal is reached, individuals become autonomous and responsible (Wallace, 1986;

Wubbolding, 1988, 1991). **Responsible behavior** allows individuals to take charge of their actions and obtain their goals; it also keeps them from interfering with others or getting into trouble. In addition, it leads to the formation of a **success identity**, which enables clients to live more productive and harmonious lives. Glasser (1981) contends that to help people "we must help them gain strength to do worthwhile things with their lives and at the same time become warmly involved with the people they need" (p. 48). Reality therapy strives to prevent problems from occurring.

A second goal is to help clients clarify what they want in life; it is vital for individuals to be aware of their life goals if they are to act responsibly. In assessing goals, reality therapists help their clients examine personal assets as well as environmental supports and hindrances. It is then the responsibility of clients to choose behaviors that fulfill personal needs. Glasser (1976) lists six criteria with which to judge whether a person is choosing a suitable and healthy behavior.

1. The behavior is *noncompetitive.*
2. The behavior is *easily completed without a great deal of mental effort.*
3. The behavior *can be done by oneself.*
4. The behavior **has** *value for the person.*
5. The client believes that *improvements in lifestyle will result from the behavior.*
6. The client *can practice the behavior without being self-critical.*

Another goal of reality therapy is to help clients *formulate a realistic and viable plan* to achieve personal needs and wishes. Poor mental health is sometimes the result of not knowing how to achieve what has been planned. Glasser advocates that plans be as specific and concrete as possible. Once a plan is formulated, alternative behaviors, decisions, and outcomes are examined; often a contract is written. The focus is on helping individuals become more responsible and realize that no single plan is absolute. According to Wubbolding (2007), a viable plan has eight features and can be represented by the acronym SAM I2 C3:

- **Simple**—clear, understandable
- **Attainable**—can be accomplished by the client
- **Measurable**—tangibly such as recording what was done, when
- **Immediate**—can be started on right away
- **Involving** the clinician in some appropriate way such as giving feedback
- **Controlled** by the client—not under the control of someone else
- **Committed** to be kept by the client realizing change is important
- **Consistent** in that the client will keep at it and repeated needed changes

An additional goal of reality therapy is to have counselors establish meaningful relationships with their clients (Glasser, 1980, 1981). Such relationships are based on understanding, acceptance, empathy, and a willingness to express faith in a client's ability to change. Counselors help their clients establish boundaries for behaviors but do not give up on their clients if they are unable to complete a behavior. Often, to facilitate effective relationships, those who work from a reality therapy basis risk disclosing personal information to clients.

Another goal of reality therapy is to focus on behavior and the present. Glasser (1988) believes that **behavior**—that is, thought and action—is interrelated with feeling and physiology. Thus, a change in behavior also brings about other positive changes. Basically, Glasser emphasizes now activities because they can be controlled by clients, who have no control over the past.

Finally, reality therapy aims to eliminate both fear of punishment and excuses from clients' lives. Clients often use the excuse that they cannot formulate and carry out a plan because they fear being punished by either their counselors or outside people if they fail. Reality therapy helps clients formulate new plans if old ones do not work. The emphasis is on planning, revision, and eventual success, regardless of setbacks. The entire procedure empowers clients and enables them to be more productive.

Assess your comprehension of the Goals by taking this quiz.

Personal Reflection

What "now activities" are you engaged in? How are you enjoying them? How productive are they for you?

Process and Techniques

Reality therapy relies on **action-oriented techniques** that help clients realize that they have choices in how they respond to events and people and that others do not control them any more than they control others (Glasser, 1998). Some of the more effective and active techniques are: teaching, employing humor, confronting, role playing, giving feedback, formulating specific plans, and making contracts.

Interventions and Direct Services

Understanding and Mastery: Skills to facilitate appropriate direct services and interventions related to specific client or client group goals

Critical Thinking Question: How are Glasser's interventions similar and different from those you have seen in other theoretical approaches?

Reality therapy relies heavily on **teaching** as a primary technique. Glasser (1965) states that "the **specialized learning situation** . . . is made up of three separate but interwoven procedures" (p. 21). First, there is **involvement** between counselors and clients in which clients begin to face reality and see that a behavior is unrealistic. Second, therapists reject the **unrealistic behavior** of their clients without rejecting the clients as persons. Finally, counselors teach clients better ways to fulfill needs within the confines of reality. One strategy that counselors use is **positiveness**, in which they talk about, focus on, and reinforce positive and constructive planning and behaving (Gilliland & James, 2003).

In reality therapy, **humor** is the ability to see the absurdity within a situation and view matters from a different and amusing perspective. It is an appropriate technique if used sparingly. Most clients do not instinctively see difficult situations as funny; yet if counselors offer a well-timed remark, clients may come to see some silliness in their behavior. The ability to laugh at oneself promotes the ability to change because the situation can be seen in a new and often insightful way. Humor should never be used as a sarcastic put-down, because use in this way usually leads to a deterioration of the therapeutic relationship and adversely affect the process of change.

In **confrontation**, counselors challenge clients about certain behaviors as a way of helping clients accept responsibility for their actions. This procedure does not differ much from the confrontation used in other approaches. **Role playing** in reality therapy is also similar to that employed in other counseling approaches. However, its purpose in reality therapy is to help clients bring the past or future into the present and assess how life will be different when they start behaving differently. Role plays are almost always followed by counselor feedback. After specific plans are formulated for improving their lives, clients develop contracts to carry out these plans in a timely and systematic way.

Reality therapy uses the **WDEP system** as a way of helping counselors and clients make progress. In this system, the *W* stands for **wants**; at the beginning of the counseling process, counselors find out what clients want and what they have been doing to get it (Wubbolding, 1988, 1991, 2000). Counselors, in turn, share their wants for and perceptions of clients' situations. The *D* in WDEP involves clients' exploration of the **direction** of their lives. The effective and ineffective self-talk that clients use is discussed. Strategically incorporated in these two steps are establishing a relationship and focusing on present behavior.

The *E* in the WDEP process stands for **evaluation**, which is the cornerstone of reality therapy. In this procedure clients are helped to evaluate their behaviors and determine how responsible their personal behaviors are. Behaviors that do not contribute to meeting client needs often alienate clients from themselves and significant others. If clients recognize a behavior as unproductive, they may be motivated to change. But if there is no recognition, the therapeutic process may break down. It is crucial, therefore, that clients, not counselors, do the evaluation.

The final letter *P*, of the WDEP system stands for **plan**, which clients make to change behaviors. The plan stresses actions that clients will take, not behaviors that they will eliminate. The best plans are simple, attainable, measurable, immediate, and consistent (Wubbolding, 1998, 2000). They are also controlled by clients and are often supported by written contracts in which responsible alternatives are spelled out.

Clients are then requested to make a commitment to the action plans. Therapists make it clear that no excuses will be accepted for failing to carry out plans of action; neither will there be blame or punish. Thus, responsibility is placed entirely on clients. If they fail to accomplish their plans, Glasser thinks they should suffer the natural or reasonable consequences of that failure (Evans, 1982).

According to Glasser (1965, 1980), reality therapists should not give up on their clients even if they fail to accomplish their goals. Instead, counselors should stubbornly and tenaciously encourage their clients to make new plans or revise old ones. Most clients, who are used to being put down or abandoned when goals are not achieved, find in Glasser's approach an opportunity to alter that cycle of failure.

Assess your comprehension of the <u>Process and Techniques</u> by taking this quiz.

Personal Reflection

Do you think there are some clients that counselors should give up on? When have you been tenacious and made new plans instead of giving up?

Multicultural Issues

Multiculturalism deals with culture, gender, disability, sexual orientation, socioeconomic disadvantage, and the world of military service. Reality therapy respects cultural differences. Clients "decide on the changes they wish to make that are consistent with their own cultural values" (Sharf, 2012, p. 445). Thus, reality therapy focuses on the responsibility of clients to themselves, others, and society. This emphasis puts it in accord with American-Indian, Asian, and Asian-American value systems (Ivey, D'Andrea, & Ivey, 2012). In addition, reality therapy has actually been used with a wide range of people from varied cultures, including African-American, Korean, Latino, and Saudi Arabian. However, reality therapy "does not take into account environmental forces such as discrimination and racism that affect people from different cultures" (Sharf, 2012, p. 445).

In regard to gender issues, reality therapy emphasizes the empowerment of clients to make choices regardless of their gender. This approach may be especially good for men who are achievement oriented because it concentrates on specific plans and behaviors without broaching the area of feelings and emotions, which many men eschew. However, this therapy may be limited in what it can do for women because it does not advocate for social change or address societal ills, such as sexism.

Evaluation of the Theory

Strengths and Contributions

First of all, reality therapy is *versatile*. It can be applied to many different disorders and populations; it is especially appropriate in treating conduct disorders, substance-abuse disorders, impulse-control disorders, personality disorders, and antisocial behavior. It can also be employed in individual counseling with children, adolescents, adults, and the aged as well as in group, marriage, and family counseling. This approach has such flexibility that it is helpful in almost any setting that emphasizes mental health and adjustment, such as hospitals, mental health clinics, schools, prisons, rehabilitation centers, and crisis centers (Glasser, 1986, 2000; Seligman, 1997).

A second advantage of reality therapy is its *concreteness*. Both counselors and clients are able to assess how much progress is being made and in what areas, especially if a goal-specific contract is drawn up. When clients are doing well in modifying one behavior but not another, increased attention can be given to the underdeveloped area.

Another advantage of reality therapy is that it *promotes responsibility and freedom* within individuals without blaming or criticizing or attempting to restructure entire personalities. To act in a responsible manner is "to fulfill one's needs, and to do so in a way that does not deprive others of the ability to fulfill their needs" (Glasser, 1965, p. 13). Many individuals need help in becoming responsible, and reality therapy provides this assistance.

Reality therapy also addresses the **resolution of conflict**. Glasser (1984) believes that conflict occurs on two levels, true and false. On the **true** level, conflict develops over interpersonal disagreements about change. In such cases no single solution exists, and people should expend their energy in other, nonconflict areas. In **false** conflict, however, such as losing weight, change is possible if persons are willing to give the effort. Responsible behavior in such situations can bring resolutions.

An additional strength of reality therapy is its stress on the **present**; current behavior is most amenable to clients' control. Reality therapists are not interested in the past.

Furthermore, reality therapy emphasizes **short-term treatment**. It is usually limited to a relatively few sessions, which focus on present behaviors. Clients work with conscious and verifiable objectives that can be achieved quickly. This approach is especially valuable in a time-limited, managed care environment.

One other strength of reality therapy is that it has national training centers. The Institute for Reality Therapy in Los Angeles and the Center for Reality Therapy in Cincinnati promote a uniform educational experience among practitioners employing this theory. The centers also publish professional literature.

Finally, reality therapy has contributed to counseling by successfully challenging the medical model of client treatment. The rationale and positive emphasis of this approach are refreshing alternatives to pathology-centered models.

Limitations and Criticisms

By emphasizing so strongly the here and now of behavior, reality therapy tends to ignore other concepts, such as the *unconscious* and *personal history*. However, people may sometimes be informed by the unconscious, for example, in dreams; or persons may need to relive and resolve past traumas. Reality therapy makes little allowance for these situations.

A second limitation of reality therapy is its belief that all forms of mental illness are attempts to deal with external events (Glasser, 1984). Mental illness does not just happen, Glasser contends; persons choose mental illness to help control their world. Thus, Glasser ignores biology as a factor in mental illness, a stance considered by some critics to be naive and irresponsible.

Reality therapy is also criticized for being too simple because it has few theoretical constructs. Even though it is becoming more sophisticated by virtue of its link to choice theory, reality therapy does not deal with the full complexity of human life, preferring to ignore most developmental stages. Thus, its critics state that the theory behind the therapy lacks comprehensiveness.

Another limitation is that reality therapy is susceptible to becoming overly moralistic, a potential difficulty rather than a certain disadvantage. Glasser (1972) asserts that reality therapy was never intended to function in this way. Therapists who practice reality therapy are not to judge clients' behaviors; clients judge their own behaviors. The role of therapists is to support their clients in a personal exploration of values. Nonetheless, overzealous practitioners may impose their values on clients.

Yet another limitation of reality therapy is its dependence on establishing a good counselor-client relationship. Without sufficient involvement, counselors may settle for general client goals, force a plan, or proceed too quickly to commitment (Wubbolding, 1975).

A related limitation of reality therapy is its dependence on verbal interaction and two-way communication. As a consequence, it may falter in helping clients who, for any reason, cannot adequately express their needs, options, and plans (James & Gilliland, 2003).

Finally, reality therapy keeps changing its focus and emphasis, despite an initial denial of that charge by Glasser (1976). Acceptance is now emphasized more than it previously was. Furthermore, the integration of control theory

Assess your comprehension of the <u>Evaluation of the Theory</u> by taking this quiz.

and then its replacement by choice theory as the bedrock of the approach necessarily altered the theory's earlier focus. Thus far there has been no attempt to document these changes and to note which emphases are most essential to the practice, leaving reality therapy less well understood and utilized than it might otherwise be.

Treating Linda with Choice Theory/Reality Therapy

Conceptualization

From the perspective of reality therapy, Linda is avoiding making choices. She has let others decide for her, such as whether to have a baby. Thus, she has a number of excuses as to why her life has been relatively unproductive. In addition, Linda has not taken care of her psychological need for belonging, power, freedom, and fun. By neglecting these needs, Linda has taken on a failure identity.

However, Linda can choose to be different. She can choose to be in noncontrolling relationships with her family and friends. Furthermore, she can choose to take other constructive action and stop failing and depressing herself. If she makes these choices, Linda can become more autonomous, responsible, and successful. She can also clarify what she wants in life and find internal and external support for realistic pursuit of her goals. Thus, her mental health can improve, and she will be able to live in the present in a productive way.

Treatment Process

As a reality therapist, you are active in Linda's treatment process. You base your work on a good, strong, and trusting client-counselor relationship. You try to teach her how she can reject unrealistic behaviors without rejecting herself or being rejected by you. And you reinforce her positive and constructive plans and behaviors.

You use humor with Linda as she gains insight into herself and sees the folly of her ways. However, you are mostly serious and confront Linda with the fact that she is responsible for her actions, especially now in the present. You role-play with her how she can act responsibly.

After you confront, you use the WDEP system to help Linda articulate her wants and the direction she wishes to travel. You help her evaluate behaviors that will contribute to her growth, and then you support her in formulating a plan for moving on. As a part of this process, you draw up a contract with Linda to help her see how she is carrying out her ambitions. Even though Linda has been discriminated against in the past and treated in sexist ways, you do not dwell on what has been or what might recur. Instead, you encourage and support her as she begins anew.

When Linda fails to carry out some part of her plan, such as returning to college, you do not blame or punish her. Instead, you help her formulate another plan. For Linda the ultimate achievement is to become more responsible and free and to accomplish that within a relatively brief period of time.

Summary and Conclusion

Reality therapy is an ever-evolving system of counseling that began with William Glasser in the 1960s. It focuses on present situations that clients wish to modify or change. Counselors work to establish collaborative relationships with their clients and use those relationships to help clients develop plans involving choices that are concrete and goal oriented. Excuses and blame are not a part of the process, and counselors do not give up on their clients.

Counselors use a number of techniques to help clients reach their goals. Besides strong relationships and persistence, counselors also teach, use humor, confront, and role-play with clients. Wubbolding's WDEP system—wants, direction, evaluation, plan—is sometimes used as a guide to help counselors evaluate what they need to do to help their clients be successful. If all goes well, clients become more focused and skilled in reaching realistic and productive goals.

Recall what you learned in this chapter by reviewing and completing the Chapter Review.

CHAPTER 8

Behavioral Therapies

Comstock Images/Thinkstock

Chapter Outline

Behavioral theories and the origins of behavioral therapy date back to the beginning of the 20th century. They focus on how to reinforce, extinguish, or modify a broad range of behaviors. Over the years these approaches have become quite popular because people who seek counseling often have difficulties that are due to behavioral deficits, excessive behaviors, or a repertoire of inappropriate behaviors.

The term **behavioral** encompasses a wide range of ideas, practices, and theories. In its infancy (1900s–1930s), behaviorism was concerned almost entirely with external observations and was promoted as a scientific approach to the study of human life. The first major advocate for behaviorism was John B. Watson (1913, 1925), who used his work with a child named Little Albert to demonstrate that human emotions are amenable to *conditioning* (Watson & Raynor, 1920). After World War I, behaviorist ideas were explored by researchers such as Mary Cover Jones (1924), who demonstrated how a process known as *counterconditioning* can be employed to help people overcome phobic reactions.

In the 1940s and 1950s behaviorism achieved even more prominence. In this period, behavioral therapists were seen as scientific practitioners who based their work on research. Prominent behaviorists included B. F. Skinner (1953) and his work in operant conditioning, Joseph Wolpe (1958) and his study of respondent conditioning, Hans Eysenck (1960) and his treatment of abnormal behavior, and Albert Bandura (Bandura & Walters, 1963) and his study of the effects of vicarious learning. During the 1950s the term **behavior therapy** was introduced to describe diverse behavioral approaches to resolving client problems (Yates, 1970).

John Krumboltz (1966) is credited as being one of the major personalities to popularize behaviorism in counseling. He drew upon Bandura's earlier work and revolutionized the counseling profession of his time with behavioral concepts such as observational learning (Hosford, 1980). Krumboltz's ideas, as well as behaviorism in general, gained widespread acceptance in the 1970s. By the late 1980s behavioral approaches to therapy had generally split into three main theories: the stimulus-response model, applied behavior analysis, and social-cognitive theory.

This chapter examines the dominant forms of behavioral counseling approaches, except cognitive-behaviorism, which is covered in the next chapter. As a school of thought, behaviorists "stress instrumental rationality, control over emotions, enhanced human liberty, efficiency in ways of achieving self-defined goals, and opposition to irrational authority or arbitrary privilege" (Christopher, 1996, pp. 19–20).

Major Theorist: B. F. Skinner

B. F. (Burrhus Frederick) Skinner (1904–1990) was born in Susquehanna, Pennsylvania. He was the older of two sons, but his younger brother died at the age of 16. Skinner's home environment was warm, comfortable, and stable, imbued with the virtues of small-town, middle-class America at the turn of the century (Skinner, 1976). His parents did not use corporal punishment.

Skinner's father, a wealthy attorney, wanted his son to become an attorney also, but Skinner showed skills in other areas, such as an early facility with mechanical devices. The young Skinner made roller skate scooters, blow guns, model airplanes, and a flotation system to separate green from ripe elderberries (Skinner, 1967). These inventions were precursors of later devices, such as the infant air crib and the Skinner Box. Skinner was also interested in animal behavior and was highly impressed by a troupe of performing pigeons at a country fair. He later used pigeons to demonstrate aspects of his theory, teaching them to do a variety of tasks. In addition, Skinner enjoyed music and played the saxophone in a jazz band.

As a young adult, Skinner wanted to be a writer. He majored in English literature at Hamilton College, where he earned Phi Beta Kappa honors and graduated in 1926. Back home, he set about the task of writing, having been encouraged in his efforts by Robert Frost. After a year, he moved to New York's Greenwich Village to live among writers and benefit from a stimulating environment. There he discovered the works of Ivan Pavlov and John B. Watson, as well as those of Bertrand Russell and Francis Bacon. Soon he gave up his writing ambitions to become a psychologist, although he had never taken a psychology course in college. He was accepted for graduate study at Harvard, where he received a master's degree in 1930 and a Ph.D. in 1931. After another five years of postdoctoral training, he joined the faculty of the University of Minnesota in 1936, the same year in which he married Yvonne Blue.

Skinner's first book, *The Behavior of Organisms* (1938), was followed by other major works, and he rapidly developed a national reputation. He left Minnesota for the University of Indiana in 1945, where he chaired the department of psychology until he returned to Harvard in 1948. At Indiana, he wrote an influential futuristic novel, *Walden Two* (1948), which describes a utopian society functioning without punishment and following the principles of learning.

The writing process itself was a remarkable experience for Skinner, filled with much emotion (Elms, 1981). At Harvard he was prolific. His best book on theory, *Science and Human Behavior* (1953), was published while he was there; it describes how learning principles can be applied to all areas of society. *Beyond Freedom and Dignity* (1971), also influential, outlined the steps necessary for civilization to survive and flourish. In the early 1980s Skinner wrote about how behavioral principles could be applied to problems of the aged (Skinner & Vaughan, 1983).

Overall, Skinner can be classified as a **behavioral determinist** because of his emphasis on learning as the primary determinant of human actions. He died at the age of 86, a much admired and respected pioneer in the helping professions (Fowler, 1990).

View of Human Nature/Personality

Despite the great diversity of thought among behaviorists, certain characteristics are basic to their overall view of human nature and the development of personality. Rimm and Cunningham (1985) list some commonalities that behaviorists share:

Human Systems

Understanding and Mastery: Theories of human development

Critical Thinking Question: What behaviors do you think human services practitioners must foster most in their clients? Why?

- Behaviorists assume that all *behavior is learned*, whether it is adaptive or maladaptive.
- Behaviorists believe that *learning can be effective in changing maladaptive behavior or acquiring new behavior.*
- Behaviorists *reject the idea that the human personality is composed of traits.*

Personal Reflection

Reading is a learned behavior. Think of how you were taught to read. What behaviors were involved for you and your teacher?

As mentioned earlier, the three main approaches in contemporary behavioral therapy are the stimulus-response model, applied behavior analysis, and social-cognitive theory. These ways of learning are used by all organisms, although only human learning is addressed here.

The Stimulus-Response Model

The **stimulus-response (S-R) model** is basically **classical conditioning**, sometimes called **respondent learning**. In this model the person need not be an active participant to learn because learning occurs through the association of two stimuli, also known as the **conditioning of involuntary responses**.

The best-known example of S-R learning is Pavlov's famous experiments with his laboratory dogs. Pavlov found that when a dog's food was paired with the sound of a bell, the dog would associate the bell with food and would begin to salivate in response to the bell before the food was served. The bell, initially a neutral stimulus, became a **conditioned,** or learned, **stimulus (CS)** because of its association with an **unconditioned,** or natural, **stimulus (UCS)**, that is, the food. Salivating at the sound of the bell became a **conditioned,** or learned, **response (CR)**, as opposed to the **unconditioned response (UCR)** of naturally salivating when presented with food. S-R learning in this case is represented in the following sequence (Holden, 1993b):

CS does not initially elicit CR; UCS elicits UCR
CS + UCS elicit UCR

CS + UCS presented simultaneously or
CS followed immediately by UCS CS + UCS repeated several times
CS elicits CR

In a similar way, many human emotions, such as phobias, arise because of **paired associations**. For example, a person may have an accident after eating a certain food. The association of the food with the accident, even though the two are unrelated, may result in that person's eventual fear or avoidance of the food. (I, as your author, had that experience when I had an appendectomy shortly after eating jelly beans. Now I don't eat jelly beans). Clients often associate feelings with certain events and vice versa. The sound of music, the smell of certain odors, the sight of certain colors, and the touch of a stranger are experiences to which individuals may react emotionally because of S-R learning. Once learned, these associations can be unlearned and replaced in a process known as **counterconditioning**.

Applied Behavior Analysis

Applied behavior analysis is a direct extension of Skinner's (1953) radical behaviorism (Wilson, 2011). It is based on operant conditioning. According to that theory, learning occurs only when a person is involved as an active participant with the environment. **Operant conditioning**—along with its successor, applied behavior analysis—focuses primarily on how individuals operate in the environment. In general, the idea is that a person learns to discriminate between behaviors that bring rewards and those that do not and is then likely to increase behavior that is rewarded and decrease behavior that is either punished or not reinforced. Thus, "applied behavior analysis makes use of reinforcement, punishment, extinction, stimulus control, and other procedures derived from laboratory research" (Wilson, 2011, p. 198).

Skinner's (1953) basic premise is the foundation on which applied behavior analysis is built: When a certain behavior is followed closely by a **reinforcer**, or reward, chances increase that the behavior will recur in similar or identical circumstances. Individuals do not shape their environments as much as they are shaped by them through rewards and punishments. In other words, the consequences of a behavior determine whether that behavior will be learned or repeated.

Social-Cognitive Theory

In **social-cognitive learning**, people acquire new knowledge and behavior by observing other people and events without engaging in the behavior themselves and without any direct consequences to themselves. Synonyms for social-cognitive theory include **observational learning, imitation, social modeling,** and **vicarious learning**.

"The social-cognitive approach depends on the theory that behavior is based on three separate but interacting regulatory systems (Bandura, 1986). They are (a) external stimulus events, (b) external reinforcement, and (c) cognitive mediational processes" (Wilson, 2011, p. 198). In social-cognitive learning "the behavior of an individual or a group, the model, acts as a stimulus for similar thoughts, attitudes, or behavior on the part of another individual who observes" (Perry & Furukawa, 1980, p. 131). Learning to drive a car, use the correct fork at a dinner party, give oneself positive messages, and react appropriately to a new client are often learned in this way. Learning through social-cognitive processes emphasizes the self-regulation of behavior and deemphasizes the importance of external reinforcers. Thus, learning may be independent of reinforcement (Olson & Hergenhahn, 2011). The advantages of social-cognitive learning are many, but chief among them is saving time, energy, and effort in acquiring new skills. In addition, social-cognitive theory is easily administered and is directed toward positive behavioral change. It is visually appealing and is of little or no risk to clients.

Bandura (1969) found that models closest to the observer's age, gender, race, and attitude have the greatest impact. **Live models, symbolic models** (i.e., those in films and videos), and **multiple models** (i.e., groups of people) are equally effective in producing desired behavior change. In addition, **covert models** are quite effective, whereby a client imagines a model performing a socially desired activity (Cautela, 1976).

Interventions and Direct Services

Understanding and Mastery: Skills to facilitate appropriate direct services and interventions related to specific client or client group goals

Critical Thinking Questions: Of the three ways of promoting behavioral change in clients and client groups (stimulus-response model, applied behavior analysis, and social-cognitive theory) which one do you think would be most effective and why?

Personal Reflection

Think of how you behave in certain situations, such as at parties or when attending an athletic or artistic event. Where did you learn to act as you do? Is some of your behavior a result of copying behaviors you once witnessed?

Assess your comprehension of the **View of Human Nature/Personality** by taking this quiz.

Role of the Counselor

Behaviorists concentrate on behavioral processes, that is, processes closely associated with overt behavior. Counselors who take a behavioral approach help clients learn new, appropriate ways of acting or modify or eliminate excessive actions; adaptive behaviors replace those that are maladaptive. Generally, behaviorally based counselors are active in sessions and serve as learning specialists (Krumboltz, 1966) so that clients can learn, unlearn, or relearn specific ways of behaving. In this process, counselors function as consultants, teachers, advisers, reinforcers, and facilitators (James & Gilliland, 2003). They may also instruct or supervise support people in a client's environment who are assisting in the change process. An effective behaviorist operates from a broad perspective, involving the client in every phase of the counseling. Counselors who are oriented toward social-cognitive learning serve as models for emulation, whereas those who lean toward S-R or applied approaches are more direct and prescriptive in offering assistance.

Counselors using a behavioral approach differ widely in their use of psychological tests and diagnoses. Most employ some form of client assessment device, but often these instruments measure behavior and action. Rarely do counselors use paper-and-pencil personality tests. For diagnosis, they describe clients according to the behaviors they display, many of which are listed in the DSM.

Goals

Behaviorists focus on changing, modifying, or eliminating behaviors; they set up well-defined therapy goals with their clients. Basically, behavioral counselors want to help clients achieve personal and professional objectives that are definable. Thus, the focus is on helping clients acquire healthy, constructive ways of acting. Just eliminating a behavior is not enough; unproductive actions must be replaced with productive responses.

In reaching mutually agreed-upon goals, counselors and clients follow four specific steps (Blackham & Silberman, 1979):

1. **Define the problem.** If a problem is to be solved, it must be stated concretely. Therefore, clients are asked to specify when, where, how, and with whom the problem arises. Counselors may benefit from actually observing the problem behavior.
2. **Take a developmental history.** It is useful for both clients and counselors to know whether the presenting problem is organically based and how clients have handled past circumstances.
3. **Establish specific goals.** Behavioral therapists help clients break down goals into small, achievable units. Counselors also set up learning experiences for clients to develop any needed skills (Krumboltz & Thoresen, 1976). For example, if a woman wishes to complete college, she must first select and then pass courses during a school term. She may also need to learn new study habits and new ways of interrelating with others, such as roommates.
4. **Determine the best methods for change.** Usually several behavioral methods can help clients reach desired goals. If one method does not work, it can be modified, or a new one can be generated and tried. Continual assessment of the effectiveness of methods is critical.

In general, behavioral counselors specialize in helping clients learn how to set up and achieve specific goals and the subgoals that go with them. Counselors are concrete, objective, and collaborative in their work in order to help clients define and reach the goals they are seeking.

> ### Planning and Evaluation
>
> *Understanding and Mastery: Skills to develop goals, and design and implement a plan of action*
>
> **Critical Thinking Question:** How do you think the four specific steps model for changing mutually agreed-upon behaviors would work if the specific goal to be achieved did not have subgoals?

Assess your comprehension of the <u>Goals</u> by taking this quiz.

Process and Techniques

Behavioral therapy is a process; it takes time and dedication. Accentuating, eliminating, adding, or modifying behaviors requires a collaborative effort between therapist and client. Behaviorists concentrate on the here and now as opposed to the then and there of behavior. Therefore, they focus on presenting symptoms and concerns and ways in which they can be immediately treated.

Behavioral counselors have at their disposal some of the best-researched and most effective counseling techniques available. They stress the importance of obtaining empirical evidence and scientific support for any techniques they use. A sample of behavioral procedures is discussed here, although behaviorally oriented publications offer many additional techniques.

General Behavioral Techniques

General behavioral techniques are applicable to all behavioral theories, although a given technique may be more applicable to a particular approach at a given time or in a specific circumstance.

USE OF REINFORCERS   **Reinforcers** are those events that, when they follow a behavior, increase the probability of the behavior's recurring. A **positive reinforcer** is valued and considered pleasurable by the person affected. Certain events and objects frequently serve in this capacity, such as social recognition, money, and food. A **negative reinforcer** is an aversive stimulus, the removal of which is contingent upon performance of a desired action; that removal is reinforcing for the person involved. For example, when a mother nags her son until he washes the dishes, the nagging could be viewed as a negative reinforcer, especially if the son values peace. In behavioral counseling, positive reinforcers are used more frequently than negative ones.

A reinforcer may also be either primary or secondary. A **primary reinforcer** is one that is valued intrinsically, such as food. A **secondary reinforcer**—for example, money or some other token—acquires its value by being associated with a primary reinforcer. Clients know best what activities or items are most reinforcing for them.

SCHEDULES OF REINFORCEMENT   When a behavior is first being learned, it should be reinforced every time it occurs—that is, by **continuous reinforcement**. After a behavior is established, however, it should be reinforced less frequently—that is, by **intermittent reinforcement**. Schedules of reinforcement operate according to either **ratio** (the number of responses between reinforcers) or **interval** (the length of time between reinforcers). Both ratio and interval schedules are either fixed or variable. A **fixed-ratio schedule** delivers reinforcement based on the number of responses made, for instance, being paid for the number of items produced. A **fixed-interval schedule** occurs on a regular time schedule, such as a salary payment every two weeks. A **variable-ratio schedule** offers reinforcement irregularly, as a slot machine does, but averages out to a given figure. A **variable-interval schedule** follows an irregular time schedule so that reinforcement takes place unpredictably; for example, the boss might congratulate an employee twice in one day and then not again for a month. A counselor who knows what type of schedule a client prefers can set up reinforcers accordingly.

SHAPING   **Shaping** occurs when behavior is learned gradually in steps through successive approximation. When clients are learning new skills, counselors may help break down behavior into manageable units. Clients may actually practice a behavior or may imagine doing more of a task than they had previously done (i.e., focused imagery). Before undertaking shaping, however, counselors and clients need to be aware of the specific response sequence they wish to establish—that is, what follows what and how, a process known as **chaining**. When carefully planned, such a procedure usually leads to new or improved behaviors.

GENERALIZATION   **Generalization** involves the display of behaviors in environments other than those in which the behaviors were originally learned. Generalizing behaviors and transferring them to another setting require a number of procedures, including the assignment of behavioral homework, training significant others to reinforce appropriate behaviors, and consulting with clients about particular problems in making behavioral switches (Rose, 1983).

MAINTENANCE **Maintenance** is defined as consistent performance of desired actions without depending on anyone else for support. Maintenance emphasizes increasing a client's self-control and self-management (Thoresen & Mahoney, 1974). When clients learn to modify their own behaviors, **self-monitoring** occurs in two related processes: **self-observation** and **self-recording** (Goldiamond, 1976). Self-observation requires that clients notice particular behaviors that they exhibit; self-recording focuses on keeping track of these behaviors. Self-monitoring interferes with learned habits by having clients count the occurrences of specific behaviors, which are normally done without thought. Such self-monitoring increases client awareness of targeted behaviors and the ways in which they occur. In the management of weight control, for example, individuals monitor their calorie intake and their reactions to eating certain foods.

Personal Reflection

Many specialized behaviors, such as swinging a golf club or playing a musical instrument, are learned gradually and involve shaping, generalization, and maintenance. What skills have you learned in this way?

EXTINCTION **Extinction** is the elimination of a behavior by withdrawal of its reinforcement. Few individuals continue doing something that is not rewarding. For example, when clients are no longer reinforced for talking about the past, they stop bringing it up. Thus, talking about that subject has disappeared and is said to be extinct.

PUNISHMENT **Punishment** is the presentation of an aversive stimulus in order to suppress or eliminate a behavior. A counselor might punish a client with a critical statement, such as, "I don't want to hear you talk like that." Usually, however, behavior therapists do not use punishment in their treatment of clients. Holden (1993a) identifies the differences in behavioral consequences, which are summarized in Table 8.1.

Specific Behavioral Techniques

Specific behavioral techniques are refined behavioral methods that combine general techniques in precise ways. They are found in different behavioral approaches but are used only after rapport and trust have been established between counselors and clients.

Table 8.1	The Effect of Behavioral Consequences on Behavior	
Use of Pleasurable Stimulus	**Use of Aversive Stimulus**	**Effect**
Positive reinforcement (response followed quickly by pleasurable stimulus)	Negative reinforcement (response followed quickly by termination of aversive stimulus or response precludes aversive stimulus)	Increased rate or strength of response
Extinction (response no longer followed by pleasurable stimulus)	Punishment (response followed quickly by aversive stimulus)	Decreased rate or strength of response

Source: From Samuel T. Gladding. *Counseling: A Comprehensive Profession* (4th ed., p. 267). Copyright 2000. Reprinted by permission of Pearson Education, Inc., Upper Saddle River, NJ.

BEHAVIORAL REHEARSAL **Behavioral rehearsal** consists of practicing a desired behavior until it is performed in the way a client wishes (Lazarus, 1985). The process involves gradually shaping a behavior and getting corrective feedback. It is frequently used after clients have viewed a model enacting the desired behavior. In such cases, especially with complex behavior, clients who wish to acquire the behavior will practice in a counselor's presence what they have observed. Clients then receive feedback and suggestions and make modifications accordingly. Clients also receive homework designed to help them practice the new behavior outside the counselor's office. Practice in real-life conditions often leads to success and generalization; if not, modifications can be made during the next counseling session (Kipper, 1986). Behavioral rehearsal is sometimes called **role-playing** because clients are practicing new roles. Improvisational role-playing of new behavior is an effective mechanism for change (Zimbardo & Leippe, 1991).

Interventions and Direct Services

Understanding and Mastery: Skills to facilitate appropriate direct services and interventions related to specific client or client group goals

Critical Thinking Question: What are the advantages and disadvantages of using behavioral rehearsal over environmental planning and vice versa?

ENVIRONMENTAL PLANNING In **environmental planning** a client sets up part of the environment to promote or limit certain behaviors (Krasner & Ullmann, 1973). For example, if a client associates painful memories with a certain place, a daily schedule might be designed to avoid that setting. Similarly, to control a situation and therefore promote desirable interaction, a client might arrange a room or chairs in a certain way.

SYSTEMATIC DESENSITIZATION **Systematic desensitization** is designed to help clients overcome anxiety in particular situations. Clients are asked first to describe a situation that causes anxiety and then to rank this situation and related events on a hierarchical scale, from aspects that cause no concern (0) to those that are most troublesome (100) (see Table 8.2). The higher up the scale an event or situation is the more anxious

Table 8.2	Anxiety Hierarchy
Amount of Anxiety (%)	**Event**
90	Relating to my spouse
85	Relating to my in-laws
80	Relating to my newborn child
75	Relating to my dad
70	Relating to my mother
65	General family relations and responsibilities
60	Being a project manager at work
50	Work in general
40	Coming to counseling
35	Personal finances
20	Having fun (being spontaneous)
10	Going to sleep

Source: From Samuel T. Gladding. *Counseling: A Comprehensive Profession* (5th ed., p. 217). Copyright 2004. Reprinted by permission of Pearson Education, Inc., Upper Saddle River, NJ.

clients are about it. To help clients avoid anxiety and face situations, counselors teach them to relax physically or mentally. Then the hierarchy is reviewed, starting with low-anxiety items. When clients' anxieties begin to mount, they are helped to relax again. The underlying idea is that people cannot feel anxious and relaxed at the same time, a phenomenon called **reciprocal inhibition** (Wolpe, 1958).

ASSERTIVENESS TRAINING   The major tenet of **assertiveness training** is that people should be free to express thoughts and feelings appropriately without feeling undue anxiety (Alberti & Emmons, 2008). The technique consists of counterconditioning anxiety and reinforcing assertiveness. Clients are taught that everyone has the right, not the obligation, of self-expression. Clients then learn the differences among aggressive, passive, and assertive actions. Clients tell their counselors at the beginning of the counseling relationship what their objectives are, such as being able to speak out at public meetings. Counselors then give their clients feedback, both positive and negative, about present behaviors. The next steps involve modeling the desired behaviors and having clients role-play them. Counselors reinforce these behaviors and help shape their clients' actions. Finally, clients receive homework to be completed between sessions (Bellack & Hersen, 1998). Assertive behaviors should be shaped gradually to keep clients encouraged and on track. The objective is for individuals to feel good about their ability to express themselves, not to become aggressive and manipulative.

CONTINGENCY CONTRACTS   **Contingency contracts** spell out the behaviors to be performed, changed, or discontinued; the rewards associated with the achievement of these goals; and the conditions under which rewards are to be received. Most often, contracts are used with children rather than adults, who may find them offensive (see Figure 8.1). The contracts are frequently written out as quasi-formal documents.

IMPLOSION AND FLOODING   **Implosive therapy** involves desensitizing clients to a situation by having them imagine an anxiety-producing situation that may have dire consequences, without having been taught to relax first (as in systematic desensitization). This technique should not be used by beginning counselors or with clients who have heart conditions. In **flooding**, which is less traumatic, the imagined anxiety-producing scene does not have dire consequences. Instead, clients are overwhelmed with images of anxiety-producing stimuli.

Contingency Contract Week One (must earn 5 points for a reward)							
	Make bed	Clean room	Hang up clothes	Pick up toys	Set table	Read a book	Goal
George	✓	✓		✓	✓	✓	Pizza
Will		✓		✓			Baseball game
Ann	✓	✓	✓	✓	✓	✓	Spend-the-night party

FIGURE 8.1

Contingency Contract.
Source: From *Family Therapy: History, Theory, and Practice* (3rd ed., p. 183) by Samuel T. Gladding. Copyright 2002. Reprinted by permission of Pearson Education, Inc., Upper Saddle River, NJ.

AVERSIVE TECHNIQUES   Although most behaviorists recommend that positive techniques be employed first, sometimes it is necessary to use **aversive techniques**, such as punishment. Such techniques, which vary in their severity, are useful when one behavior must be eliminated before another can be taught.

Among the most powerful aversive techniques are time-out, overcorrection, and covert sensitization. **Time-out** separates clients, usually children, from the opportunity to receive positive reinforcement. It is a mild aversive technique that requires careful monitoring and is most effective when employed for short periods of time, such as five minutes. One example is separating a child from classmates when he or she misbehaves. **Overcorrection** is a technique in which clients first restore the environment to its natural state and then make it better. For example, children who throw food in the lunchroom might be required to clean up their mess and then wax the floor. **Covert sensitization** eliminates undesirable behavior by associating it with unpleasantness. It is used in treating clients who have problems with smoking, obesity, substance abuse, and sexual deviation.

In the long run, aversive stimuli are usually not effective by themselves:

- Their negative emotional effects soon dissipate.
- They may interfere with the learning of desired behaviors.
- They may encourage escape, which, when successful, becomes a positive reinforcement.

Furthermore, ethical and legal concerns are associated with all aversive techniques. Before administering them, counselors and therapists should obtain written permission for their use, especially if minors are involved, and be sure that they are adequately trained and supervised.

Assess your comprehension of the <u>Process and Techniques</u> by taking this quiz.

Multicultural Issues

Multiculturalism deals with culture, gender, disability, sexual orientation, socioeconomic disadvantage, and the world of military service. Like most approaches, behavioral therapy has strengths and weaknesses when it comes to working with clients from cultures that differ from that of the counselor. A behavioral approach may help clients be more specific about what they want to do within their subcultures and larger cultural groups. Thus, clients in a behavioral orientation may define more precisely the behaviors that are oppressive for them and may then be better able to address these behaviors, especially if they learn new ways of responding. The drawback to such work, however, is that counselors must become even more attuned to culture-specific behaviors and ways to address them appropriately.

In regard to gender, behavior therapy "terms and techniques are free of reference to gender" (Sharf, 2012, p. 320). In addition, the behavioral approach allows clients to acquire new skills that may enhance their status across gender lines. Observational learning may be especially powerful in helping clients make changes related to nontraditional gender-role behavior, such as that involved in careers (Bussey & Bandura, 1999).

Evaluation of the Theory

Strengths and Contributions

Behavioral therapy works well with clients who are predominantly goal and action oriented, with a need for achievement and results. It is also a good approach with clients who are interested in changing either a discrete response or a limited number of behaviors.

A second strength of behavioral therapy is that it deals directly with symptoms; it is objective in defining and addressing problems. Thus, it demystifies the process of counseling and makes it possible for clients and outside evaluators to assess levels of change in a measurable way. Moreover, by working directly with symptoms, counselors are often able to assist clients immediately. Because behavioral approaches focus on the here and now, clients do not have to examine the past to obtain help in the present, thus saving time and money.

Another positive aspect of behavioral counseling is its appropriateness in working with certain disorders, for example, attention-deficit disorders, conduct disorders, eating disorders, substance abuse disorders, psychosexual dysfunction, impulse control disorders, and phobic disorders (Seligman, 1997). Behavioral approaches are also useful in addressing difficulties associated with anxiety, stress, assertiveness, parenting, and social interaction (Seligman, 1997; Hackney & Cormier, 2012).

In addition, behavioral therapy offers numerous techniques for counselors to use. Behavioral techniques, which more than doubled from 1969 to 1976, continue to increase. And therapists can employ these techniques in numerous settings, including institutions such as mental hospitals or sheltered workshops. Many behaviorally oriented counseling journals are also available, such as the *Journal of Applied Behavior Analysis*.

Another strength of behavioral therapy is that it is based on **learning theory**, which is a well-formulated way of documenting how new behaviors are acquired (Krumboltz & Thoresen, 1976; Thoresen, 1969). Furthermore, learning theory continues to evolve and generate pragmatic applications for treatment in a wide variety of areas (Rescorla, 1988).

Behavioral therapy is also buttressed by the Association for the Advancement of Behavior Therapy (AABT), which publishes ethical guidelines for its members (Azrin, Stuart, Risely, & Stolz, 1977). The AABT promotes the practice of and education about behavioral counseling methods, while protecting the public from unscrupulous practitioners.

Finally, behaviorism is supported by exceptionally good research on how techniques and processes affect the process of counseling. Thus, novice counselors can follow one of many research designs. A common denominator among all behavioral approaches is a commitment to objectivity and evaluation.

Limitations and Criticisms

Behavioral therapy does not deal with the total person, just with explicit behaviors. Critics contend that many behaviorists, such as B. F. Skinner, have taken the person out of personality and replaced it with an emphasis on laws that govern actions in specific environments. This emphasis may be too simplistic in explaining complex human interaction (Olson & Hergenhahn, 2011).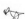

A second criticism is that behaviorism is sometimes applied mechanically. Goldstein (1973) notes that "the most common error of neophyte behavior therapists is to start employing techniques too quickly" (p. 221). Even though most behaviorists are careful to establish rapport with their clients and make counseling a collaborative effort, those who do not initially stress the counselor–client relationship have hurt the approach's image.

A third limitation of the behavioral approach is that it is best demonstrated under controlled conditions that are difficult to replicate in normal counseling situations. Implicit in this criticism is an uneasiness that much of behavioral theory has been formulated using other animal forms, such as rats and pigeons. Many counselors wonder whether a behavioral approach can work with human clients who operate in less than ideal environments.

Another weakness of behaviorism is that techniques may be ahead of theory (Thoresen & Coates, 1980). A proliferation of new methods has been generated by behavioral counselors, however, the theory that should underlie these methods has not kept pace.

Yet another criticism is that behaviorism ignores clients' past histories and unconscious forces. Although it may work quite well with someone who clearly has a behavioral concern, those who wish to resolve past issues or deal with insight from the unconscious may not be helped.

A related concern is that behaviorism does not consider developmental stages (Sprinthall, 1971). Skinner (1974) notes that a child's world does develop, but he and many other behaviorists think that developmental stages do little to explain overt behavior.

Assess your comprehension of the <u>Evaluation of the Theory</u> by taking this quiz.

Finally, critics charge behaviorists program clients for minimum or tolerable levels of behavior, reinforce conformity, stifle creativity, and ignore client needs for self-fulfillment, self-actualization, and feelings of self-worth (James & Gilliland, 2003).

Treating Linda with Behavioral Therapy

Conceptualization

From a behaviorist point of view, Linda has been reinforced for being passive, dependent, depressed, and submissive. She has been punished when assertive. Thus, the behaviors Linda has learned have prevented her from utilizing many of her talents and have resulted in her now being isolated, relying on things she can manipulate, such as, the pages of books and the remote control of the television.

Linda has lacked models of strong and competent women in her life. Her mother was rather withdrawn, her sisters have achieved very little, and Linda has never had a woman supervisor. Overall, Linda lacks the behaviors that would help make her successful as a person and a professional.

Treatment Process

As a behavioral therapist, you want to help Linda learn new, appropriate ways of acting, replacing maladaptive behaviors with adaptive ones. Thus, you function as a consultant, teacher, adviser, reinforcer, and facilitator. Initially, you work with Linda to identify behaviors she wants to acquire and those she wants to eliminate. For instance, Linda reveals that she would like to be more assertive instead of passively accepting the dictates of others and then getting angry about it. Linda also wants to explore how to make the most of her talents and possibly gain new job skills.

You set up specific and mutually agreed-upon goals by concretely defining the problem (i.e., a lack of adequate social and vocational skills), taking a developmental history, establishing specific goals, and determining the best method for change. In Linda's case you believe that an assertiveness training course offered by a community agency would be helpful, as would an assessment of her vocational interests and skills. As an active learning specialist you set up both experiences.

During therapy sessions you discover reinforcers for Linda and begin to help her shape and generalize the assertive behavior she wants by role-playing different scenarios with her. You also set up a self-observation and self-monitoring schedule for Linda to use outside counseling sessions so that she becomes ever more aware of her behavior. In addition, you encourage Linda to reinforce herself when she realizes that she is speaking up for herself or when she takes positive steps to acquire additional vocational skills.

As therapy continues, Linda becomes more independent and joins a number of community organizations in which she has an interest. She finds out how best to use the business skills she already has and takes some additional courses at a nearby college. Without being aggressive or passive, she lets her family know how she wants to relate to them and even plans some of the regular Sunday outings so that they are fun for her and educational for her family. Overall, behavioral therapy helps Linda become a more accomplished person.

Summary and Conclusion

Behavior therapy is a diverse way of working with clients to help them improve their personal and interpersonal skills. Through behavioral therapy, individuals learn how to manage excessive behaviors, extinguish unwanted behaviors, and learn new behaviors. The three primary approaches to behavioral change are the stimulus-response model, applied behavior analysis, and the social-cognitive theory. Behaviorists employ many general techniques with their clients, including the use of reinforcement, shaping, generalization, extinction, and problem-solving rehearsals. They also use specialized and refined techniques such as environmental planning, systematic desensitization, assertiveness training, contracts, implosion, flooding, time-out, and overcorrection.

A real strength of behavioral therapy is its solid learning theory base; excellent research supports the behavioral approaches. In addition, behavioral therapy is extolled for dealing directly with symptoms and behaviors, working in the present, being relatively brief, demystifying the counseling process, having a plethora of available techniques, and being buttressed by a professional association of practitioners and researchers in the field—the Association for the Advancement of Behavior Therapy. On the other hand, behaviorism is limited by conducting some of its research with animals, ignoring clients' histories and the unconscious, dismissing developmental stages as unimportant, and reinforcing conformity.

Recall what you learned in this chapter by reviewing and completing the **Chapter Review**.

Cognitive and Cognitive-Behavioral Therapies

B. Leighty/Photri Images/Alamy

Chapter Outline

Cognitions are thoughts, beliefs, and internal images that people have about events in their lives. Cognitive counseling theories—*cognitive therapy (CT)* and *cognitive behavioral therapy (CBT)*—focus on mental processes and their influence on mental health. A common premise of all cognitive approaches is this: How people think largely determines how they feel and behave (Beck & Weishaar, 2000). As Burns (1980) points out, "Every bad feeling you have is the result of your distorted negative thinking" (p. 28). Therefore, most cognitive theorists agree with the biblical verse from Proverbs 23:7, "As people think, so shall they be," and with Shakespeare's Hamlet, who said, "There's nothing either good or bad but thinking makes it so." In short, cognitive theorists and clinicians believe that if individuals change their ways of thinking, their feelings and behaviors will be modified as a result.

Cognitive approaches to counseling are relatively new; they came into prominence in the 1970s and have remained influential. Among the best-known cognitive theories are Aaron Beck's cognitive therapy and David Burns's new mood therapy. Cognitive-behavioral therapeutic approaches emerged slightly later, using behavioral tasks to modify faulty perceptions and interpretations of important life events (Bankart, 1997). Researchers and practitioners such as Donald Meichenbaum (1977, 1985) and Neil Jacobson have been among the most prominent cognitive-behaviorists. Their work emphasizes the importance of mental processes in human behavior and views thoughts as a type of behavior. The essence of the cognitive behavioral approach is the blending of behavioral and cognitive strategies to help people make needed changes in their lives. Thus, cognitive-behaviorists form a bridge between counselors who are exclusively focused on either cognitive or behavioral changes.

Major Theorists: Aaron Beck and Donald Meichenbaum

A prolific writer of more than 400 articles and 15 books, Aaron T. Beck (1921–) is a Philadelphia psychiatrist who was originally trained as a psychoanalyst. He developed a cognitive approach to mental disorders in the late 1950s and early 1960s, emphasizing the importance of cognitive thinking, especially dysfunctional thoughts, which are unproductive and unrealistic, and which may produce depression (Weinrach, 1988; J. Beck, 2011).

A professor emeritus now, Beck served for many years as the director of the Center for Cognitive Therapy at the University of Pennsylvania's Department of Psychiatry. There he refined his theory and rigorously tested it (see Beck, 1991; Newman & Beck, 2009). In the process he found that cognitive therapy is effective as a short-term treatment for a number of problems and disorders, especially for depression and general anxiety (Beck & Alford, 2009; Clark & Beck, 2012). In these maladies there are "interpretations and expectations that lead to the painful effects of sadness and anxiety, to avoidance and inhibition" (Weinrach, 1988, p. 161). Thus, cognitive counselors trained in Beck's methodology try to help clients become more realistic in their interpretation of events by generalizing less in the case of depression or projecting less in the case of anxiety. This approach uses a Socratic method that is problem oriented, educational, brief, and collaborative. In short, Beck's approach emphasizes that affect and behavior are determined by the ways in which people mentally structure their worlds, especially their thinking.

Donald Meichenbaum (1940–) is one of the founders of CBT. He was born and reared in New York City, where he observed many people talking to themselves. He concluded that helping people talk to themselves differently and constructively might be an excellent goal for therapy and might bring about behavioral changes (Meichenbaum, 1995, 1997).

Meichenbaum is the author of numerous articles, chapters, and books, some of which are now considered classics in the field of therapy, such as *Cognitive-Behavioral Modification: An Integrated Approach* (1977) and *Stress Inoculation Training* (1985). He is especially noted for his work on treating individuals with anger and aggressive behavior and adults with posttraumatic stress disorder. In a survey reported in the *American Psychologist*, North American clinicians voted Meichenbaum one of the 10 most influential psychotherapists of the 20th century. He has served on the editorial boards of numerous journals and has lectured and consulted worldwide. Prior to retirement, Meichenbaum was a professor of psychology at the University of Waterloo in Waterloo, Canada, where he also had a private practice as a clinical psychologist.

View of Human Nature/Personality

A particular concern of cognitive and cognitive-behavioral therapies is the impact of thinking on personality. These counseling approaches are usually employed with individuals who are not visibly impaired but who suffer from dysfunctional automatic thoughts specific to an event and schemata, which are general rules about themselves or the world associated with an event (Holden, 1993b; J. Beck, 2011). These individuals often engage in *self-statements* that affect their behaviors in much the same way as statements made by another person (Corey, 2013). For instance, a guest who is slighted at a party may automatically think, "That person is a jerk!" The schema that follows may be, "I'm offended" or "I'm hurt."

For Beck, and cognitive therapists in general, there are a number of *cognitive distortions* to which a counselor should be attuned. These include at least nine ways of mentally assessing a situation (Arnkoff & Glass, 1992; DeRubeis, Webb, Tang, & Beck, 2010; Sharf, 2012).

- **All-or-nothing thinking** (also known as **dichotomous thinking**) occurs when people think they must do something a certain way or else they are failures. For example, in giving a speech, if all-or-nothing thinkers do not say every word written, they believe they will be seen as incompetent.
- In **selective abstraction**, individuals pick out an idea or fact to support their negative thinking. For instance, if a person who usually makes straight A's in school suddenly makes a B, that person might use the B to conclude, "I'm not really very smart."
- **Overgeneralization** makes a rule based on a few incidences or events. For example, someone may think that all white people are insensitive because of encounters with some white people who were rude and uncaring.
- **Magnification** and **minimization** are two sides of the same thought process. In **magnification** a cognitive distortion occurs when an imperfection is exaggerated beyond reality. For instance, a high school student could fail a test and conclude, "I will never be able to get into a good college." In **minimization** a person downplays good points or notable achievements. The student who is an accomplished artist may not apply to appropriate colleges, thinking, "I am not up to the quality of these colleges."
- **Personalization** occurs when an event that is unrelated to a person is distorted and made to appear as if it is related. For example, a woman may begin to think that just the elevators in her office complex are slow even though she uses them only at peak times.
- **Labeling** and **mislabeling** are common cognitive distortions that arise when people characterize themselves in certain ways. For instance, a man who goes to a batting cage to hit balls and misses most of them during his first visit may label or mislabel himself as a poor hitter, instead of a person needing more practice.
- **Catastrophizing** is similar in both Beck's and Ellis's theories. Basically, it involves mentally distorting an event so that one becomes fearful of it. For example, if a shy but accomplished young man is attracted to an outgoing, sophisticated, and good-looking young woman, he may say to himself, "She is far superior to me in every way. I cannot ever talk to her, let alone ask her out for a date." Thus, he precludes any possible relationship and becomes completely discombobulated any time he is near her.

- **Mind reading** refers to the tendency of some people to guess what others are thinking about them. An older adult may believe that others who see him think, "There is an incompetent old fool who is good for nothing." Therefore, he fails to interact with people in his environment and becomes a recluse.

- **Negative predictions** are beliefs that something bad is going to happen. They may have little basis in fact, but they influence a person's actions just the same. For instance, a person may believe, "I will get sick if I eat chicken, because I once got sick after a meal that included chicken." Thus, the prediction keeps that person from eating chicken, which, in reality, would have no negative impact.

Human Systems

Understanding and Mastery: Theories of human development

Critical Thinking Question: How can negative predictions impact the behaviors of an individual or a group when confronted with change or a new challenge?

Personal Reflection

When have you seen people display any of the distorted cognitions just described? All-or-nothing thinking, overgeneralization, and negative predictions seem to be especially prevalent in society.

Assess your comprehension of the **View of Human Nature/Personality** by taking this quiz.

Role of the Counselor

The role of cognitively oriented counselors is to collaborate with clients (Beck, 1976), sharing the responsibility to select goals and bring about change. In this relationship, therapeutic personnel function as experts on cognitions, behaviors, and emotions and as educators. Clients collaborate by participating in assignments. Initially, cognitively oriented counselors do not try to disprove beliefs but let clients examine the functionality of their beliefs. Beck's model is exploratory in working with clients and Socratic in letting them assess what is correct and incorrect in their belief systems (Holden, 1993a). Thus, cognitive therapy is ever evolving so that as new data come in, the counselor-client team can make new strategies.

Overall, cognitively based helping requires empirical testing on the part of clients to understand how functional or dysfunctional their beliefs are. Counselors, especially those who are cognitive-behavioral, may use diagnoses, such as those in the DSM, in working with clients. However, diagnoses are employed only as a way of working with clients to overcome a disorder, such as post-traumatic stress.

Planning and Evaluating

Understanding and Mastery: Skills to develop goals, and design and implement a plan of action

Critical Thinking Question: How might you empirically test how functional or dysfunctional a client's beliefs are?

Goals

Both cognitive and cognitive-behavioral approaches to helping employ specific learning experiences to help teach clients ways to monitor their negative or automatic thoughts (J. Beck, 2011). Clients are taught to recognize the relationship between these thoughts and their emotions and behaviors. In addition, human service practitioners with this

Assess your compre-
hension of the Goals by
taking this quiz.

orientation help clients compile evidence for and against their distorted automatic thoughts. Ideally, clients are freed to alter their distorted beliefs and to substitute reality-based interpretations for unrealistic thoughts.

In order to help clinicians achieve these goals, profiles and treatment plans have been developed, especially by Beck, for disorders such as depression (Beck, Rush, Shaw, & Emery, 1979), suicide, and anxiety (Dattilio & Padesky, 1990). However, goals are constantly reexamined and modified to fit particular clients; cognitive approaches are personally tailored to individual situations.

Process and Techniques

Cognitive and cognitive-behavioral therapy are specific and goal directed (Sharf, 2012), emphasizing the modification of thoughts to bring about therapeutic change. One way to organize thoughts is to evaluate them in three categories: cold, warm, and hot cognitions. A **cold cognition** is basically descriptive and nonevaluative, such as "I lost my job." A **warm cognition** emphasizes preferences and nonpreferences, such as "I lost my job and I really don't want to have to start looking for another one." **Hot cognitions** "are heavily laden emotional-demand statements" (James & Gilliland, 2003, p. 238) that may reveal varied distortions, such as overgeneralizing, catastrophizing, magnification, and all-or-nothing thinking—for example, "I must get a job just like the one I lost." Hot cognitions usually lead to dysfunctional behaviors because they are filled with both demands and distortions.

A cognitive approach to change must first establish a relationship between client and counselor and then implement cognitive strategies in a basic four-step procedure (Burns, 1989; Schuyler, 1991). These four steps and the premises behind them are at the heart of change.

The first step is to use standardized guidelines for understanding in a concrete manner the events in clients' lives, that is, what is happening in their environments. The second step is to set up a way of recording or reflecting clients' thoughts about these events in order to understand their cognitions in a clear, precise way. Often thoughts are written down so that they can be seen in as concrete a manner as possible.

In the third step, counselors and clients work to find a means to identify and challenge distorted thoughts. For instance, if a client believes that no one likes her, an empirical test might be set up whereby she records all positive as well as negative interactions. The final step is to implement new ways of thinking that are realistic and productive. Thus, the client might change her thinking from "Nobody likes me" to "Some people like me and some do not." This process frees her to act more positively with specific individuals and with people in general.

Cognitive Techniques

The following are among the most prevalent cognitive techniques in use:

- **Specifying automatic thoughts.** As mentioned earlier, **automatic thoughts** are cognitions that occur without effort. They are usually distorted and lead to emotional responses that are not healthy. Therefore, a major focus of cognitive therapy is to identify—that is, specify—and then correct such thoughts.
- **Homework.** As with other types of therapy, much change that occurs in cognitive therapy happens outside actual counseling sessions. Thus, clients may practice

giving themselves different thoughts at home, on the job, or in particular settings. Such practice makes it easier for clients to achieve the desired changes in their thinking.

- **Cognitive interventions**. A number of processes occur under the heading of cognitive interventions. All of them focus on bringing cognitive distortions into greater awareness—for example, challenging absolutes, reattribution, labeling of distortions, and challenging all-or-nothing thinking.
- **Cognitive rehearsals**. Because practice makes perfect, it is important for clients to consistently rehearse healthy thoughts. They may do so covertly or overtly, privately through mental rehearsal, or publicly, as in a gathering of friends. Cognitive rehearsals ensure that clients will say to themselves and others the right words in the right way—at least most of the time.
- **Scriptotherapy**. In the process of writing, which is scriptotherapy, individuals improve their thoughts by expressing them concretely. Pennebaker (1990), among others, has noted both mental and physical changes in clients who write about stressful situations in their lives.

Personal Reflection

How helpful do you find it to write your thoughts down? Look at what you write and how you write about success and disappointment in your life.

Cognitive-Behavioral Techniques

Some of the most exciting new techniques in counseling have been originated by cognitive-behaviorists (Craighead, Craighead, Kazdin, & Mahoney, 1994; Mahoney, 1995). Cognitive-behavioral techniques are "usually active, time-limited, and fairly structured. They are designed to enlist the client" and others in "a collaborative process" (Meichenbaum, 1986, p. 147). Although "there is no single definition of cognitive-behavioral theory … the individual theories are tied together by common assumptions, techniques, and research strategies" (Kalodner, 1995, p. 354). Thus, CBT approaches maintain a diversity of views about the role that cognitions play in behavior change, but all agree that cognitions play a part in such change.

CBT procedures emphasize the present, the environment, and learning. Common to cognitive-behavioral intervention is "a directive style; structured, goal-directed, and time-limited treatment; use of homework assignments and skill practice; and a focus on problem-solving ability" (Kalodner, 1995, p. 364). Dozens of interventions can be included under the cognitive-behavioral banner—for example, "cognitive restructuring, problem-solving, relaxation training, behavioral and imaginal rehearsal, self-monitoring, self-reinforcement, and efforts at environmental change" (Meichenbaum, 1985, p. 21). Following are some of the interventions most common to cognitive-behavioral approaches to counseling:

- **Self-instructional training.** One of the best methods for changing clients' cognitions and behaviors is a process known as self-instructional training (Meichenbaum, 1977). In this procedure, counselors perform a task or engage in appropriate behaviors while verbalizing aloud through self-talk the reasons behind what they are doing. Clients then do the same task or behavior and also give themselves instructions aloud. Next, they engage in these actions while whispering self-instructions and then finally perform the behaviors while silently repeating the reasons behind what they are doing. These covert messages thus become the basis for the clients' behaviors, and in the future they may communicate with themselves in this manner. As a strategy, self-instructional training is especially powerful and popular in working with impulsive, defiant, or attention-deficit children and adolescents (Barkley, 1987; 1991; Kendall, 2007).

- **Stress-inoculation training**. Stress inoculation is a preventive technique, like medical inoculation, in which individuals are taught sets of coping skills to help them handle stressful events. First, clients are helped to understand the nature of stress and coping. Second, clients learn specific coping skills and are reinforced for using the ones they already possess. The final phase emphasizes practice: Clients use coping skills in clinical settings and real situations. Overall, stress inoculation involves focusing on what lies ahead, grouping stressful events into manageable doses, thinking of ways to handle small stressful events, and practicing coping skills (Meichenbaum, 1985; 1986). The major drawback to this procedure is that its initial results sometimes do not generalize into permanent behavior changes (Arnkoff & Glass, 1992). Therefore, follow-up and booster sessions are often necessary.

- **Thought stopping**. Thought stopping helps clients who ruminate about the past or who have irrational thoughts to stop such self-defeating behavior and live more productively. Counselors initially ask their clients to think in the self-defeating manner and then, in the midst of such thoughts, suddenly yell, "Stop!" The shout interrupts the thought process and makes it impossible to continue. There are several components of the thought-stopping process (Cormier & Cormier, 1998); basically, it teaches clients to progress from outer to inner control of negative thought patterns. It also helps clients replace self-defeating thoughts with assertive, positive, or neutral ones.

Interventions and Direct Services

Understanding and Mastery: Skills to facilitate appropriate direct services and interventions related to specific client or client group goals

Critical Thinking Question: How difficult do you think it is to teach someone to cognitively change or restructure their thoughts?

- **Cognitive restructuring**. Among the most effective cognitive-behavioral techniques is cognitive restructuring, which includes stress inoculation and thought stopping. In cognitive restructuring, clients are taught to identify, evaluate, and change self-defeating or irrational thoughts that negatively influence their behavior. This process is accomplished by getting them to vocalize their self-talk and then change it, when necessary, from negative to neutral or positive. This technique is similar to Ellis's (1962) and Beck's (1976) proposals for modifying thought processes.

Assess your comprehension of the <u>Process and Techniques</u> by taking this quiz.

Multicultural Issues

Multiculturalism deals with culture, gender, disability, sexual orientation, socioeconomic disadvantage, and the world of military service. Cognitive therapy and CBT approaches are applicable to multicultural populations because they let clients take the lead in assessing whether their thoughts and beliefs are appropriate to their cultures. A number of studies have shown the positive use of cognitive counseling approaches with a variety of populations including African American and Latino men and with Malaysians (Sharf, 2012).

Cognitive therapy and CBT approaches may also be appropriate for both men and women in dealing with gender-specific concerns. By examining their beliefs, men and women may come to better understand the cognitive distortions that hinder their overall functioning. The only major drawback in this regard is that some clients may become dependent on their counselors to structure sessions and help them examine their beliefs, thus failing to become empowered. This potential may be of special concern to women who are not assertive.

Evaluation of the Theories

Strengths and Contributions

Cognitive therapy and CBT are both focused on teaching clients how to identify and monitor their thoughts and behaviors and also to change or modify them. For instance, Clark and Beck (2012) have published an anxiety and worry workbook that provides readers with practical strategies for identifying their anxiety triggers and challenging the thoughts and beliefs that lead to distress. In addition, cognitive and cognitive behavioral therapists have published workbooks for clients and instructional guides for clinicians in numerous private and public settings including schools (Creed, Reisweber, & Beck, 2011). Overall, both approaches are proactive, providing training to clients that helps them prepare for and then successfully deal with a variety of specific and general problems.

Another contribution of these counseling theories is that they demystify the process and techniques associated with choice and change. Clients realize that in order to become someone different and act in a more functional manner, they have to think, behave, and feel in ways that are different from those of the past.

Cognitive therapy and CBT are also generally empowering for clients. When they learn new ways to think and behave, they are free to generalize their learning to new situations and end their treatment. For example, CBT has been found to be an excellent treatment for all types of eating disorders with those receiving help generalizing their behaviors to not only eat a variety of foods but to eating out in public at restaurants (Fursland, Byrne, Watson, La Puma, Allen & Byrne, 2012).

Furthermore, cognitive therapy and CBT are applicable to a wide range of client disorders, such as depression, guilt, phobias, distress, and pain. Because they work with children, adolescents, adults, and the aging, they are beneficial for a large group of clients. Cognitive therapy and CBT have published a plethora of research documenting the effectiveness of these approaches (Clark & Beck, 2010; Dobson, 2010) and comparing cognitive-behavioral therapy with other brief therapeutic approaches such as short-term psychoanalytic psychotherapy (STPP) (Bhar & Beck, 2009).

Finally, cognitive and CBT approaches have set up training centers like the Academy of Cognitive Therapy (Dodson, Beck, & Beck, 2005) to identify and credential mental health professionals who demonstrate competence in cognitive therapy. By setting up training centers, cognitive counseling has ensured its future thus strengthening its place as a major player in professional therapeutic circles.

Limitations and Criticisms

In order to receive the maximum benefit from these approaches, clients need to have average to above-average intelligence. Individuals who fall too far below average in their cognitive abilities have more trouble using the various techniques. Furthermore, clients cannot be psychotic or disabled by present problems if they are to succeed with cognitive or cognitive-behavioral approaches. Both cognitive and CBT methods depend on clients being able to think clearly.

Another drawback is that clients must be willing and able to complete systematic homework assignments. Change comes about as a result of practice, and clients must be willing to work on their own as well as with their therapists.

In addition, clients must possess a repertoire of behavioral skills and responses or be able to learn such behaviors rapidly. Clients who cannot or will not apply what they know or learn are not good candidates for these approaches.

Finally, cognitive therapy and CBT do not explore to any great extent the past influences in clients' lives, including the unconscious or underlying conflicts. Even though surface thoughts and behaviors may be of greatest concern and may be most susceptible to change, previous difficulties and the history behind them may be pertinent as well.

Assess your comprehension of the <u>Evaluation of the Theory</u> by taking this quiz.

Personal Reflection

Homework is helpful in learning. If you have to memorize something you know repetition over time helps and that often means doing homework. When have you engaged in homework to master a behavioral or a cognitive-behavioral skill?

Treating Linda with Cognitive and Cognitive-Behavioral Therapy

Conceptualization

From a cognitive and cognitive-behavioral perspective, Linda is having difficulty with her life because of her thinking. She is using self-statements that are demoralizing or depressing. In many ways she is repeating in her own mind what her father, her former husband, and even some of her bosses have said to her, for example, "You are no good unless you obey us" or "Women are inferior and will never amount to anything." These thoughts have become automatic and have prevented Linda from doing anything constructive with her life. In fact, these thoughts have led her to contemplate suicide. Thus, Linda has labeled herself a failure and has acted accordingly. She has sabotaged her own life by not venturing out or speaking out. Indeed, she has engaged in catastrophizing and negative predictions to the point that these mental distortions now control her life.

Treatment Process

As a cognitive or cognitive-behavioral therapist you work in collaboration with Linda to select goals and to bring about change. You encourage Linda to examine her beliefs functionally, using a Socratic method to determine which beliefs are correct and which are incorrect. For instance, in mulling over the idea that women are inferior and will never amount to anything, Linda quickly dismisses such a notion as she thinks of famous historical and contemporary women who have been high achievers. As you engage Linda in this way, you are also helping her see the link between thoughts and feelings; if she gives herself negative messages, she is going to depress herself. You urge Linda to keep a written record of her thoughts so that she can see what messages she is sending herself.

In addition to helping Linda decipher and challenge the automatic negative thoughts that are most pervasive in her life, you help her cognitively rehearse healthy thoughts. You use the CBT technique of self-instructional training, in which you perform a task or engage in appropriate behavior while verbalizing aloud the reasons behind what you are doing. Linda then does the same task or behavior, at first giving herself instructions aloud and then performing the action while whispering self-instructions. Finally, she does the task silently.

You also teach Linda stress inoculation as a preventive technique. In this procedure, you teach her a set of coping skills to help her handle stressful events like interacting with sexist men and her father. In addition, you instruct Linda on how to stop thoughts so that she does not persist in her negative thinking. By the end of therapy, Linda is engaged in healthy thinking, and her actions reflect a woman who is much more self-confident and realistic about who she is and what she can do.

Summary and Conclusion

Cognitive therapy and CBT approaches to treatment are some of the most creative and effective in counseling. They are based on the belief that cognitions are directly related to behaviors and in the case of CBT that beliefs are behaviors. As a rule, cognitive and cognitive-behavioral therapies are straightforward and successful with a wide variety of clients; the results can be seen in a timely and concrete way. In addition, the number of sessions involved is usually minimal, and the outcomes are usually long-lasting.

Although Beck's approach to cognitive therapy provides a common ground for linking psychodynamic and behavior therapies (Beck & Weishaar, 2000), cognitive therapy and CBT are distinct in their emphasis. They focus on the present as opposed to the past, and they target specific behaviors instead of general ways of acting. Furthermore, they continue to evolve in their techniques and processes. A common misconception of these approaches is that they neglect emotions; however, they do deal with the affective by attending to the cognitive and cognitive-behavioral aspects of life first.

Overall, Beck's cognitive approach and Meichenbaum's cognitive-behavioral therapy are among the most used and useful theories in practice today. They will most likely continue to gain in popularity because of their pragmatic nature and their applicability to the concerns of many clients. Their suitability for people of both genders, all ages and stages of life, and multiple cultures adds further to the prestige and practicality of these counseling approaches.

Recall what you learned in this chapter by reviewing and completing the **Chapter Review**.

CHAPTER 10

Lisa F. Young/Shutterstock

Rational Emotive Behavior Therapy

Rational emotive behavior therapy (REBT) was originally known as **rational therapy** (Backx, 2011) and then **rational-emotive therapy** but changed its name when its founder, Albert Ellis (1995), decided that his approach needed to better reflect what the theory actually did, that is, focus on behavior as well as cognitions. Although the name change came in 1993, the various forms of REBT have been evolving for decades (Dryden, 1994).

REBT is sometimes considered a cognitive-behavioral therapy, even though it began to evolve long before the term *cognitive behavioral* was formulated. Initially, it was more similar to the cognitive therapy of Aaron Beck than to any other counseling approach. However, because of its unique history, founder, and recent developments, it is treated on its own here.

Major Theorist: Albert Ellis

Albert Ellis (1913–2007), the founder of rational emotive behavior therapy (REBT), was once described by Weinrach (1980) as "abrasive, impatient, and lacking in some of the basic social graces that my mother spent hours indoctrinating me with" but also as "brilliant, sensitive, perceptive, humorous, and stimulating" (p. 152). That Ellis fit both of these descriptions is partially the result of his life experience.

Ellis was born into a Jewish family in Pittsburgh, Pennsylvania; his parents eventually had a daughter and another son. Early in his life, Ellis's family moved to New York City, where he spent most of the rest of his life. Ellis described his father in positive and neutral terms, although the elder Ellis was often absent from home. From his father Ellis thought he acquired his intelligence, drive, and persistence (Newhorn, 1978). His mother was quite independent for her time, often idiosyncratic in her behavior as well as happy and nonsmothering. Ellis described her way of parenting as benign neglect (Dryden, 1989).

At the age of 5 Ellis almost died from tonsillitis and later suffered from acute nephritis and diabetes (Morris & Kanitz, 1975; Dryden, 1989). He thought most members of his family were pretty crazy and by the age of 7 he was largely on his own (Weinrach, 1980). Ellis's parents' divorced when he was 12 years old, which caused him to give up plans to be a Hebrew teacher. Instead, he became a self-described probabilistic atheist—someone who does not believe that God exists but would accept empirical evidence to the contrary.

Ellis's dream as an adolescent was to become a writer. He planned to make enough money to retire early in life and then devote his time to writing. In 1934, he graduated in business from the City College of New York and worked in the business world until the mid-1940s. When not working, he wrote fiction, but his literary efforts proved unsuccessful, and he decided to study psychology. From Columbia University, Ellis received a master's degree in 1943 and a Ph.D. in clinical psychology in 1947.

Ellis wanted to become a psychoanalytic clinical psychologist, a wish that frustrated him at first because institutions that specialized in such training admitted only medical professionals. He finally succeeded in obtaining his own analysis from the Karen Horney group and practiced classic psychoanalysis in the early 1950s. However, dissatisfied with that approach, Ellis formulated and began practicing his own theory in 1955 (Backx, 2011).

Rational emotive behavior therapy was primarily a cognitive theory in the beginning. Its main tenets were first published in Ellis's *Reason and Emotion in Psychotherapy* (1962). REBT has since broadened its base considerably and now includes behavioral and emotional concepts.

Ellis established a nonprofit institute to promote REBT—the Albert Ellis Institute. A prolific writer, he produced more than 500 articles, 50 books, and numerous films and tapes. Up until his death, Ellis's weekly schedule included as many as 80 clients for individual sessions and up to eight group sessions. Annually, he gave about 200 workshops and talks. Yet despite such a work load, Ellis did not consider himself a compulsive professional because he did not have to work or prove himself (Weinrach, 1980). He relaxed by reading, listening to music, and socializing.

Ellis married twice and stated that he learned something about himself and the nature of women from each marriage. From 1964, he had a solid love/companionship relationship with Janet Wolfe, who helped him build the Albert Ellis Institute (Dryden, 1989). Besides being a devout practitioner of his own theory, Ellis was recognized in professional circles in many ways, including being named Humanist of the Year by the American Humanist Association. Although he was flamboyant in a humorous and startling manner, Ellis was affectionate and warm too (Dryden, 1989). Indeed, he was a man of contrasts who saw ways of combining ideas that, on the surface, might appear to clash, such as religion and REBT (Powell, 1976).

View of Human Nature/Personality

REBT assumes that people are both "inherently rational and irrational, sensible and crazy" (Weinrach, 1980, p. 154). According to Ellis (1995), this **duality in people** is biologically inherent and is perpetuated unless a new way of thinking is learned (Dryden, 1994). **Irrational thinking**, or as Ellis defines it, **irrational Beliefs (iBs),** may include the invention of upsetting and disturbing thoughts. These fallacies, which have been used in formulating various tests, have been correlated "with various kinds of emotional disturbance" (Ellis, 1984, p. 266). Ellis organizes irrational beliefs under three main headings:

1. "I absolutely must perform important tasks well and be approved by significant others, or else I am an inadequate, pretty worthless person!"
   • Result: severe feelings of anxiety, depression, and demoralization, often leading to severe inhibition.
2. "Other people, especially my friends and relatives, truly must treat me kindly and fairly, or else they are rotten, damnable people!"
   • Result: severe feelings of anger, rage, fury, often leading to fights, child abuse, assault, rape, murder, and genocide.
3. "The condition under which I live absolutely must be comfortable, unhassled, and enjoyable, or else it's awful, I can't stand it, and my life is hardly worth living!"
   • Result: severe feelings of low frustration tolerance, often leading to compulsion, addiction, avoidance, inhibition, and public reaction. (Ellis, 1996b, p. 77)

Although Ellis did not deal with the developmental stages of individuals, he thought that children are more vulnerable to outside influences and irrational thinking than adults are. He believed that human beings are by nature gullible, highly suggestible, and easily disturbed. Overall, people have within themselves the means to control their thoughts, feelings, and actions, but they must first realize what they are telling themselves (i.e., **self-talk**) to gain command of their lives (Ellis, 1962). This matter is one of personal, **conscious awareness**; the unconscious mind is not involved.

Ellis believed that it is a mistake for people to evaluate or rate themselves beyond the general idea that everyone is a fallible human being. He especially discouraged the use of any form of the verb *to be* (e.g., is, was, am, has been, being) to describe a person. He reasoned that human problems do not come from the id, as Freud envisioned, nor from the what if, but rather from the *is;* the verb *to be* makes it difficult to separate people from their actions. Therefore, Ellis advocated that individuals speak and think of their behavior as separate from their personhood—for example, "I act badly" rather than "I am bad" (Ellis & Harper, 1975). Avoiding the verb *to be* fosters a more rational thought process and gives a person the freedom to change, to focus on altering specific behaviors instead of overhauling personality.

Human Systems

Understanding and Mastery: Theories of human development

Critical Thinking Question: How are the premises of REBT similar to and different from cognitive and cognitive-behavior therapy?

Personal Reflection

What do you think of Ellis's idea about calling yourself a fallible human being and not using the verb *to be* to describe yourself? What are the strengths to such an approach? What are the drawbacks?

Assess your comprehension of the <u>View of Human Nature/Personality</u> by taking this quiz.

103

Role of the Counselor

In the REBT approach, counselors are active, direct, provocative, and confrontational (Backx, 2011). They are instructors who teach and correct clients' cognitions. Countering a deeply ingrained belief requires more than logic; it requires consistent attention and repetition (Krumboltz, 1992). Therefore, REBT therapist must listen carefully for illogical or faulty statements from their clients and must challenge them. In the process, they show concern and care for their clients by "attending to their behavior, by frequently asking questions for clarification, by recalling personal details about the client and his or her problems, by the use of gentle humor, and by active attempts to help the client solve difficult issues" (Vernon, 1996, p. 122).

Ellis (1980) and Walen, DiGuiseppe, & Dryden (1992) have identified several characteristics desirable for REBT counselors. They should be bright, knowledgeable, empathetic, respectful, genuine, concrete, persistent, scientific, interested in helping others, and involved in using REBT themselves. They should also adopt the humanistic core REBT philosophies of unconditional self-acceptance, unconditional other-acceptance, and unconditional life-acceptance (Ellis & Ellis, 2011). A counselor's main assessment instrument is the evaluation of a client's thinking. Some formal tests may be employed to measure rational and irrational thinking, but the evaluation process is primarily accomplished in counselor-client sessions. As a rule, REBT practitioners do not rely heavily on the diagnostic categories in the DSM.

Intervention and Direct Services

Understanding and Mastery: Skills to facilitate appropriate direct services and interventions related to specific client or client group goals

Critical Thinking Question: Why is it important that human services practitioners or other helping professionals use REBT in daily life if they are going to practice it?

Goals

The primary goals of REBT focus on helping people realize that they can live more rational and productive lives. In general, rational emotive behavior therapy constitutes "an attempt to correct mistakes in a client's reasoning as a way of eliminating undesirable emotions" (Cohen, 1987, p. 37).

REBT is heavily influenced by **stoic philosophy**, and Ellis was fond of quoting a 1st-century Stoic, Epictetus: "Men feel disturbed not by things, but by the views which they take of them." Thus, individuals often disturb themselves by changing wishes and desires into demands. Ellis points out that when people use words such as *must, should, ought, have to,* and *need,* they make demands of wishes and think irrationally. For individuals who think that wishes must or should occur, a wish unfulfilled results in a catastrophe. REBT helps clients stop catastrophizing and making such demands. Clients in REBT may express some negative feelings, but a major goal is to help them avoid a more emotional response than is warranted by the event.

Information Management

Understanding and Mastery: Obtain information through interviewing, active listening, consultation with others, library or other research, and the observation of clients and systems

Critical Thinking Question: As a human services practitioner what would you especially listen for in interviewing clients to determine if they were rational or not?

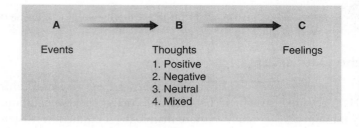

FIGURE 10.1
The ABC Model of
Human Interaction.
Source: From *Group
Work: A Counseling
Specialty* (4th ed.,
p. 439) by Samuel T.
Gladding. Copyright
2003. Reprinted by
permission of Pearson
Education, Inc., Upper
Saddle River, NJ.

Another goal of REBT is to help people change self-defeating habits of thought or behavior. One way this goal is accomplished is through the **ABCs of REBT**: *A* signifies an activating experience, *B* represents how the person thinks about the experience, and *C* is the emotional reaction to *B* (see Figure 10.1).

Many clients believe that an experience directly causes feelings—a concept called **cognitive bypass**. Left out of this conceptualization is the thought process that leads to the development of emotions. For example, a person may lose a job or an opportunity and then assert that the experience caused depression. REBT helps people recognize their emotional anatomy, that is, how feelings are attached to thoughts.

Thoughts about experiences may be characterized in four ways: *positive, negative, neutral,* or *mixed*. A positive thought leads to **positive feelings**. For example, if a host at a party reminds a man that he has had too much to drink, the man may think about the host's care and concern on his behalf and have positive emotions. On the other hand, the man may think that the host is criticizing him and has no right to do so, resulting in **negative feelings** about that same experience. If the latter thought process occurs, the man becomes angry. With a **neutral thought** the man might simply note the host's actions and move on to another thought, having no emotional reaction. **Mixed thoughts** occur when a person has both negative and positive thoughts at once—for example, "I'm glad something was said, but I dislike the way it was said." The resulting feeling is ambivalence.

REBT encourages clients to be more tolerant of themselves and others, for everyone is a fallible human being. People are encouraged through REBT to achieve personal goals, rather than dwell on mistakes or miscues. Such goals are accomplished when individuals learn to think rationally in order to change self-defeating behavior.

Assess your comprehension of the Goals by taking this quiz.

Personal Reflection

Keep a chart for a couple of days on how often you use "*must, should,* and *ought*." See if you can avoid using these words and what a difference it makes.

Process and Techniques

The two primary emphases of REBT are *teaching* and *disputing*. Before any changes can be made, clients must learn the basic ideas of REBT and understand how thoughts are linked to emotions and behaviors. Consequently, REBT is highly didactic and very directive. In the first few sessions, counselors teach their clients the anatomy of an emotion; that is, feelings are a result of thoughts, not events, and self-talk influences emotions. This process, generally known as **rational emotive education (REE)**, has had a high success rate with children, adolescents, and adults with a wide variety of problems and from a wide range of backgrounds (Wilde, 1996).

It is also critical in the REBT process that clients be able to dispute irrational thoughts. Disputing thoughts and beliefs takes one of three forms—*cognitive, imaginal,* or *behavioral*—and is most effective when all three forms are used (Walen et al., 1992). **Cognitive disputation** involves the use of direct questions, logical reasoning, and persuasion. Direct questions challenge clients to prove that their responses are logical. Sometimes these inquiries use the word *why*, which is seldom employed in other counseling approaches because it puts many people on the defensive and closes off exploration. However, why questions help REBT clinicians cut through defenses and educate clients to new ways of thinking, feeling, and behaving. For example, counselors might ask, "Why must you?" or "Why must that be so?" These inquiries help clients learn to distinguish between rational and irrational thoughts and appreciate the superiority of rational thoughts.

Another form of cognitive disputation involves the use of **syllogisms**, "a deductive form of reasoning consisting of two premises and a conclusion" (Cohen, 1987, p. 37). Syllogisms help clients and counselors more thoroughly understand inductive and deductive fallacies that underlie emotions. For example, in irrational can't-stand-it-ism, the process might go as follows (Cohen, 1987, p. 39):

Major premise: "Nobody can stand to be lied to."
Minor premise: "I was lied to."
Conclusion: "I can't stand it."

Certainly, being lied to is not pleasant, but it is often a part of life, and concluding "I can't stand it" is silly, false, and illogical.

Imaginal disputation depends on a client's ability to imagine and employs a technique known as **rational emotive imagery (REI)** (Maultsby, 1984). REI may be used in one of two ways. First, a client may be asked to imagine a situation in which she is likely to become upset and to examine her self-talk during that imagined situation. Then she is asked to envision the same situation but to be more moderate in her self-talk this time. Second, a counselor may ask a client to imagine a situation in which he feels or behaves in a different way from that of a real occurrence. The client is then instructed to examine the self-talk he used in this imagined situation. REI takes practice.

The **emotional control card (ECC)** is a device that helps clients reinforce and expand the practice of REI (Sklare, Taylor, & Hyland, 1985). Wallet-sized ECCs list four emotionally debilitating categories—*anger, self-criticism, anxiety,* and *depression* (Ellis, 1986). Under each category are a list of inappropriate or self-destructive feelings and a parallel list of appropriate or nondefeating feelings. In potentially troubling situations clients can refer to the cards and change the quality of their feelings about the situations. At their next counseling sessions the clients can discuss the use of the cards in cognitively restructuring their thoughts from irrational to rational.

Behavioral disputation involves behaving in a way that is the opposite of the client's usual way of acting. Sometimes behavioral disputation takes the form of **bibliotherapy**, in which clients read a self-help book such as those distributed by the Albert Ellis Institute. At other times behavioral disputation includes role playing and completing a homework assignment in which clients do activities they previously considered impossible. In both cases clients bring their completed assignments to their scheduled counseling sessions and evaluate them with their counselors.

If disputation of irrational beliefs (iBs) is successful, a new and effective philosophy will emerge (Ellis, 2011). This philosophy will include a new **cognitive Effect (cE),** which is a restatement of original rational Beliefs (rBs). For example, "It is not awful, merely inconvenient, that I was rejected by a particular person."

Ellis (2011) has devised a number of homework assignments, such as **shame attack exercises,** to help clients learn to behave differently. These exercises usually include an activity that is harmless but dreaded, such as introducing oneself to a stranger or asking for a glass of water in a restaurant without ordering anything else. By participating in such exercises, clients learn the ABCs of REBT on a personal level and come to realize more fully that the world does not stop if a mistake is made or if a want remains unfulfilled. Clients also learn that others are fallible human beings and need not be perfect. And finally, clients learn that goals can be achieved without awfulizing or terriblizing personal situations.

In addition, Ellis frequently used puns and other humorous devices to help his clients see how irrational thinking develops and how silly the consequences of such thinking are. He cautioned clients not to "should on themselves" and advised them to avoid "musterbation." He has even composed a number of songs to help remind himself and others to think rationally.

Other REBT counselors, such as Richard Watts (1996), have also written **rational emotive behavior therapy songs** to common tunes—"I've Been Working on the Railroad," "Jimmy Cracked Corn," "Twinkle, Twinkle, Little Star," and "O Suzannah." These songs address cognitively distorted thoughts in a humorous and therapeutic way.

Personal Reflection

Pick a familiar tune and write lyrics that are humorous and rational, such as the following ones to the song of "I've been working on the railroad."

"I've been working on my thinking all the live long day.
I've been working and not drinking and I believe that it's okay.
Can't you see me speaking rationally to everyone I meet
Don't you know I'm acting calmly and my mind is now upbeat!"

How do you think singing this song or another like it might be helpful to you or someone you work with as a human services professional? What are the drawbacks to such songs?

Two other powerful REBT techniques are **confrontation** and **encouragement.** As previously noted, REBT counselors explicitly encourage their clients to abandon thought processes that are not working. Sometimes counselors challenge, or confront, clients who claim to be thinking rationally but who are not. At other times counselors encourage clients to continue working from an REBT base even when they are discouraged. Confrontation need not be done in the style of Ellis—that is, vigorously confronting and attacking a client's beliefs (Johnson, 1980). Instead, counselors can be empathetic and insistent at the same time.

Assess your comprehension of the <u>Process and Techniques</u> by taking this quiz.

Multicultural Issues

Multiculturalism deals with culture, gender, disability, sexual orientation, socioeconomic disadvantage, and the world of military service. Almost from its beginning, REBT has been concerned with its effectiveness as a multicultural approach. In the 1970s, Ellis (1977) provided research data on the effectiveness of REBT with different types of clients in specific settings across the life span. In addition, REBT counselors are generally sensitive to their clients' cultures and adjust their actions to respect those they are helping (Sharf, 2012). James and Gilliland (2003) summarize REBT effectiveness with minority culture clients and reveal that it is usually positive.

REBT is also sensitive to the needs and specific concerns of women. Because REBT practitioners realize that women may be stereotyped according to their gender and gender roles, REBT counselors give female clients a voice as to what they will work on (e.g., assertiveness, career, life change, stress) and how (e.g., in a group or individually).

Self-Development

Understanding and Mastery: Awareness of diversity

Critical Thinking Question: Is thinking enough to become aware of diversity or do other factors, such as behavior, have to be a part of the process?

Evaluation of the Theory

Strengths and Contributions

One of the major strengths of REBT is that it is clear, easily learned, and effective. Most clients have few problems in understanding the principles or terminology of REBT. Furthermore, Roush (1984) reports that REBT is effective with many different types of individuals, including adolescents, and can be used as a preventive approach to mental health in educational settings (Banks, 2011). Furthermore, Seligman (2001) notes that REBT is appropriate for the treatment of affective disorders, anxiety disorders, and adjustment disorders.

A second strength of REBT is that it can easily be combined with other behavioral techniques to help clients experience more fully what they are learning (Ellis, 2002). REBT is like cognitive-behavioral counseling in that it borrows and integrates other techniques that are compatible with its theoretical foundation.

Another asset of REBT is that it is relatively short-term, usually lasting 10 to 50 sessions. Thereafter, clients can continue to use the approach on a self-help basis. Thus, the economy and efficiency of REBT is impressive (Ellis, 1996b; Ellis & Ellis, 2011).

Moreover, REBT has generated a great deal of literature and research for clients and counselors. Few other theories have developed as much bibliotherapy material; Ellis was a prolific writer and researcher, as are many other REBT practitioners today. Each year the Albert Ellis Institute produces a catalog filled with an array of books, booklets, audiotapes, and videotapes on rational emotive behavior therapy. In addition, Ellis's institute is constantly engaged in empirical studies on the use of REBT with a wide variety of clients.

A final strength of REBT is that it has continued to evolve over the years as its processes and techniques have been refined. An example of this evolution is found in the difference between inelegant and elegant REBT (Dryden, 2010). **Inelegant REBT**, which developed first, focuses on the activating event and the distortions that clients usually have about such events (Ellis, 1977, 1995, 2011). It does not give clients any coping strategies for dealing with situations in which perception matches reality. Instead, clients are encouraged to assure themselves that they will do better in the future or that they are good persons. **Elegant REBT**, on the other hand, concentrates on the beliefs of clients and focuses on their taking responsibility for their own feelings. In the process clients realize that success in everything is not essential and that catastrophe does not result from every unfulfilled want.

Limitations and Criticisms

One drawback to REBT is that it cannot be used effectively with individuals who have mental problems or cognitive limitations, such as those with schizophrenia and those with severe thought disorders. Nor is it productive with people who are severely mentally impaired. A person who is intellectually bright benefits most from this approach.

Another limitation of REBT is that it may be too closely associated with its founder, Albert Ellis; many individuals have difficulty separating the theory from Ellis's eccentricities. Although Johnson (1980) urges counselors to adapt the theory and its techniques to their own personalities and individual styles of counseling, some therapists still eschew the approach because of its connection with Ellis.

REBT also has limited usefulness if its practitioners do not combine its cognitive base with more behavioral and emotive techniques. Ellis says that REBT has always been a diverse approach, and he advocates its use in various settings (Weinrach, 1980). Indeed, the theory is now much broader than it was originally, but some counselors still concentrate on the cognitive side of REBT, thus limiting its effectiveness.

Furthermore, REBT's direct and confrontational approach to clients may be a limitation for some individuals. There is the potential for counselors to be overzealous and pushy, with the result that clients may resist change more strongly than might otherwise be the case and/or drop out of treatment.

Yet, another drawback to REBT is its lack of a strong research base. The theory makes sense intuitively but it has not been well researched. Research on the effectiveness of REBT pales when compared to Beck's Cognitive Therapy which is similar in its emphasis on the therapeutic importance of changing client thinking.

Finally, REBT's emphasis on changing thinking may not be the simplest way of helping clients change their behaviors or emotions. Gestalt theorists would challenge REBT and charge that emotions should be experienced before interventions are made.

Assess your comprehension of the Evaluation of the Theory by taking this quiz.

Treating Linda with Rational Emotive Behavior Therapy

Conceptualization

From the perspective of rational emotive behavior therapy (REBT), Linda is demonstrating her inherently rational and irrational sides through her thoughts, feelings, and behaviors. This duality is to be expected, but Linda is unduly upsetting herself with her irrational beliefs that life is not worth living and that she is worthless. Linda's negative self-talk is dangerous to her well-being, as is her assessment of herself as inadequate.

Treatment Process

As an REBT therapist, you work actively to teach Linda the ABCs of REBT. You show her that events do not cause feelings but thoughts do and she has a choice as to how she is going to think—with positive, negative, neutral, or mixed thoughts. Right now she is engaged almost exclusively in negative thinking. As a user of REBT yourself, you show genuine concern for Linda and build rapport with her by asking questions and using gentle humor. You even give her a personal example of how REBT has helped you.

You talk with Linda about how the use of words such as *must*, *should*, *ought*, *have to*, and *need* make demands of wishes and lead to irrational thinking. You also work with her on not responding more emotionally to an event than is warranted. You then teach Linda how to dispute thoughts—cognitively, imaginally, and behaviorally. She decides that she will dispute cognitively, and when things do not go her way, she will ask herself *why* questions, for example, "Why must things go my way?" By engaging herself in this way, she empowers herself.

To help Linda even more, you give her some of the bibliotherapy writings from REBT practitioners. You also encourage her to monitor her thoughts regularly and to challenge irrational ones. Treatment ends when Linda is more rational in her thinking and playful in her outlook. Through REBT she is able to see that the world will not end if her family does not become more functional or her workplace more friendly. On the other hand, she has become more aware that she can take control of her thoughts and the emotions and behaviors that go with them. She uses this knowledge to explore new vocational possibilities, new clubs and community activities in which she has an interest, and new and appropriate relationships with men.

Summary and Conclusion

Rational emotive behavior therapy is a popular approach in human services professions that makes use of affective, behavioral, and cognitive methods to help bring about change. A primary focus of this approach is teaching clients to realize that feelings are derived from thoughts, not events.

REBT stresses role play and homework assignments as well as recognition of thoughts. Disputations are employed to counteract faulty, irrational thinking and help clients take control of their lives. REBT is both a psycho-educational and a psychotherapeutic means of promoting change in clients.

Recall what you learned in this chapter by reviewing and completing the **Chapter Review**.

Transactional Analysis

Pixland/Thinkstock

Some clinicians classify transactional analysis (TA) as an almost purely cognitive theory with a linkage to psychoanalysis. Others consider it a versatile and comprehensive system of psychotherapy (Widdowson, 2010). TA was formulated by Eric Berne in the early 1960s and rose to prominence after the publication of two best-selling books: Berne's *Games People Play* (1964) and Thomas Harris's *I'm OK, You're OK* (1967). Although Berne was fearful that the popularity of these books would undermine the seriousness of his work, it simply made the theory more attractive and familiar to the general public.

Since the 1970s, TA has not been as popular in the United States as it has been in some other countries. One explanation is that the theory has not continued to evolve much and research supporting it has been sparse. In addition, TA has suffered from the rise of cognitive therapy and rational emotive behavior therapy (REBT), both of which have had stronger proponents and a plethora of research supporting their use. Nevertheless, TA is still used by a number of practitioners and is important to understand.

Major Theorist: Eric Berne

Eric Berne (1910–1970) was born in Montreal, Canada, where his father was a doctor and his mother, a writer and an editor. Berne was five years older than his only sibling, a sister. He was close to his father, who died at the age of 38, when Eric was only nine years old. Berne followed in his father's footsteps, earning a medical degree from McGill University in 1935. He then completed a psychiatric residency at Yale, set up a private practice in Connecticut and New York, became a U.S. citizen, and married. During World War II, he served as an army psychiatrist in Utah, where he started practicing group therapy.

After the war, Berne settled in Carmel, California, where he separated from his wife and completed his first book, *The Mind in Action* (1947), which was a critical survey of psychiatry and psychoanalysis. In California he resumed the psychoanalytic training he had started before the war, part of which was his own analysis, supervised by Erik Erikson. Erikson insisted that Berne not remarry until after the analysis was finished, and Berne complied. He remarried in 1949 and fathered two children, as he had in his first marriage. He built a study in his house away from the noise of the children and, in 1950, began a demanding schedule that included consultations and practice in Carmel, San Francisco, and Monterey. His only breaks occurred on Friday nights, when he played poker at his house.

In 1956 Berne was turned down for membership in the Psychoanalytic Institute, a rejection that proved to be a turning point in his life. He reacted by disassociating himself from psychoanalysis and devoting his time to the development of TA, which has a psychoanalytic aspect.

Dusay (1977) describes the formulation of TA in four phases. In the first phase (1955–1962), Berne developed the concept of **ego states**. His ideas were influenced by his clients' descriptions of behaving like **a parent**, **an adult**, **or a child**—the three ego states (as represented in the following diagram with the parent ego state on top and the child ego state on the bottom).

(P)   Parent
(A)   Adult
(C)   Child

In the second phase (1962–1966), Berne concentrated on transactions and games. The International Transactional Analysis Association was created in 1964, and Berne published the popular book *Games People Play*. In the third phase (1966–1970), he emphasized the reasons some individuals choose to play certain games in life. In the fourth phase (from 1970 on), he and his followers emphasized action and energy distribution.

Berne was involved in the first three phases of TA development. After a second divorce in 1964, he spent a great deal of time writing; at one point he was working on the manuscripts of six books and editing the *Transactional Analysis Bulletin*. He also gave numerous lectures and seminars. Berne's third marriage was short-lived; he died of a heart attack at the age of 60.

View of Human Nature/Personality

Transactional analysis is an **optimistic theory**: It assumes that people can change despite any unfortunate events of the past. According to Barrow (2007), TA is a kind of positive psychology because of its emphasis on optimism among other things. Regardless, besides stressing optimism, TA is also **antideterministic**, proposing that people have choices in their lives and that what was once decided can be redecided at a later date. As James and Jongeward (1971) emphasize, "Transactional analysis is a rational approach to understanding behavior and is based on the assumption that all individuals can learn to trust themselves, think for themselves, make their own decisions, and express their feelings" (p. 12).

TA focuses on four major methods of understanding and predicting human behavior:

- **Structural analysis**—understanding what is happening within the individual
- **Transactional analysis**—describing what happens between two or more people
- **Game analysis**—understanding transactions that lead to bad feelings
- **Script analysis**—understanding an individual's life plan

Structural Analysis

In structural analysis each person is considered to have three functional ego states—child, parent, and adult. Berne (1964) defines an **ego state** as "a consistent pattern of feeling and experience directly related to a corresponding consistent pattern of behavior" (p. 364). He notes that the findings of Wilder Penfield and his associates (1952; 1954) support this definition. Penfield, a neurosurgeon, found that an electrode applied to different parts of the brain evokes memories and feelings long forgotten by the person. The implication is that the brain functions like a tape recorder to preserve complete experiences in a sequential form recognizable as ego states.

The child ego state, the first to develop, is that part of the personality characterized by childlike behaviors and feelings. Childlike behavior might be described as inquisitive, affectionate, selfish, mean, playful, whiny, and manipulative. The **child ego state** consists of two subdivisions—the natural, or free, child and the adaptive child (see Figure 11.1). The **natural child** is the part of the person that is spontaneous, impulsive, feeling oriented, and often self-centered and pleasure loving. The natural child is also intuitive, creative, and responsive to nonverbal messages. The **adaptive child** is the compliant part of the personality that conforms to the wishes and demands of parental figures. These adaptations of natural impulses occur in response to traumas, natural life experiences, and training.

The **parent ego state** incorporates the attitudes and behaviors of parental figures—that is, the dos, shoulds, and oughts (see Figure 11.2). Outwardly, these messages are expressed through critical or nurturing behavior. Parental messages are present throughout a person's life; any response to a thoughtful question that occurs within 10 seconds usually comes from the parent ego state. This ego state also consists of two subdivisions. The **nurturing parent** is the part that comforts, praises, and aids others. The **critical parent** is the part that finds fault, displays prejudices, disapproves, and prevents others from feeling good about themselves. These two parts are revealed in nonverbal behaviors such as pointing a finger at someone and in verbal statements such as, "That's too bad, but don't worry."

FIGURE 11.1
The Child Ego State.

FIGURE 11.2
The Parent Ego State.

The **adult ego state** is not subdivided or related to a person's age. It is the objective, thinking, data-gathering part of a person. The adult ego state tests reality, much as the ego does in Freud's system. The adult is rational and organized, functioning in some ways like a computer by processing data without feelings and expressing itself through phrases such as "I understand" and "I'm going to."

Sometimes the different ego states operate simultaneously. For example, a woman may observe an attractive man and go through the following self-dialogue: "He is really good-looking and well-spoken [adult], but he's probably stuck up [critical parent]; although I've heard he's very sensitive [nurturing parent]. I wonder how I could attract him and get him to notice me [natural child]. Oops! I'd better stop looking and get back to work, or my boss will get mad at me [adaptive child]."

A major focus of TA is determining which ego state(s) a person is using. Although TA does not favor one ego state over another, the theory stresses the importance of being able to balance responses when necessary and appropriate. Those who constantly exhibit just one ego state do not function as well as those who are more flexible.

One way of assessing which ego state(s) a person employs most is through the use of an **egogram** (Dusay & Dusay, 1989). An egogram remains fixed unless an individual invests energy in changing response patterns. The egogram of a person who responds primarily from the adult ego state is shown in Figure 11.3.

> ### Human Systems
>
> *Understanding and Mastery: Theories of human development*
>
> **Critical Thinking Question:** As a human services practitioner how might you help clients who mostly respond from a single TA ego state such as their critical parent?
> •

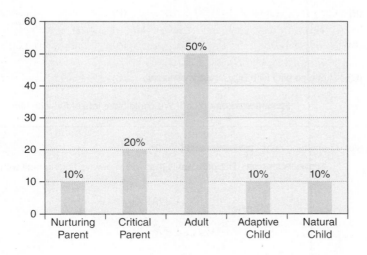

FIGURE 11.3
An Egogram.
Source: From Counseling: A Comprehensive Profession (4th ed., p. 248) by Samuel T. Gladding Copyright 2000. Reprinted by permission of Pearson Education, Inc., Upper Saddle River, NJ.

Personal Reflection

Make an egogram of your speech in different situations such as asking for a favor, ordering a meal, and recapping your day to a friend. What do you notice about the TA ego states you tend to use in these situations?

••

Transactional Analysis

The second way of understanding and predicting human behavior involves ego state transactions. In contrast to the intrapersonal focus of structural analysis, transactional analysis is interpersonal. Transactions may occur on one of three levels: complementary, crossed, or ulterior. In a **complementary transaction** both persons are operating either from the same ego state (e.g., child to child, adult to adult) or from complementary ego states (e.g., parent to child, adult to parent). In such cases, responses are predictable and appropriate.

An adult-to-adult transaction might look like it's shown in Figure 11.4.

A child-to-child transaction would involve more playfulness, as shown in Figure 11.5.

A parent-to-parent transaction, however, would be more nurturing or critical, as shown in Figure 11.6.

In a **crossed transaction**, an inappropriate ego state is activated, producing an unexpected response. Crossed transactions hurt, prompting individuals to withdraw from each other or switch topics. In a crossed transaction, one person might be operating

FIGURE 11.4
Adult-to-Adult
Transaction.

FIGURE 11.5
Child-to-Child
Transaction.

FIGURE 11.6
Critical Parent-to-
Parent Transaction

(P)

(A) You're capable of carrying them yourself.

(C) Can you help me carry these heavy bags?

(P)

(A)

(C)

(P)

(A) Do you want to come in and listen to some music?

(C) Want to come in and have some fun together?

(P)

(A)

(C)

FIGURE 11.7
Crossed Transaction.

FIGURE 11.8
Ulterior Transaction.

from a child ego state and hoping for a complementary parent ego state response but might receive instead a comment from the other person's adult ego state, as shown in Figure 11.7.

An **ulterior transaction** is one in which two ego states operate simultaneously and one message disguises the other. Ulterior transactions appear to be complementary and socially acceptable even though they are not. For example, at the end of a date one person might say to the other, "Do you want to come in and listen to a little music?" On the surface, this question might seem to be coming from an adult ego state but in reality is masking a child ego state: "Want to come in and have some fun together?" (see Figure 11.8).

Game Analysis

Games are ulteriorly motivated transactions that appear complementary on the surface but end in bad feelings. Games confirm and reinforce script decisions (Tyrangiel, 2011). People play games to structure time, achieve recognition, make others predictable, and prevent intimacy. Because intimacy involves risks, games keep people safe from exposing their thoughts and feelings. There are first-degree, second-degree, and third-degree games; and all have predictable ends. Berne (1964) offers examples of each degree.

First-degree games are played in social circles with anyone who is willing to participate. They generally lead to mild upsets. An example of a first-degree game is **Seducto**, which can be exciting and fun initially. In this game, a male and a female enjoy an evening flirting with each other until one turns the other down and both leave feeling slightly uncomfortable.

A **second-degree game** occurs when the players go after bigger stakes, usually in more intimate circles, and end up with bad feelings. An example of a second-degree game is **Uproar**, in which two persons get angrier and angrier until one or both get very upset about being called a name or put down.

A **third-degree game** usually involves injury; the players end up in jail, the hospital, or the morgue. An example of this game is **Cops and Robbers**, in which people dare those in authority to catch them and yet leave clues about where they can be cornered. With each increasing degree there is greater danger of permanent damage. Very few games have a positive or neutral outcome (Berne, 1964).

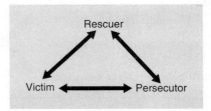

FIGURE 11.9
Karpman Triangle.
Source: From *Counseling: A Comprehensive Profession* (4th ed., p. 250) by Samuel T. Gladding. Copyright 2000. Reprinted by permission of Pearson Education, Inc., Upper Saddle River, NJ.

Individuals who play games operate from one of three positions: victim, persecutor, or rescuer (Karpman, 1968). To keep games going, people often assume new roles. For example, in the game Why Don't You/Yes, But, one person plays the rescuer, responding to a complaint from the victim by saying, "Why don't you . . . ?" The victim answers, "Yes, but . . . ." When this game becomes tiresome, the rescuer may switch off to a persecuting role and respond sarcastically to the victim's complaint: "Ain't it awful!" Figure 11.9 represents the three positions that people assume during game interactions. The list of possible games is almost endless, and it is easy for individuals to get hooked into playing them. In the long run, however, game players avoid meaningful and healthy human interactions.

Personal Reflection

What games have you observed in your life? Are there some games that are more prevalent than others in certain situations? Describe their dynamics and give them a name.

Script Analysis

Berne contends that everyone makes a **life script**, or life plan, by the age of 5. These scripts, which determine how individuals interact with others, are based on interpretations of external events. **Positive messages** given to children function as permissions and do not limit them in any way. **Negative messages**, or injunctions, are more powerful and may become the basis for destructive scripts. Many parental injunctions begin with *don't*: "Don't question," "Don't contradict," "Don't play with them." Unless people make conscious attempts to overcome such injunctions, they may experience negative consequences.

Most life scripts revolve around giving and receiving **strokes** (i.e., verbal or physical recognition). Berne points out that negative strokes, or punishments, are better than no strokes at all, that is, being ignored. Strokes result in the accumulation of either good or bad feelings, known as **stamps**. When individuals collect enough stamps, they cash them in on certain behaviors. For example, a teenager may collect enough bad feelings from frequent failing grades to justify quitting school or enough good feelings from studying hard to justify attending a party. Healthy people give and receive positive strokes most often.

The following negative scripts are common:

- **Never scripts:** Individuals never get to do what they want (e.g., "Marriage is bad; never get married").
- **Until scripts:** Individuals must wait until a certain time to do something they want to do (e.g., "You cannot play until you have all your work done").

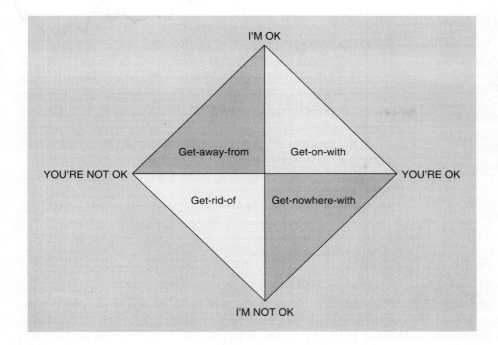

FIGURE 11.10
OK Positions.
Source: From *Counseling: A Comprehensive Profession* (4th ed., p. 252) by Samuel T. Gladding. Copyright 2000. Reprinted by permission of Pearson Education, Inc., Upper Saddle River, NJ.

- **Always scripts:** Individuals tell themselves that they must continue doing what they have been doing (e.g., "You should always continue a job once you've started it").
- **After scripts:** Individuals expect difficulty after a certain event (e.g., "After age 40, life goes downhill").
- **Open-ended scripts:** Individuals do not know what they are supposed to do after a given time (e.g., "Be active while you're young").

There are also **miniscripts** that focus on minute-by-minute occurrences. Some of the most common miniscripts are "Be perfect," "Be strong," "Hurry up," "Try harder," "Please someone." These five messages, called **drivers**, allow people to escape their life scripts, but the escape is only temporary.

The ideal life script in TA terms is informed by the position **I'm OK; you're OK** (i.e., a get-on-with position) (Harris, 1967). But people may operate from three other positions: **I'm OK; you're not OK** (i.e., a get-away-from position); **I'm not OK; you're OK** (i.e., a get-nowhere-with position); and **I'm not OK; you're not OK** (i.e., a get-rid-of position). Figure 11.10 shows these positions.

Everyone operates from each of these four positions at various times, but well-functioning individuals learn to recognize unhealthy positions and modify their thoughts and behaviors accordingly. Berne holds that life scripts can be rewritten if people become more conscious of what they are thinking and make concerted efforts to change.

Assess your comprehension of the <u>View of Human Nature/Personality</u> by taking this quiz.

Personal Reflection

What miniscripts are you likely to give yourself when encouraged? When discouraged? When in doubt? When happy? When mad?

Role of the Counselor

TA treatment assigns counselors the initial role of teacher. They must explain to their clients the language and the concepts of TA, a new way of thinking about self. There-after, counselors contract with clients for specific changes and help them achieve them. Counselors also help their clients obtain the tools, or skills, necessary for change and empower them through various techniques.

TA counselors do not rely heavily on formal psychological tests, although they do assess client functioning. However, assessment is usually done through an egogram or another less formal method. The purpose is to determine how clients are spending time and from which ego states they are operating. Diagnosis based on DSM categories is not stressed and is only done if absolutely necessary.

Goals

The primary goals of TA focus on transforming clients from frogs into princes and princesses. It is not enough that clients learn to adjust, as in psychoanalysis. Instead, the emphasis is on attaining health and autonomy. Counselors help their clients identify and restore distorted or damaged ego states, develop the capacity to use all ego states, use the adult ego state with its reasoning powers, alter inappropriate life scripts, and adopt a position of "I'm OK; you're OK" (Berne, 1966).

In becoming autonomous, clients exhibit more awareness, intimacy, and spontaneity; become free of games; and eliminate self-defeating scripts. They become more in touch with their past but, at the same time, are freed from previous negative influences. One of Berne's most important contributions was to depathologize mental health issues by helping people see that the psychological symptoms they developed were the best options they had in childhood to try to take care of themselves (Steward & Joines, 2011). A major emphasis of TA is on learning about the self in order to decide what changes to make and whom one wishes to become (Goulding & Goulding, 1997).

Process and Techniques

Transactional analysis has initiated a number of techniques for helping clients reach their goals. Most TA counselors begin with analysis—structural, transactional, game, and/or script—as described earlier. Other techniques include the following:

- **Treatment contract**—emphasizes agreed-upon responsibilities for both counselors and clients (Dusay & Dusay, 1989); reveals when counseling goals have been reached
- **Interrogation**—involves speaking to a client's adult ego state until an adult response is given; can be confrontational; can be ineffective, supplying only historical material
- **Specification**—identifies the ego state that initiated a transaction; takes place on an adult-to-adult level
- **Confrontation**—involves pointing out inconsistencies in client behavior or speech

- **Explanation**—teaches the client about some aspect of TA; occurs on an adult-to-adult ego state level
- **Illustration**—enlightens the client or elaborates on a point; may speak to both the child and the adult ego states
- **Confirmation**—points out recurrence of previously modified behavior; can be effective only when the client has a firmly established adult ego state
- **Interpretation**—explains to the child ego state of the client the reasons for the client's behavior; can be effective only when the client has a functioning adult ego state
- **Crystallization**—involves an adult-to-adult transaction in which the client becomes aware that game playing may be given up; frees the client; completes the TA process

Almost all of the techniques in TA involve some combination of questioning, confrontation, and dialogue. The following questions are among those most frequently asked by TA counselors:

What are the nicest and worst things your parents ever said to you? What is your earliest memory?

What is the family story about your birth? What is your favorite fairy tale, story, or song? How would you describe your mother and father?

How long do you expect to live?

To be most effective, TA counselors must always carefully assess the ego strengths of individual clients. Clients are usually capable of making new decisions about life once they discover different aspects of themselves.

Transactional Analysis was divided into three main schools of treatment in the 1970s: the **classical San Francisco** school (with an emphasis on explanation, diagrams, contracts, and behavioral change), the **cathexis** school (which emphasized confrontation and reparenting), and the **redecision** school (which emphasized the child's compliance with injunctions and the power to make new decisions) (Barnes, 1977). Today there are over a dozen TA schools each representing a particular theoretical slant, for example, psychodynamic transactional analysis, constructivist transactional analysis, relational transactional analysis, and body-centered transactional analysis (Erskine, 2009). All of these schools use contracts as their primary method of intervention and have autonomy as the final goal of treatment.

Interventions and Direct Services

Understanding and Mastery: Skills to facilitate appropriate direct services and interventions related to specific client or client group goals

Critical Thinking Question: Since almost all techniques in TA involve some combination of questioning, confrontation, and dialogue, think which of these ways is easiest for you and which is hardest as well as how you can make your weakest way of communicating stronger.

Assess your comprehension of the Process and Techniques by taking this quiz.

Multicultural Issues

Multiculturalism deals with culture, gender, disability, sexual orientation, socioeconomic disadvantage, and the world of military service. Transactional analysis appears as an appropriate theory to use in many of these cultures. Indeed, there are TA associations in 65 countries, from Argentina to Ukraine. TA has an appeal in countries with diverse populations, largely because the contract basis acts as a safeguard against therapists imposing their values on clients. In addition, the cognitive nature of TA and the instructive methods it uses are appealing to some cultural groups within the United States, such as African-Americans, Latinos, and Asian-Americans (Henderson & Thompson, 2011).

Likewise, TA seems to be an appropriate theory for work on gender-sensitive issues. The emphasis on empowerment and contracts strengthens the position of women in TA therapy. Furthermore, the exploration of life scripts and family messages may help both men and women explore their roles and decide whether they wish to make any changes in what they do and how they do it.

Evaluation of the Theory

Strengths and Contributions

Transactional analysis uses terms that are easily understood and clearly defined. Consequently, it can be used in varied settings with varied populations—for example, with students who want to overcome math anxiety (Eisenberg, 1992). Another strength of TA is that it is easily and effectively combined with other more action-oriented counseling theories. The use of TA and Gestalt therapy together has been especially powerful (James & Jongeward, 1971).

One other positive aspect of TA is that it puts the responsibility for change on clients. Individuals can choose to change or remain the same, but it is their decision, not their therapists'. In addition, TA is goal directed. The contractual nature of the counseling process makes it possible for both counselors and clients to know when treatment should be terminated (James & Gilliland, 2003).

A final benefit of TA is a worldwide association that sponsors certification, conferences, and publications related to the theory. The International Transactional Analysis Association (ITAA) is active in training and certifying its members and in publishing a scholarly journal, the *Transactional Analysis Journal*.

Limitations and Criticisms

Transactional analysis has been criticized for its cognitive orientation; to understand is only the beginning of change. Although TA promotes understanding, it is limited in its effectiveness unless it is used with another more action-oriented theory.

The TA approach is also criticized for its simplicity, structure, and popularity. TA is so widely known that some people use the terminology but do not practice the theory. These individuals intellectualize their problems but take few actions to modify them. Moreover, TA terms such as "I'm OK; You're OK" have become so popular that they sometimes lose their punch.

A further criticism is that TA does not emphasize the authenticity of the counselor. Counselors and clients are seen as equals, and little attention is paid to the person of the counselor in the process.

A more serious criticism of TA is that the research behind it is relatively weak. Methodological improvements are needed to study populations receiving TA treatment (Miller & Capuzzi, 1984). In addition, some clinicians charge that the approach has not developed much since Berne's death in 1970. Although distinct emphases and schools of TA have emerged, few new ideas have been conceptualized. And there are no prominent new theorists or disciples of TA on the national or international scene. Unless there is renewal within the theory and those who practice it, TA will lose prominence as a counseling modality.

Assess your comprehension of the Evaluation of the Theory by taking this quiz.

Treating Linda with Transactional Analysis

Conceptualization

From a TA perspective, Linda has made some decisions that have not been very productive. Many of these decisions have been made out of her adaptive child ego state, the compliant part of the personality that conforms to the wishes and demands of parental figures. She has conformed to the wishes and demands of her father, her former husband, and her bosses at work. She has not found any of this acquiescent behavior satisfactory; in fact, it has been just the opposite, and hence her involvement with escape literature and movies. Basically, Linda has an overdeveloped child ego state and an underdeveloped adult ego state.

In addition, Linda does not operate on a complementary level in her interpersonal relationships. Instead, her responses are crossed, as when unequals speak. Most of the time these transactions leave Linda dissatisfied and discouraged. She feels that others talk down to her, and she is frustrated. Consequently, Linda plays games, most of which have left her with bad feelings, except for her most recent third-degree game involving suicide, which could have left her in the morgue. Linda feels like a victim in the games she plays and in life.

You also note that Linda has injunctions in her life, such as "Don't be too competent." Therefore, Linda's life is limited in how much she can achieve. Because Linda has received mainly negative strokes in her life, she has followed negative scripts that have allowed her to distance herself from her family, divorce her husband, and find fault with her work. Her miniscript has been to please others. She is definitely in the I'm-not-OK position, as are most of those with whom she associates.

Treatment Process

As the TA therapist you are first of all a teacher. You explain to Linda the language and concepts of TA and the ways in which she can use these tools to think about herself. You want Linda to achieve a healthy lifestyle, to develop a strong adult ego state, and to adopt a position of I'm OK; you're OK. You want Linda to become autonomous and exhibit more awareness, intimacy, and spontaneity; become free of games; and eliminate self-defeating scripts. Therefore, you draw up a treatment contract with Linda with mutually agreed-upon goals and responsibilities.

When necessary, you confront Linda about inconsistencies in her behavior, explaining, illustrating, confirming, and interpreting as appropriate. Almost all of the TA techniques you use involve some combination of questions, confrontation, and dialogue. The techniques are aimed at helping Linda gain insight into not only what she is doing now but also how she can transform herself in time. To help her in this pursuit, you use some Gestalt techniques that add action and emotion to the thought process. In the end, Linda is able to experience what it is like to be talking to others from an adult ego state and to be successful instead of frustrated and angry.

Summary and Conclusion

Transactional analysis was formulated in the 1960s by Eric Berne. It parallels psychoanalysis with its emphasis on ego states, yet it has a number of other assumptions and practices that differ from those of psychoanalytic theory. For instance, TA holds that people can change if they gain insight into their thinking process; thinking influences feeling and behavior. The unconscious is not important. The TA approach also stresses that therapy is a learning process and that counselors operate in the role of instructors. TA theory emphasizes the importance of clients' homework outside formal therapeutic sessions and requires clients to learn new vocabularies. TA can be used in a number of settings and with a variety of client problems.

Although TA has strengths, it likewise has limitations. TA is so cognitively based and has so few techniques that TA counselors often must combine their theory with other approaches, such as Gestalt, to make it more active and strong. In addition, the TA research database is not strong. Many clinicians think that TA has stagnated in its development and that its popular appeal weakens its impact on clients and its status in the world of therapy.

Recall what you learned in this chapter by reviewing and completing the Chapter Review.

CHAPTER 12

Feminist Therapy

Elenathewise/Fotolia

Feminist therapy is a growing approach in counseling. Feminist views of counseling sprang from the emergence of the women's movement in the late 1960s and 1970s and the development of **feminist theory**, which begins "with the experience of women and uses women's values and beliefs as the assumptive framework" (Nwachuku & Ivey, 1991, p. 106).

Initially, the **feminist movement** was seen as a challenge to patriarchal power. However, as feminism has grown, its focus has centered more on the development of females as individuals, with common and unique qualities (Brown, 2010). In a society in which women face discrimination and subordination because of their gender, feminist therapy offers women a nonsexist, active way of addressing social ills and creating a positive sense of self (Miller, 1986; Okun, 1990; Ballou, M., Hill, M., & West, 2008).

The infusion of feminist theory into counseling was gradual at first. It started to escalate after the publication of Carol Gilligan's *In a Different Voice* (1982) as the distinctions between and commonalities of women and men were more clearly defined. This approach encourages women and men to become aware of socialization patterns and personal options in altering traditional gender roles. Furthermore, it encourages clients to become involved not only in personal but also in social change activities that stress equality as a way of life (Enns & Hackett, 1993). Overall, the major goals of **feminist counseling** besides equality are change, balancing independence and interdependence, empowerment, self-nurturance, and valuing diversity (Herlihy & McCollum, 2011). Feminist counseling

Chapter Outline

emphasizes analyzing the meaning of power and privilege in each person's life and its placement of that life into the larger social and political context as a strategy for understanding both distress and good function (Brown, 2010).

Major Theorist: Carol Gilligan

Feminist therapy can claim a number of individuals as its founders; the translation of feminist theories into therapy has seen a number of proponents. Carol Gilligan, Rachel Hare-Mustin, Paula Caplan, Laura S. Brown, Annette Brodsky, Lenore Walker, Carol Travis, Phyliss Chesler, Pam Remer, Mary Gergen, and Carol Enns all stand out as persons who have helped in this process. However, Gilligan is briefly highlighted here.

Carol Gilligan (1936–) was born in New York City. She majored in literature at Swarthmore College, from which she graduated summa cum laude. From there she went on to receive a master's degree in clinical psychology from Radcliffe and a doctorate in social psychology from Harvard.

Gilligan began teaching at Harvard in 1967 and in 1970 became a research assistant to Lawrence Kohlberg. She disagreed with Kohlberg's focus on males and issues pertinent to them in his moral development research. Consequently, Gilligan's primary focus came to be the moral development in girls, especially the impact of caring and relationships. In 1982 she published *In a Different Voice: Psychological Theory and Women's Development* and came to be known as the founder of **difference feminism**.

Gilligan is considered to be a pioneer of gender studies, particularly the psychological and moral development of girls. In 1997 she was appointed to Harvard's first position in gender studies and coordinated the formation of the Harvard Center on Gender and Education. In 2002 Gilligan left Harvard to join the faculty of New York University in an interdisciplinary position with the Graduate School of Education and the School of Law.

The recipient of numerous awards, Gilligan was named one of *Time* magazine's 25 most influential people in 1996. She has authored and coauthored numerous books and publications and has been instrumental in her research on adolescence, moral development, women's development, and conflict resolution. As a feminist, scholar, professor, and author, she has helped to form a new direction for women.

View of Human Nature/Personality

Feminist theory and the therapy that has sprung from it are not **monolithic**; diverse views about human nature exist among feminist counselors. Various feminist theories have been described as liberal, cultural, radical, or socialist, with each having its unique emphasis. Yet the different points of view share some beliefs in common about people and the nature of problems within society.

Feminist counselors believe that women have been constrained and oppressed in society (Ballou, Hill, & West, 2008). Their strengths have been devalued, and they have been socialized to take care of others and deny their own needs. Thus, many problems that women experience are the result of sociopolitical

> ## Human Systems
>
> *Understanding and Mastery: Theory of human development*
>
> Critical Thinking Question: How are the premises of feminist theory similar and different from the counseling theories covered thus far?

and cultural forces. In addition, feminist counselors believe that clients know what is best for their lives; for example, women should determine their sexual and procreative lives.

Another assumption underlying the feminist approach is that societal relationships and institutions, as well as gender relationships, are primarily based on noncooperative values. If society and its individuals are to be more mentally healthy, values must change and society must become more nurturing, cooperative, and relational. Individual change will best occur through social change (Okun & Kantrowitz, 2008).

Assess your comprehension of the **View of Human Nature/Personality** by taking this quiz.

Role of the Counselor

Counselors who work from a feminist perspective play a number of roles in the treatment of their clients. As educators, counselors demystify what counseling is and inform clients about how the therapeutic process works. Furthermore, feminist therapists assume an egalitarian and collaborative role and often use self-disclosure to reduce the power differentiation between client and counselor.

Counselors also attempt to make the client active in the therapeutic process focusing on the inner power a client has that may have been previously unrecognized or discounted. Through open dialogue a feminist helps the client make goals and follow through on them, often using contracts to make therapy more overt and concrete.

In addition, feminist counselors challenge the traditional ways of assessing psychological health. They do not usually make diagnoses using the latest Diagnostic and Statistical Manual (DSM) but rather include clients in the assessment and treatment process. Somewhat like Adlerian therapists, feminists have their own descriptive terms to define the concerns and problems that clients bring. They tend to reframe and relabel disorders that are especially prevalent in women—for example, depression, eating disorders, and posttraumatic stress—as ways of coping or responding to unfair societal norms and standards.

Planning and Evaluating

Understanding and Mastery: Skills to develop goals, and design and implement a plan of action

Critical Thinking Question: How would you go about demystifying the helping process for clients who do not understand what you are doing or why you are doing it?

Personal Reflection

How might you reframe or relabel depression? How about anxiety? What are the challenges of trying to reframe or relabel a disorder? How could it be harmful as well as helpful?

Goals

Counselors with a feminist focus have a number of goals and objectives:

- To **develop client awareness** of the gender-role socialization process and internalized gender-role messages and replace them with functional beliefs
- To **foster personal empowerment** and the development of a wide range of freely chosen behaviors
- To **help clients acquire skills** to bring about change in the environment

- To promote and **foster equality in society** and in male–female relationships
- To enable clients to **balance independence and interdependence**
- To assist clients in becoming more **self-nurturing**
- To **value diversity** in all of its forms, especially in regard to gender, culture, and lifestyle (Enns, 1997)

Assess your comprehension of the <u>Goals</u> by taking this quiz.

Process and Techniques

Because many women who seek help do not recognize that the origin of their problems lies in the inferior status of women in society, part of the counseling process begins with education. Counselors emphasize the value of social, political, and economic action as a major part of treatment. Feminists adapt interventions from a wide range of theoretical orientations, usually explaining the possible effects of and the rationale for their use.

- **Gender-role analysis.** Gender-role expectations begin early in life and impact the way individuals behave. In gender-role analysis, counselors help clients ferret out messages they have been given by significant others about how they should behave or appear. For example, clients may have internalized messages such as "Be passive" or "Be pretty." These messages are assessed for their positive and negative impacts, and statements or self-statements are identified that clients may want to change. A plan is then developed to implement the desired changes.
- **Gender-role intervention.** In gender-role intervention, counselors conduct a social analysis of the implications of gender roles and other social expectations for clients. This process provides a broader framework within which clients can assess individual psychological problems; it gives clients insight into ways that social issues may be impacting them. For example, social expectations that women should be thin may be linked to difficulties clients are having regarding body image, weight, and self-esteem.
- **Power analysis.** In power analysis, counselors help clients recognize the difference in power between men and women in society. Power refers to the ability to access resources in order to effect change on a personal and/or external level (Worrell & Remer, 2003). As clients analyze power differences, therapists help them identify alternate kinds of power they may possess and ways to make appropriate changes. For instance, clients may not be able to individually control a chaotic situation, such as verbal or physical abuse. However, they may be able to call in allies to help rectify the situation, or they may leave the environment, but under no circumstances should they internalize the abusive messages.
- **Power intervention.** Power intervention is more spontaneous than other techniques. It involves strengthening or empowering clients by reinforcing their statements or giving them information (Sharf, 2012). Through power intervention clients become more self-sufficient, confident, courageous, and competent. For example, if clients are reinforced for being forthright in giving feedback to people who have acted inappropriately, they will most likely continue that behavior and gain enhanced status in their environments.
- **Assertiveness training.** One of the ways that clients may be empowered is by being taught how to be assertive, that is, stating what one wants in a clear and direct

way. Assertiveness is different from aggression or passivity. For instance, the assertive statement "I want to go home now" differs significantly from the aggressive statement "I'm leaving you dull, boring losers" or the passive statement "I can't make up my mind whether to go or stay. What do you think I should do?" Like many other forms of behavior, assertiveness can be taught through role-playing and modeling. It is a skill that must be evaluated culturally and exercised in sensitive, sensible, and appropriate ways.

- **Reframing and relabeling.** The techniques of reframing and relabeling are used in a number of therapeutic approaches to help clients see situations from another perspective and thereby attribute a different meaning to certain behaviors. For example, behaviors that might be seen as pathological, such as depression, can be relabeled as coping mechanisms or as reactions to an oppressive policy or practice within society. In feminist therapy, societal expectations are frequently explored, leading clients to understand themselves better. The result is often "a shift from blaming oneself to looking at society for an explanation" (Sharf, 2012, p. 506).

- **Bibliotherapy and scriptotherapy.** Reading and writing can help reinforce therapeutic explorations. Therefore, feminist therapists often encourage their clients to read books or magazines or view appropriate media material, such as films, to assist them in understanding themselves and society better. Journaling or keeping a log of what is being learned or thought or felt can be therapeutic, too. Materials either read or written can be the grist for much discussion in counseling sessions.

- **Demystifying therapy/self-disclosure.** When clients do not understand how counseling works, a power differentiation is created, with the professional in charge of the therapeutic process being most powerful. To break down this barrier, feminist therapists are clear, open, and direct in explaining what counseling is and how it works. They inform clients about the parameters of the process and work with them in an egalitarian way. One helpful strategy is **self-disclosure**, in which the counselor shares with the client personal thoughts and feelings that are educative and yet revealing of the counselor as an individual.

- **Group work/social action.** Although therapeutic groups—such as support, self-help, and advocacy groups—are not always a part of feminist therapy, they can be useful adjuncts to this approach (Corey, 2013). Such groups help connect clients with one another and promote unity among the women involved. These groups may benefit clients who are in therapy or may be a powerful follow-up after counseling ends. Similarly, joining a social action organization may help clients help themselves and others by working to change society's stereotypes of women.

Personal Reflection

Assertiveness can change the way a woman feels about herself and the way others feel about her. What are the positives in being assertive as opposed to being passive or aggressive? Is there a downside to being assertive?

Assess your comprehension of the <u>Process and Techniques</u> by taking this quiz.

Multicultural Issues

Multiculturalism deals with culture, gender, disability, sexual orientation, socioeconomic disadvantage, and the world of military service. Using this criteria feminist counseling is seen as a multicultural form of therapy. Its concepts and strategies apply equally to individuals and groups regardless of age, race, culture, gender, or sexual orientation. Issues related to various forms of discrimination are important topics of discussion within this approach. Initially, feminist therapy focused mainly on middle-class white women; however, since the 1990s it has become much more encompassing. In essence, feminist counseling is an intentionally multicultural approach to therapy (Brown, 2008).

Gender issues are highlighted in feminist therapy, and nonsexist development is stressed. For example, in the area of career development feminist thought focuses on requirements for work instead of stressing traditional work roles by gender. Men as well as women may profit from feminist therapy by becoming more attuned to themselves and to gender-prescribed roles that inhibit their growth and restrict their relationships.

> ### Client-Related Values and Attitudes
>
> *Understanding and Mastery: The worth and uniqueness of individuals including ethnicity, culture, gender, sexual orientation, and other expressions of diversity.*
>
> **Critical Thinking Question:** How does feminist theory promote the worth and uniqueness of individuals, especially women?

Evaluation of the Theory

Strengths and Contributions

Feminist therapy has paved the way for gender-sensitive counseling practices (Corey, 2013). It has helped therapists from many other theoretical persuasions consider potential bias, especially toward women, in many traditional therapeutic practices. Feminist therapy was originally developed to address the negative effects of societal sexism on the lives of women and later was expanded to focus on the impacts of all forms of oppression on people's lives (Remer, 2008). This awareness has made it possible for clinicians to be fairer in their work with individuals, groups, couples, and families.

A second contribution of the feminist approach is its effectiveness "with women who are motivated for change and empowerment" (Austin, 1999, p. 69). Feminist therapy gives women a way of moving past passivity and traditionally ascribed roles. It opens up women to explore the inequality of power differentials in gender interactions. Furthermore, it explores the potency of power in relationships and society and the ways in which women can become more powerful through assertive means. It also advocates **self-acceptance**, including one's body, and teaches clients not to devalue or discount themselves because they are female or imperfect.

Another contribution of feminist counseling is its stress on the varied roles men and women may have and the limited flexibility society promotes because of gender-ascribed behaviors. Through its emphasis on social and political realities that create problems for women and men, feminist therapy addresses oppressive factors in the fabric of society and takes the blame off women for many of their difficulties.

In addition, feminist counseling highlights the importance of interpersonal relationships and behaviors such as cooperation and self-disclosure. Feminist therapists demystify the counseling relationship and stress the egalitarian nature of counseling. This approach allows greater focus on the change process itself.

Men may benefit from feminist counseling practices, too, when they are sensitized to the plight of women and to the limitations that men face when they are forced to maintain a masculine role (Levant, 2001). These insights help men realize how gender-role stereotypes negatively impact society as a whole.

Finally, feminist therapy is extremely flexible and inclusive and can be combined with many other ways of working with clients. Few, if any, counseling theories cannot incorporate feminist principles, ideas, and techniques and thereby broaden their work with diverse client groups in various stages of life and perhaps stimulate positive social change.

Limitations and Criticisms

The major drawback to feminist therapy is that there is little controlled outcome research on it. "The effectiveness of feminist therapy, both in relative and absolute terms, has not been rigorously evaluated" (Prochaska & Norcross, 2010, p. 393). Therefore, it is impossible to state whether feminist therapy is appropriate for certain clients with specific conditions and concerns.

Another limitation of feminist therapy is the difficulty of finding adequate training. The Stone Center at Wellesley College is conducting some work on what it is like to be female in society and what difficulties women in the United States face in therapeutic situations. However, the Stone Center is not a training center for feminist therapy (Sharf, 2012).

Yet another criticism of feminist therapy is that it does not take a neutral stand on issues. Instead, it actively advocates for "definite change in the social structure, especially in the area of equality, power in relationships, the right to self-determination, freedom to pursue a career outside the home, and the right to an education." Although nothing is inherently wrong with any of these goals, feminist therapists need to be cautious to avoid pushing their own agenda on their clients (Corey, 2013). Some clients who come for counseling are not interested in changing social structures.

A final criticism of feminist therapy is its lack of agreement on whether the approach is a theory or a philosophical orientation. In recent years, advocates of this approach have asserted that it is a theory (e.g., Enns, 1997; Crawford, 2012). However, as such, it differs significantly from other mainstream theories except for existentialism, which also is criticized for its emphasis on philosophy and its lack of concrete approaches originating from the theory itself.

Assess your comprehension of the Evaluation of the Theory by taking this quiz.

Treating Linda with Feminist Therapy

Conceptualization

From a feminist perspective, Linda has not been able to reach her potential because she grew up in a patriarchal culture that limited her growth and development as a person because she is female. Thus, she is stuck in a limiting, gender-stereotyped role in which she is stymied in her attempts to achieve and is devalued as a woman. Sociopolitical and cultural forces have conspired to keep her pigeonholed in taking care of others' needs but not her own. Linda knows in some ways that life is not working for her, but she needs to clarify exactly what she wants.

Treatment Process

As a feminist therapist you work as an educator, a collaborator, and a partner with Linda. You explore with her the ways in which her strengths and abilities have been discounted or devalued, such as her father's negative stereotyping because of her gender. You work with Linda to define her concerns and goals as concretely as possible. Some of your goals for her include becoming aware of society's and her own internalized messages regarding women and men, becoming more empowered and developing skills that will help her grow, balancing independence with dependence, becoming self-nurturing, promoting and fostering equality in society, and valuing diversity.

To help Linda reach these goals, you conduct a **gender-role analysis** in which Linda focuses on identifying limiting or enabling messages in her life that were given by significant others. Thereafter, you perform a gender-role intervention, which gives Linda insight into ways that social issues may be impacting her. Next, you repeat the analysis and the intervention focusing on the topic of power. In this process, you help Linda identify the power she has and reinforce herself for becoming more self-sufficient, confident, courageous, and competent.

You also teach Linda assertiveness through role playing and modeling. In this way, she is freed to ask for what she wants without being aggressive or passive. Furthermore, she learns how to reframe and relabel situations so that she does not pathologize herself. In addition, you encourage Linda to read books and magazines or view films that can assist her in understanding herself and the role of women in society. And you suggest that she keep a log of what she is learning, thinking, and feeling. Finally, you advise her to join a support group with other women to advocate for and promote equality within society. Linda finds that idea intriguing and begins to explore what it means to be a woman in the 21st century and what possibilities are available to her. A bonus from her support group is that she forms new friendships with others with whom she has much in common and learns helpful information about jobs and education, too.

Personal Reflection

What do you think of feminist therapy compared with other therapies covered in this text? What are the strengths of this approach? What are the limitations?

Summary and Conclusion

A recent phenomenon growing out of the women's movement of the late 1960s and 1970s, feminist therapy is a multifaceted approach to counseling rather than a well-formulated set of constructs (Enns, 1997). It questions and challenges the attitudes of traditional counseling theories, which often advocate maintaining the status quo of a male-dominated, hierarchical society.

According to feminist therapy, gender-role expectations have a profound impact on human development. Because women and men are socialized differently, models of psychological development based on male development fail to recognize that women's identity develops in a context of connectedness and relationship with others (Miller, 1991; Jordan, 2000). Feminist counselors seek to empower women to change the social contexts that suppress them (Austin, 1999), working through gender and power analysis and intervention as well as universal interventions such as bibliotherapy and reframing/relabeling. The result is greater personal and social sensitivity and often social activism.

In feminist therapy, external forces are recognized as the root of women's problems. Clients learn self-appreciation and self-value, and they learn to change their environments rather than adjust to them. They also learn to advocate for social change and to develop egalitarian, rather than hierarchical, relationships.

Recall what you learned in this chapter by reviewing and completing the Chapter Review.

CHAPTER 13

Bowen Family Systems Therapy

Paul Thomas/Photodisc/Thinkstock

Chapter Outline

Family counseling is a relatively recent approach to working with clients. It grew out of the need to help families readjust to life after the upheaval of World War II. At its inception, family therapy was considered radical. Most early theories dealt with how an entire family operates and interacts, both internally and externally. Such approaches differed significantly from other commonly accepted theories of the time, which were more individually oriented.

One of the oldest and most distinguished theories of working with families is Bowen family systems therapy. Murray Bowen and Michael Kerr have been its chief architects and advocates, but Bowen himself was the major originator of this philosophy. Nonetheless, many of its concepts have been popularized by other authors, such as McGoldrick (2011) and Friedman (1985).

This chapter covers Bowen family therapy, which can be used with individuals, couples, and families. Chapter 14 addresses strategic family therapy, an equally established approach and one that has some of the versatility of the Bowen approach but a different philosophy and methodology. These two family therapies, along with solution-focused therapy, represent the innovation and creativity connected with counseling families and the individuals in them.

Major Theorist: Murray Bowen

Murray Bowen (1913–1990) was the oldest of five children in a tightly knit family that resided for several generations in a small town in Pennsylvania. After growing up, Bowen moved away and kept a formal distance from his parents, maintaining family relations on a comfortable but superficial level. Bowen was a psychiatrist who became interested in working with families while he was employed at the Menninger Clinic. As early as 1951, he began to require that mothers of disturbed children live in the same hospital setting as their offspring during treatment (Guerin, 1976). From this experience, he became interested in studying mother-patient symbiosis, that is, the intense bond that develops between a parent and a child that does not allow either to differentiate from the other (Bowen, 1960, 1961).

In 1954 Bowen joined Lyman Wynne at the National Institute of Mental Health (NIMH), where he continued to study the dynamics of families with schizophrenic children. Bowen worked with the research team at NIMH on a pilot project to hospitalize and treat all members of such families as part of treatment. He recognized during this time that the characteristics exhibited by a schizophrenic family were similar to symptoms in many dysfunctional families. A few years later, Bowen moved to Georgetown University, where he researched family dynamics and developed his therapeutic approach.

For Bowen, therapy and theory cannot be separated without doing a disservice to each. He preferred to think of himself as a theorist, one who stood alone in conceptualizing "the family as a natural system ... which could only be fully understood in terms of the fluid but predictable processes between members" (Wylie, 1991, p. 26). Thus, Bowen viewed himself as a scientist in search of universal truths, and his theory "constantly strives to make continuous what other theories dichotomize"—for example, nature/nurture, male/female, physical illness/emotional illness (Friedman, 1991, p. 136).

During his years at Georgetown, especially in the 1970s, Bowen completed his most productive personal and professional work. Personally, he removed himself from the triangulation with his parents by returning home and reacting cognitively and neutrally to a number of emotional issues that family members presented to him (Anonymous, 1972). Professionally, he clarified his theory (Bowen, 1978); began the Georgetown Family Center Symposium; expanded the Georgetown Family Center to new, off-campus quarters; and initiated the American Family Therapy Association "in order to restore a serious research effort in family therapy" (Wylie, 1991, p. 77).

View of Human Nature/Personality

Bowen was influenced by events in his own life, especially his difficulties with his family of origin. Thus, his personal situation had a major impact on what he proposed in regard to the development of others (Anonymous, 1972; Papero, 1991). Basically, Bowen states that individuals who do not examine and rectify patterns passed down from previous generations are likely to repeat these behaviors in their own families (Kerr, 1988; 2003). This possibility is particularly likely if family members, especially those of different generations, are either emotionally overinvolved with each other or emotionally cut off from each other. Bowen concerns himself with the family's emotional system and its impact on family members' personalities.

A key element of Bowen family therapy is that "there is a **chronic anxiety** in all of life that comes with the territory of living" (Friedman, 1991, p. 139). This anxiety is both emotional and physical and is shared by all living organisms. Some individuals are more affected than others "because of the way previous generations in their families have channeled the transmission" of this anxiety to them (Friedman, 1991, p. 140).

If anxiety remains low, few problems exist for individuals or families; the family emotional system is undisturbed. However, when anxiety rises, some predictable patterns occur.

To address chronic anxiety and emotional processes in families and society, Bowen emphasizes a number of basic concepts through which therapists can understand the dynamics within a family: differentiation, multigenerational transmission process, nuclear family emotional system, family projection process, triangles, sibling position, and societal regression (Bowen, 1978; Kerr, 1981, 2003; Gilbert, 2006).

Differentiation refers to the ability of persons to distinguish themselves from their family of origin on an emotional and an intellectual level and to balance the intrapsychic and interpersonal dimensions of the self (Bowen, 1978; Kerr, 2003). Differentiated people can recover emotional equilibrium quickly after stress passes (Greene, Hamilton, & Rolling, 1986). They are **autonomous**, which is the ability to think through a situation clearly. For instance, Peleg-Popko (2004) found family differentiation (specifically, adolescents' relationships with their mothers) to be negatively correlated with levels of test and trait anxiety and positively correlated with cognitive performance.

Undifferentiated or fused is the opposite of differentiation. It implies an emotional dependence on family members, even if living away from them. Undifferentiated people are vulnerable to stress and are much more prone to physical and social illnesses than others (Hooper & Doehler, 2011). In such situations, family members may exhibit dysfunctional behaviors, such as bulimia, which are more likely to become chronic when they occur. "Theoretically, at least four factors influence a person's level of differentiation: emotional reactivity, emotional cutoff, fusion with others, and the ability to take an *I-position*" (Tuason & Friedlander, 2000, p. 27). It is through the process of differentiation that families and the individuals in them are able to change. People vary in the level of self-differentiation they can achieve at any one time; the concept itself denotes a process (Bowen, 1965).

Another of Bowen's basic concepts deals with the coping strategies and patterns that tend to be passed on from generation to generation, an important phenomenon known as the **multigenerational transmission process**. Families that present a problem have had the forces of several generations shaping and carrying it along. In marriage, people tend to select partners at their own level of differentiation (Bowen, 1976), from which union a nuclear family emotional system evolves.

Spouses with equally high levels of identity are able to establish and maintain clear individuality "and at the same time to have an intense, mature, nonthreatening, emotional closeness" (Bowen, 1965, p. 220). Indeed, research shows that couples that are less reactive, cutoff, or fused and that are able to relate from an *I-position* "experience the greatest levels of marital satisfaction" (Skowron, 2000, p. 233). This result is particularly true if the male partner remains emotionally present and available.

On the other hand, spouses with equally low levels of differentiation have difficulty establishing intimacy because they have developed only **pseudoselves**, that is, pretend selves (Kerr, 1988, p. 43). The pseudoselves fluctuate according to situations and usually result in the fusion of these selves into a "common self with obliteration of ego boundaries between them and loss of individuality to the common self" (Bowen, 1965, p. 221). Couples tend to produce offspring with the same level of differentiation that the parents have, a process Bowen describes as **family projection** (Kilpatrick, 1980).

To rid themselves of anxiety, spouses with low self-differentiation keep an emotional distance from each other. When anxiety becomes too great, it is frequently manifested in one of four ways: (1) marital conflict, (2) physical or emotional illness in one spouse, (3) projection of the problem to the children, or (4) a combination of these (David, 1979).

When working with individuals and couples, Bowen family therapists look for **triangles** (Kerr, 2003), which can occur between people or between people and things. A triangle consists of a state of calm between a comfortable twosome and an outsider (Anonymous, 1972); it is "the basic building block of any emotional system and the smallest stable relationship system" (Kilpatrick, 1980, p. 168). The original triangle is between a child and parents. Some triangles are healthy; others are not. In the latter case, triangles are a frequent way of dealing with anxiety, allowing tension between two persons to be projected onto another person or object. In stressful situations, anxiety can spread from one central triangle within the family to interlocking triangles outside the family, especially in work and social systems (Kerr, 1988, 2003).

> ### Human Systems
>
> *Understanding and Mastery: Theories of human development*
>
> **Critical Thinking Question:** Why is differentiation so important for the health and well-being of persons and for society?

Personal Reflection

Where have you observed triangles in your community outside of couple relationship? How prevalent are they? What does that tell you about the health and well-being of where you live?

Bowen therapists also examine **sibling positions** because people can develop fixed personality characteristics based on their functional birth order in the family (Toman, 1961). The more closely a marriage replicates a couple's sibling positions in their families of origin, the better the chance for success. For example, if a youngest son marries an oldest daughter, both have much to gain from the arrangement because the youngest son most likely enjoys being taken care of, and the oldest daughter probably enjoys taking care of someone.

By examining these processes, family members gain insight and understanding into the past and are free to choose how they will behave in the present and future. Similarly, they gain a perspective on how well society as a whole is doing. In a society under too much stress (e.g., from population growth or economic decline), societal regression occurs because too many toxic forces counter the tendency to achieve differentiation.

> **Assess your comprehension of the View of Human Nature/Personality** by taking this quiz.

Role of the Counselor

In the Bowen model, the differentiation of the therapist is crucial. Bowen family therapists must maintain a calm presence and be differentiated from their families of origin (Friedman, 1991); **objectivity** and **neutrality** are important characteristics of Bowen therapists. To be able to work with families, therapists must first undergo emotional change (Kerr, 1981), or those they work with will not be able to experience healthy shifts.

Having personally resolved family-of-origin concerns, the Bowen therapist is usually involved in coaching on more cognitive levels. Initially, family members—primarily individuals or couples—talk to the therapist or to one another through the therapist so that emotional issues do not cloud communication (Kerr, 2003). According to Bowen, therapists should not encourage people to wallow in emotionalism but should teach them by example to transcend it, behaving with reason and self-control. Therapy should be just like a **Socratic dialogue**, with the teacher, or coach, calmly asking questions until the student learns to think independently (Wylie, 1991, p. 27).

Bowen family therapy looks at boundary and differentiation issues from a historical perspective. Therapists instruct individuals to search for clues as to where various family pressures have been expressed and how effectively the family has adapted to stress since its inception, through three previous generations if possible. Individuals might draw a genogram or visit their family of origin to obtain this information. By examining family dynamics, therapists become interpreters with their clients in working through multigenerational patterns of fusion and cutoffs and then resolving areas of difficulty.

Goals

Bowen family therapy promotes differentiation in regard to self/family and also intellect/emotion. Therapists help their clients, especially couples, separate their feelings from their intellect and in the process **detriangulate**.

Another primary goal is that family members come to understand **intergenerational patterns** and gain insight into historical circumstances that have influenced the ways they currently interact (Learner, 1983). Then it is hoped that clients can focus on changing the "intergenerational inferences operating with the current family" (Smith, 1991, p. 25). Therapists can help family members differentiate from each other and become more diverse and fluid in their interactions (Bowen, 1978). At the end of treatment, individuals should be able to relate on an autonomous, cognitive level, and projective patterns of blame should be changed (Kerr & Bowen, 1988). Nuclear family members should experience greater self-differentiation.

Assess your comprehension of the <u>Goals</u> by taking this quiz.

Process and Techniques

In Bowen family therapy, the chief focus is an individual or a couple; the whole family is usually not seen, even though the emphasis is systemic (Kerr, 2003). "A theoretical system that thinks in terms of family, with a therapeutic method that works toward improvement of the family system, is 'family' regardless of the number of people in the sessions" (Kerr, 1981, p. 232). By changing just one person, therapy may directly influence an entire family. Thus, the therapist may work "with all involved family members present, with any combination of family members present, or with only one family member present." However, "since the two spouses are the two family members most involved in the family ego mass, the most rapid family change occurs when the spouses are able to work as a team in family psychotherapy" (Bowen, 1965, p. 220).

Bowen family therapy is not technique-oriented; rather it is **process-oriented**, with techniques used to help clients when needed. Bowen therapists ask questions about their clients' thoughts and give homework assignments. Among the techniques most often employed are genograms, going home again, detriangulation, person-to-person relationships, differentiation of self, and asking questions.

A **genogram** is a visual representation of a family tree, depicted in geometric figures, lines, and words (Sherman, 1993; McGoldrick, 2011) (see Figure 13.1). Genograms include information about family relationships over at least three generations. They help people gather information, hypothesize, and track relationship changes in the context of historic and contemporary events (Dunn & Levitt, 2000). "From this simple diagram, counselors and clients alike are able to view simultaneously family composition, gender, age, ethnicity, dates of birth, marriages, divorces, deaths, and other important family events" (Frame, 2000, p. 69).

The tangibility and nonthreatening nature of a genogram help clinicians gather a large amount of information in a relatively short period of time. Furthermore, genograms can increase "mutual trust and tolerance" among all involved in their construction (Sherman, 1993, p. 91). Bowen family therapy "advises people to go 'back, back, back; and up, up, up' their family tree to look for patterns, 'recycling,' getting not just information but a feel for the context and milieu that existed during each person's formative years" (White, 1978, pp. 25–26). This process promotes the shift from emotional reactivity to clear cognitions.

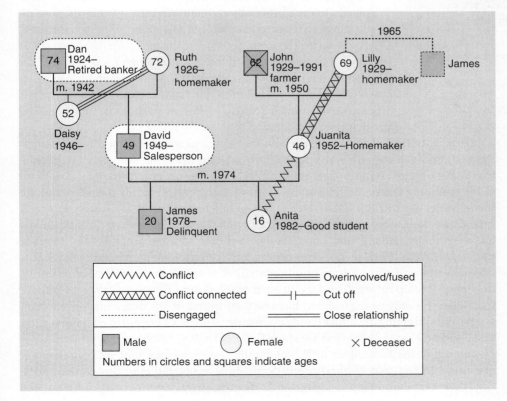

FIGURE 13.1

Family Genogram.

Source: From Family Therapy: History, Theory, and Practice (3rd ed., p. 137) by Samuel T. Gladding. Copyright 2002. Reprinted by permission of Pearson Education, Inc., Upper Saddle River, NJ.

Genograms can be color coded to indicate everything from substance abuse to forms of spirituality (Frame, 2000). Data in genograms are scanned for (1) repetitive patterns, such as triangles, cutoffs, and coalitions; (2) coincidences, such as the deaths of members or the ages of symptom onset; and (3) the impact of change and untimely life cycle transitions, such as off-schedule events (e.g., marriage, death, and the birth of children occurring at a different time than is the norm) (McGoldrick, 2011).

In going home again, the family therapist instructs the individual client or family members to return home in order to get to know better their family of origin (Bowen, 1976). With this type of information, individuals can differentiate themselves more clearly and thus can operate more fully within all family contexts of which they are a part. However, before returning home, clients may need to learn and practice how to remain calm (Bowen, 1976).

The concept of **detriangulation** involves "the process of being in contact and emotionally separate" (Kerr, 1988, p. 55). It operates on at least two levels. On one level, individuals resolve their anxiety over family situations and do not project feelings onto anyone else. On a second level, Bowen therapists help those individuals separate themselves from the tension that arises in the family, refusing to allow themselves to become targets or scapegoats for others who may be overcome with anxiety. For example, if a usually triangulated person stays rational during times of emotional stress, he or she will seldom become the focus of attention for the others in the triangle (Bowen, 1972). On both levels, individuals will be free to voice their concerns and try out new ways of acting.

In **person-to-person relationships** two family members "relate personally to each other about each other; that is, they do not talk about others (triangling) and do not talk about impersonal issues" (Piercy & Sprenkle, 1986, p. 11). For instance, a father may say to his son, "Your actions remind me of myself when I was your age." In return, the son may say, "I really don't know much about you when you were a boy. Please tell me about what you did and how you felt when you were my age." Such a process helps promote individuation, or autonomy, and intimacy.

Differentiation of self has to do with the degree to which a person is able to distinguish between the subjective feeling process and the more objective intellectual (thinking) process" (Gibson & Donigian, 1993, p. 28). This procedure may involve all of the preceding techniques plus some confrontation between family members and the therapist. As was mentioned earlier, a failure to differentiate results in **fusion**, in which "people are dominated by their automatic emotional system"; they have "less flexibility, less adaptability, and are more emotionally dependent on those around them" (Sauber, L'Abate, & Weeks, 1985, p. 43). Over generations, children most involved in family fusion move toward a lower level of differentiation of self (Bowen, 1972). For example, they may develop eating disorders. In such cases, Bowen therapists try to help these individuals (usually young women) increase their degree of self-differentiation through assertiveness training, healthier family boundaries, enhanced cognitive communication skills, and new coping behaviors for stress (Levy & Hadley, 1998).

In each of the techniques in Bowen family theory, a consistent strategy is to ask questions. In fact, asking questions is deemed the magic bullet of Bowen therapists. For instance, when major events such as deaths, births, and marriages disturb the

---

Interpersonal Communication

Understanding and Mastery: Establishing rapport with clients

Critical Thinking Question: As a Bowen family therapist, how do you think you could calm a person's anxiety in asking him or her to go home again and to have a person-to-person relationship with another family member?

equilibrium of a family, emotional shock waves may result (Bowen, 1976). Questions can help individuals involved in Bowen family therapy learn to better understand the reactions of those in their families.

Personal Reflection

How comfortable are you asking questions to members of your family? Think of some of the behavioral, cognitive, and cognitive behavioral strategies you read about earlier.

Assess your comprehension of the <u>Process and Techniques</u> by taking this quiz.

Multicultural Issues

Multiculturalism deals with culture, gender, disability, sexual orientation, socioeconomic disadvantage, and the world of military service. Bowen family therapy is flexible in its applications and can be used in many multicultural situations. For instance, it has been used with the homeless who are not mentally ill or addicted to help them break the pattern of behavior leading up to and maintaining homelessness (Hertlein & Killmer, 2004).

However, some of Bowen concepts are limited in their applicability to different cultures. On the positive side, genograms can be multicultural in nature and can include worldview and cultural factors that influence the behavior of family members (Thomas, 1998; McGoldrick, 2011). In addition, there is evidence that differentiation is applicable across cultures. However, for some groups such as Filipinos and North Americans, "psychological well-being in adulthood may well be affected by factors outside of the family, such as peer relationships, employment, or societal influences" (Tuason & Friedlander, 2000, p. 33).

The Bowen approach is somewhat controversial in regard to gender-specific issues. Bowen theory proposes that the genogram is gender neutral in its display of facts and patterns. However, Knudson-Martin (2002) suggests that many women, as well as persons from less individualistic cultures and very spiritual persons, develop a connected self that is significantly different from Bowen's image of separate selves engaged with each other. Basically, Knudson-Martin contends that Bowen theory ignores many of the positive aspects of togetherness.

Self-Development

Understanding and Mastery: Awareness of Diversity

Critical Thinking Question: How do differentiation and awareness of diversity occur simultaneously or does one precede the other?

Evaluation of the Theory

Strengths and Contributions

A strength of Bowen theory is that it calls attention to **family history**, emphasizing the importance of noticing and dealing with past patterns to enable individuals and families to avoid repeating these behaviors in the future. The genogram is a specific tool developed to plot historical linkages and as such is increasingly used by theorists of all persuasions in assessing client families.

Another strength of Bowen family therapy is that it is a well-established and heuristically appealing approach. Its emphasis on theory as well as its practical nature makes it attractive. In addition, the theory and the therapy are extensive and intertwined. The theory is a blueprint for the therapy; the therapy is consistent with and inseparable from the theory. Family therapists are indebted to Bowen for intertwining these two aspects.

A further strength is that Bowen was insightful and detailed in suggesting the course of working with families. And he established a center for educating practitioners, ensuring that the Bowen approach will continue to be learned and used.

One final contribution is that Bowen family therapy is systemic in nature, controlled in focus, and cognitive in practice, thereby giving clinicians and their clients a concrete way of evaluating progress (Bowen, 1975). Furthermore, unlike many other systemic family approaches, Bowen family therapy can be used extensively with individuals or couples. It is considered "the most comprehensive theory of individual functioning from a family systems perspective" (Skowron & Platt, 2005, p. 281).

Limitations and Criticisms

The Bowen approach is vulnerable to criticism for its failure to fully validate its intergenerational hypothesis (Tuason & Friedlander, 2000). In other words, the ideas behind this approach are intriguing but are not always verified. A related concern is that the theory underlying the approach is its own paradigm (Friedman, 1991). Thus, setting up research questions to refute or verify this approach is a challenge of the highest order.

Another drawback is that Bowen's stress on the importance of the past encourages some families or family members to examine their history rather than deal immediately with present circumstances. Such a process may promote insight but not action.

One other limitation is the time and, consequently, the financial resources that Bowen family therapy requires of its clients. Most people cannot afford to invest as heavily in this process as is necessary. Thus, the number of people who can benefit from this approach is limited.

A final criticism of the Bowen approach is the complex and convoluted nature of Bowen's writings about the continuity of and connection between theory and therapy (Kaplan, 2000). Reading Bowen is not easy.

Assess your comprehension of the Evaluation of the Theory by taking this quiz.

Personal Reflection

What do you know about your family at this point in time? What more would you like to know? How can knowledge in and of itself be therapeutic?

Treating Linda with Bowen Family Systems Therapy

Conceptualization

From a Bowen family systems perspective, Linda is most likely undifferentiated from her family of origin. Therefore, she suffers from chronic anxiety and has difficulty relating to others from an *I-position*. This inability to relate on a deep level has resulted in Linda's developing a pseudoself that fluctuates with situations. She becomes angry when threatened and either lashes out, as in her past jobs, or withdraws, as with her family finding solace in her fascination for adventure books and films. Linda's state of functioning is a result of multigenerational transmissions; she reflects the low level of differentiation in her family. If this condition is not rectified, Linda will most likely start forming triangles to scapegoat people and activities about which she becomes anxious.

Treatment Process

As a Bowen family therapist, you maintain a calm presence in the midst of Linda's anxiety because you have dealt with your own family-of-origin issues. You work cognitively with Linda as a coach, a teacher, and a catalyst, being as objective and neutral as possible. It is not necessary for Linda to bring her family to therapy because you can help her make changes and gain insight that will alter the system dynamics in her family.

Initially, you press Linda to search for clues on how her family has dealt with stress. You ask her questions. You also have her draw a genogram, a multigenerational family diagram that reveals how past generations in the family have acted and reacted in times of significant turmoil and transition. Your goal in each of these activities is to have Linda draw on historical information to influence the present. If Linda can separate her thoughts from her feelings and herself from her family, she may become more autonomous, differentiated, and healthy.

You also assign Linda homework: She is to go home again and have person-to-person relationships with as many family members as possible. In addition, she is to ask questions of her parents and siblings about relationships in the family. The hope is that she will learn information that will help her detect family patterns and then change her ways of relating. If successful, she will be able to differentiate herself from her family and form deep and lasting bonds with others. The process of therapy takes several months, but in the end Linda is calmer and has begun to think about what her next steps will be vocationally, as well as in the community and in her family.

Summary and Conclusion

Bowen family therapy is one of the most established approaches to working with individuals and families. A psychoanalytically trained psychiatrist, Murray Bowen devised his own approach to working with families, especially couples, based in part on his life experiences and in part on psychoanalytic theory.

Bowen theory emphasizes the importance of unconscious forces in family life. The therapy is systemic, although its primary clients are individuals and couples. It emphasizes the importance of historical intergenerational patterns and uses a cognitive strategy to help couples and family members differentiate and change their ways of thinking. In the process, the therapist acts as a coach, a teacher, and a catalyst.

Overall, this approach emphasizes in-depth exploration of clients' families and concentrates on long-term results. It requires a considerable investment of time and resources. Yet Bowen theory is concrete in outcome and gives its clients a way to recognize dysfunctional patterns transmitted across generations.

Recall what you learned in this chapter by reviewing and completing the Chapter Review.

CHAPTER 14

Strategic Family Therapy

Bruce Ayres/Stone/Getty Images

Chapter Outline

Erickson
Solution
Focused

Strategic family therapy is method oriented and brief in duration. Varied strategic therapies are indebted to the genius of Milton Erickson, whose work influenced their founders. Erickson's goal in treatment was change; he believed in utilizing the resources of his clients and designing a "strategy for each specific problem" (Madanes, 1991, p. 396). Erickson then gave directives and indirect suggestions to help his clients assist themselves. He did not care whether people gained insight as long as their actions produced beneficial results. "If Freud was a philosopher-priest from Vienna, Erickson was a samurai warrior from Wisconsin" (Wylie, 1990, p. 28).

Although inspired by Erickson, the ideas and techniques of strategic family therapy have been generated and refined primarily in two different centers: the Mental Research Institute (MRI) in Palo Alto, California, and the Washington School of Jay Haley and Cloe Madanes (Gardner, Burr, & Wiedower, 2006). The MRI form of strategic family therapy is the older of these therapeutic approaches. It is a descendent of the Bateson communications studies group, which was conducted in Palo Alto from 1952 to 1962. Among the most active modern proponents of this approach are Paul Watzlawick and John Weakland; other related practitioners are Lynn Hoffman, Peggy Penn, and Richard Rabkin. The Washington School, organized in the mid-1970s, is most associated with Haley and Madanes (Keim, 2000).

The strategic family therapy approaches have a history that is both long and distinguished. Haley (1963, 1973) coined the term **strategic**

therapy to describe the work of Erickson, who paid extreme attention to the details of the symptoms his clients presented. His focus, like that of most present-day strategic therapists, was to change behavior by manipulating it, not to instill insight. Erickson achieved his objectives in therapy by accepting and emphasizing the positive; framing all symptoms and maladaptive behaviors as helpful; using indirect and ambiguous directives; and encouraging or directing routine behaviors so that resistance is shown through change and not through normal and continuous actions (Haley, 1963).

Major Theorist: Jay Haley

Jay Haley (1923–2007) is one of the most distinguished and controversial pioneers in the field of family therapy. He influenced the Bateson group and the MRI group as a founding member of each and set up the Family Therapy Institute of Washington, DC, with Madanes in 1974. In addition, he served as an effective communicator between people and groups and was a strong advocate of family therapy in public and professional settings (Ray, 2007).

Haley's development is unique among family therapists; he learned from and with the three people who had the most influence on the evolution of family therapy—Erickson, Gregory Bateson, and Salvador Minuchin. Haley began his career with Bateson in 1952. Because Haley had a master's degree in communications, his chief responsibility on Bateson's research team was to take the lead in diagnosing communication patterns in schizophrenic families. As a result of that work, Haley became interested in the hypnotherapy communication process of Erickson. Haley learned hypnosis from Erickson in 1953 and later taught and practiced it (Simon, 1982). He also incorporated many of Erickson's ideas into his own concepts about therapy and learned to become a therapist under Erickson's supervision. Basically, Haley adopted and modified Erickson's individual emphasis so that it would work with families.

In 1962, after the Bateson team dissolved, Haley joined the Mental Research Institute staff and worked there until 1967. At this time, he stopped doing therapy and became primarily involved in "family research and the observation of therapy" (Simon, 1982, p. 20). He also became the first editor of the initial journal in the field of family therapy, *Family Process*, and held that position from 1962 to 1969. Haley became even more involved in supervision when he moved east to join Salvador Minuchin at the Philadelphia Child Guidance Center in 1967. With Minuchin he organized "the Institute for Family Counseling (IFC), a project training people from the Philadelphia ghetto, who had no formal education beyond high school, to be family therapists" (Simon, 1982, p. 20). This effort further established his prominence.

In 1976, he moved to the Washington, DC, area to establish the Family Therapy Institute with Madanes. Thereafter, he published two of his most influential books, *Problem-Solving Therapy* (1976) and *Leaving Home* (1980). These books spell out the essence of strategic family therapy as he viewed it, with an emphasis on power and hierarchy. Haley is described as having the skills of a power broker and a military strategist and making these skills "respectable therapeutic techniques" (Wylie, 1990, p. 28). Haley retired in 1995 and died 12 years later in La Jolla, California.

View of Human Nature/Personality

In general, strategic family therapists concentrate on the following dimensions of family life:

- **Family rules**—the overt and covert rules that families use to govern themselves
- **Family homeostasis**—the tendency of the family to remain in the same pattern of functioning unless challenged to do otherwise
- **Quid pro quo**—the tendency of family members to treat others in the way they are being treated
- **Redundancy principle**—a family's repetition of limited behavioral sequences
- **Punctuation**—the belief that what individuals say in a transaction is caused by what others say
- **Symmetrical relationships** and **complementary relationships**—relationships that are among equals (symmetrical) and among unequals (complementary)
- **Circular causality**—the idea that events are interconnected and that behaviors are caused by multiple factors

> **Human Systems**
>
> *Understanding and Mastery: Changing family structures and roles*
>
> **Critical Thinking Question:** How can a change in a family's structure or roles change the family for better or for worse?

> Assess your comprehension of the <u>View of Human Nature/Personality</u> by taking this quiz.

Role of the Counselor

As a group, strategic family therapies follow Ericksonian principles, emphasizing short-term treatment of about 10 sessions. Often, strategic therapies are characterized as **brief therapy**, referring to the clarity about what needs to be changed rather than to the time required. "A central principle of brief therapy is that one evaluates which solutions have so far been attempted for the patient's problem" (Priebe & Pommerien, 1992, p. 433). Then, different solutions are tried that are often the opposite of what has already been attempted (Watzlawick, 1978). "Brief therapists hold in common the belief that therapy must be specifically goal-directed, problem-focused, well-defined, and, first and foremost, aimed at relieving the client's presenting complaint" (Wylie, 1990, p. 29).

The roles of strategic therapists differ among the subschools. However, those who work within this methodology believe in being active and flexible with their clients. It is the therapist's responsibility to plan strategies to resolve family problems. Therefore, counselors often proceed quickly and specifically to resolve presenting problems and virtually ignore family histories and personal diagnoses (Wylie, 1990). "They are symptom focused and behaviorally oriented" (Snider, 1992, p. 20).

"The first task of the therapist is to define a presenting problem in such a way that it can be solved" (Madanes, 1991, p. 396). Thus, the therapist usually tries to define it as something that the family has voluntary control over and that involves a power struggle. The therapist tries to help family members make changes that alter family dynamics from a competitive stance, in which there are winners and losers, to a cooperative position, in which everyone wins (Watzlawick, 1983).

Most strategic therapists are overtly active and direct (Gardner et al., 2006). For instance, Haley (1990) believed that it is essential to make changes in individuals and families within the first three sessions. Thus, he worked hard at reframing a client's perceptions and the presenting complaints. Haley also strove for a unique and innovative approach in each case, tailored to the family as Erickson would have done, much as a surgeon would plan an operation. "Therapists also use structural interventions such as attempting to unbalance family systems by joining with one or more members on a conflictual point, fortifying generational boundaries, and supporting members at particular times to accomplish a specific objective" (Snider, 1992, p. 20). Families usually have homework assignments between sessions.

Interventions and Direct Service

Understanding and Mastery: Skills to facilitate appropriate direct services and interventions related to specific client or client group goals

Critical Thinking Question: What are the advantages and drawbacks of a therapist or human services practitioner acting as an expert and planning family strategies for change?

Personal Reflection

What were the overt rules in your family when you were a child? What were the covert rules? How did they contribute to the functioning of your family?

Goals

The goal of strategic family therapy is to resolve, remove, or ameliorate the problem that the family has agreed to work on (Snider, 1992). In addition, the family must learn, at least indirectly, how to address other problems in a constructive manner. Often, resolving family difficulties involves a multitude of interventions, or steps. Four common procedures help to ensure a successful outcome:

1. Defining a problem clearly and concisely
2. Investigating all solutions that have previously been tried
3. Defining a clear and concrete change to be achieved
4. Formulating and implementing a strategy for change (Watzlawick, 1978)

Overall, the emphasis in strategic therapy is on process rather than content. The methods used focus on breaking up vicious cycles of interaction and replacing them with virtuous cycles that highlight alternative ways of acting (Friesen, 1985).

Assess your comprehension of the Goals by taking this quiz.

Process and Techniques

Strategic therapists are innovative. They believe that it is not helpful to tell people what they are doing wrong or to encourage catharsis (Haley, 1976). If families are going to change, alterations in behaviors must precede new perceptions and feelings. This goal can be accomplished in an almost endless number of ways.

Each intervention in strategic therapy is tailored to the idiosyncrasies of individuals and problems. This customization makes strategic therapies some of the most technique driven of all approaches to helping. In general, strategic family therapists emphasize reframing, directives, paradoxes, ordeals, pretending, and positioning.

Reframing involves the use of language to induce a cognitive shift within family members and alter the perception of a situation. In reframing, a different interpretation is given to a family's situation or behavior, a circumstance is given new meaning, and as a consequence, other ways of behaving are explored. Reframing does not change a situation, but "the alteration of meaning invites the possibility of change" (Piercy & Sprenkle, 1986, p. 35). For instance, depression may be conceptualized as irresponsibility or stubbornness. Overall, reframing helps establish rapport between the therapist and the family and breaks down resistance. What was once seen as out-of-control behavior may become voluntary and open to change.

A **directive** is an instruction from a family therapist to a family to behave differently. "The directive is to strategic therapy what the interpretation is to psychoanalysis. It is the basic tool of the approach" (Madanes, 1991, p. 397). Many types of directives can be given, including **nonverbal messages** (e.g., silence, voice tone, and posture), **direct and indirect suggestions** (e.g., "Go fast" or "You may not want to change too quickly"), and **assigned behaviors** (e.g., when you think you won't sleep, force yourself to stay up all night). The purpose of outside assignments is to help individuals behave differently so that they can have different subjective experiences. Directives also increase the influence of the therapist in the change process and give the therapist information about how family members react to suggested changes. One example of a directive is to tell a family to go slowly in working to bring about change. If they disobey the directive, their resistance to change may dissolve. If they follow the directive, the therapist may gain more influence in their lives.

One of the most controversial and powerful techniques in the strategic approach is **paradox** (Sexton & Montgomery, 1994). Although fine distinctions can be made between them, this process is similar to prescribing the symptom. It gives families permission to do something they are already doing and is intended to lower or eliminate resistance. Haley (1976) is one of the best-known proponents of this technique, which can take many forms.

1. In **restraining**, the therapist tells the client family that they are incapable of doing anything other than what they are doing. For example, a therapist might say, "In considering change, I am not sure you can do anything other than what you are presently doing."
2. In **prescribing**, family members are instructed to enact a troublesome dysfunctional behavior in front of the therapist. For instance, parents may be asked to show how they argue with their 16-year-old about getting a driver's license. They are told to continue the argument as long as it usually lasts and to come up with the same impasses.
3. **Redefining** is attributing positive connotations to symptomatic or troublesome actions. The underlying idea is that symptoms have meaning for those who display them, whether such meaning is logical or not. In the case of a school-phobic daughter, the therapist might redefine her behavior as an attempt to keep her parents together by focusing their attention on her.

Ordeals involve helping clients give up symptoms that are troublesome to maintain (Haley, 1984). In this method the therapist assigns an ordeal, which is a constructive or neutral behavior that must be performed before one can engage in the undesirable behavior. For example, an ordeal might be to exercise before the onset of depression.

The ordeal is always healthy but is not an activity that the client wants to engage in. The hope is that the client will give up the symptom in order to avoid performing the constructive behavior.

The **pretend technique** is a gentler and less confrontational technique than most of the other procedures used in the strategic approach. Madanes (1981, 1984) is identified as the creator of this concept. Basically, the therapist asks family members to pretend to engage in a troublesome behavior, such as having a fight. The act of pretending helps individuals change by experiencing control of a previously involuntary action.

Positioning involves acceptance and exaggeration of what clients or family members are saying (Piercy & Sprenkle, 1986). If conducted properly, it helps clients see the absurdity of what they are doing, thereby freeing them to do something else. For example, if a son states that his relationship with his father is difficult, the counselor might respond, "No, it is absolutely hopeless" (Watzlawick, 1983).

Interpersonal Communication

Understanding and Mastery: Establishing rapport with clients

Critical Thinking Question: How could any of the following techniques—pretending, directives, or reframing—help or hurt in establishing rapport with a family or client family members?

Personal Reflection

Directives are preferred to many other strategic therapy techniques. They are straight forward ways of changing behaviors. When have you seen directives work in your own life or in the lives of others?

Assess your comprehension of the Process and Techniques by taking this quiz.

Multicultural Issues

Multiculturalism deals with culture, gender, disability, sexual orientation, socioeconomic disadvantage, and the world of military service. Strategic counseling has been used effectively in many cultures and subcultures dealing with problems. For example, Santisteban et al. (2003) found brief strategic family therapy to be effective in working with Hispanic youth exhibiting behavioral problems and drug use. Likewise, Soo-Hoo (1999) found brief strategic family therapy effective in working with Chinese-American families and consistent with their family values. The concept of reframing was an especially effective principle in this work.

In short, strategic family therapists seem to be sensitive to different cultures and are able to work within them. Richeport-Haley (1998) describes a brief strategic family therapy approach that can be an alternative to a culture-focused therapy. A **culture-oriented counselor** focuses on understanding cultural premises and then attempts to do therapy within the worldview of the clients. In contrast, the **strategic approach** emphasizes the structure of the family and offers techniques that can be used whatever the culture.

Strategic family therapy is also noted for its gender sensitivity as addressed by Madanes (1990). Many of today's strategic family therapy practitioners use pretend techniques, which are much gentler and more gender friendly than paradox or ordeals. Counselors

Client-Related Values and Attitudes

Understanding and Mastery: The worth and uniqueness of individuals including ethnicity, culture, gender, sexual orientation, and other expressions of diversity

Critical Thinking Question: How do you think the multiple techniques of strategic family therapy contribute to clients' attitudes of feeling valued and unique?

also pay attention to gender-related issues. For example, Madanes has devised a 16-step procedure for working with sex offenders and their victims. This approach is notable for obtaining clear facts, connecting sexuality with spirituality, and persuading the offender to seek forgiveness while kneeling before the victim.

Evaluation of the Theory

Strengths and Contributions

A major strength of strategic family therapy is its flexibility with a variety of clients. This approach has been successfully used with family members who display such dysfunctional behaviors as enmeshment, eating disorders, and substance abuse (Haley, 1980; Stanton, Todd, & Associates, 1982).

Another positive characteristic of the strategic approach is that most therapists who use it "now concede that real change is possible at the individual and dyadic level—that the entire system need not always be involved in lower-order change" (Fish, 1988, p. 15). Because significant change can be brought about without having the entire family involved in treatment sessions, the chances of a desirable outcome are increased.

A third contribution of the strategic approach is its focus on innovation and creativity. Strategic therapists trace their lineage to Erickson, who was especially skilled in devising novel ways to help his clients. Strategic clinicians have continued that effort, and through their "introduction of the novel or unexpected, a frame of reference is broken and the structure of reality is rearranged" (Papp, 1984, p. 22).

An additional strength of strategic family therapy is its ability to be employed with a number of other therapies (Haley, 1976; Alexander & Parsons, 1982; Fish, 1988; Steinberg, Sayger, & Szykula, 1997). Because many influential therapists have a historical or personal connection with strategic therapy, they continue to be influenced in their thoughts and actions by dialogue and debate with and among strategic family therapists.

Limitations and Criticisms

One aspect of strategic therapy that may be considered a limitation is its concentration on one problem. Even though the one problem approach may help families marshal their resources to deal with an identified difficulty quickly and efficiently (Snider, 1992), many families have more than one presenting problem that needs attention.

A second criticism of strategic therapy is that the approach is seen as too cookbookish and mechanical (Simon, 1984). This charge results from the prescribed methods of treatment by the MRI and Haley, although therapists who embrace this theory do experience considerable flexibility.

An additional limitation of this approach is the skill necessary to implement some of its methods. For instance, the use of paradox can be powerful in the hands of a skilled clinician, but it can be a catastrophe if employed in a naive way (Friesen, 1985). Some strategic approaches demand considerable training before practitioners can implement them properly.

Another drawback of strategic therapy concerns time and emphasis. All sub-schools within this orientation restrict the number of therapeutic sessions, hoping to motivate families to work. However, the seriousness or extent of problems may not be dealt with adequately (Wylie, 1992). It is also hoped that families will learn problem-solving skills by resolving one specific situation, although some families may not achieve this goal.

A final downside of strategic family therapy is its lack of collaborative input from clients. Some models, such as those devised by Haley, emphasize power techniques and the expertise of the therapist. All stress the creativity of the therapist to find a solution for the family. Thus, the strategic therapist who does not produce the desired results in clients usually takes the blame. This approach is the antithesis of most other forms of therapy.

Assess your comprehension of the <u>Evaluation of the Theory</u> by taking this quiz.

Personal Reflection

The strategic approach involves being in charge of the counseling session and what is done in it. How comfortable are you in such a role?

Treating Linda with the Strategic Approach

Conceptualization

From the perspective of strategic therapy, Linda is stuck in a homeostatic pattern of difficult interaction with older authority figures, especially demanding and demeaning men. Linda's husband was apparently much like her father, and she obeyed him even when it meant having an abortion that she did not want. Linda's bosses have not been any better in their treatment of Linda, displaying sexist behavior. In many ways, Linda has acted with her husband and her bosses as she did with her father.

Linda began this behavior when she followed the rule in her family that women are inferior. This pattern has led her to function below her abilities and act out in ways that are potentially harmful to her. For example, she pursued a two-year business degree instead of a four-year college degree, then started working as a secretary instead of seeking a more challenging career, and recently gave notice on one job before she found another. Linda has consistently set up complementary relationships in which she is unequal. These relationships and her associated actions have left her depressed, discouraged, and trapped in situations that are unfulfilling and disheartening. She has also followed the redundancy principle of repeating a limited number of behaviors. Because she blames others, especially her family, for where she is today, she avoids them but has not broken out of her self-defeating behavior to create new friends and opportunities.

Treatment Process

As a strategic counselor you are quite active as you begin your work with Linda. First, you evaluate the effectiveness of solutions Linda has tried so far, for example, obedience, passive-aggressive behavior, depression. You then help Linda define her problem in such a way that it becomes solvable: "The problem is being passive and not utilizing my abilities."

After the problem is defined, you give Linda a homework assignment. Because she came alone initially, you give her the task of bringing her family into therapy with her the next time. You want her family to collaborate with her to find better ways to experience life, thereby setting up a cooperative and potentially exciting relationship. Your goal is to help Linda formulate and implement a strategy for change in which she can be successful, breaking out of the vicious cycle she has been in and into a virtuous cycle.

When Linda comes in with her family, you are creative in finding a strategy that will work for everyone. You reframe the family's difficulties as members having forgotten to give positive and helpful messages to each other. As with anything forgotten, learning to remember is quite possible. This reframing of the problem from a negative to a positive and from a basis of blame to one of remembering is appealing to all family members. Therefore, you give them the following directive: During their Sunday lunch time, each person is to give to every other family member a sincere and helpful message framed in a positive manner. No one resists the assignment, and you remind them that they can pretend to be sincere if they find that aspect difficult.

The next week, the family reports that it carried out the directive. Thus, you see no need to use paradox or ordeals. You exaggerate and accept all that the family members say and compliment them on helping one another. You learn that Linda has received feedback that she is capable, smart, and able to do anything she sets her mind to. You notice that family members are sitting closer to one another and are more jovial. As the strategic therapist you are functioning as the expert, using your power as a physician does to bring about healing and growth through powerful interventions. After several more sessions, Linda and her family terminate their treatment with you. They are interacting positively and often with each other.

Summary and Conclusion

Strategic family therapy is among the most popular approaches to working with individuals and families. It was formulated in the 1960s by the Mental Research Institute (MRI) and Haley, following the creative genius of Erickson. It is short-term, specific, positive, and designed to change behaviors and thoughts often overlooked by other therapeutic approaches. As they did originally, strategic family therapists continue to limit to 10 the number of sessions in which they see a family. They work actively on clearly defined problems.

Strategic family therapists are innovative and creative. They use a variety of techniques including reframing, directives, prescribing the symptom, ordeals, pretending, and positioning. This approach is used in multicultural contexts and, thanks to the work of Madanes, is gender sensitive. Strategic family therapy emphasizes the power and expertise of the therapist.

Recall what you learned in this chapter by reviewing and completing the **Chapter Review.**

CHAPTER 15

Solution-Focused Therapy

Steve Mason/Thinkstock

One of the most recent theoretical developments in the field of counseling is the creation of solution-focused therapy. This approach grew out of strategic family therapy, particularly the Mental Research Institute (MRI) model, but departs from that tradition by concentrating on finding solutions instead of dealing with problems (Sharry, Madden, & Darmody, 2012).

One of the most experienced and articulate spokesperson for solution-focused approach was Steve deShazer, who studied with Milton Erickson. This model appeared first in deShazer's writings and those of his associates at the Brief Family Therapy Center in Milwaukee, Wisconsin (deShazer, 1982; 1985; 1988; 1991). Current advocates of the solution-focused position include Bill O'Hanlon and his associates (O'Hanlon & Wilk, 1987; O'Hanlon & Weiner-Davis, 1989), Patricia O'Hanlon Hudson (Hudson & O'Hanlon, 1991), Michele Weiner-Davis, Alan Gurman, Eve Lipchik, and Scott Miller. Solution-focused therapy has a Midwest origin with a worldwide application.

Major Theorists: Steve deShazer and Bill O'Hanlon

Although Steve deShazer and Bill O'Hanlon developed their ideas separately, the various forms of this theory spring from the work of Milton Erickson (1901–1980). Steve deShazer (1940–2005) began his career at the Mental Research Institute in the mid-1970s. In the late 1970s, he and other individuals in Milwaukee established the Brief Family Therapy

Center (Kaplan, 2000). There, deShazer first gained attention as a therapist and began to emerge as a major theorist through his writings in the 1980s. Initially, deShazer was considered a strategic family therapist influenced by the work of not only Erickson but also Gregory Bateson and the staff of the MRI. However, beginning in the 1980s and continuing until his death, deShazer's writings and presentations were distinct from the mainstream of the strategic family therapy approach.

DeShazer (1982) identified his theory as brief family therapy, sometimes called just **brief therapy**, and described it as an ecosystemic approach. Whenever possible, he employed a team, collectively known as **consultants**, that observed a session from behind a one-way mirror and transmitted messages to the therapist at a designated break time. Thus, a client benefited from multiple inputs.

Bill O'Hanlon (1953–) entered the therapeutic world because of his own life experiences. As an adolescent he was unhappy and shy; as a college student he was isolated and uncomfortable in the world. He reports that he felt like "all exposed nerve—no skin—everything hurt" (Krauth, 1995, p. 24). He experimented with drugs and noticed that "the reality we all take for granted could be changed by a couple of micrograms of something introduced into one's body" (Bubenzer & West, 1993, p. 366). He also contemplated suicide but changed his mind when a friend offered him a lifetime of free rent on a Nebraska farm if he would stay alive. This possibility changed his outlook on life and led to his interest in therapeutic work that went beyond repairing damage or dealing with pathology.

After earning a tailor-made master's degree from Arizona State University in family therapy, O'Hanlon went on to receive special tutelage under Milton Erickson in exchange for tending his garden. Erickson's influence on O'Hanlon was profound and shifted his attention to a focus on solutions. He was also influenced by MRI work. In 1980 O'Hanlon became a major proponent of solution-focused therapy, which he now prefers to call **possibility therapy** (Bubenzer & West, 1993; Krauth, 1995). He characterizes his approach as one that is pragmatic and full of Midwest values.

View of Human Nature/Personality

The view of human nature characteristic of solution-focused therapy is built on the philosophy of **social constructionism**, that is the social or cultural context of people or families. Because culture influences the way individuals view the world, therapy must incorporate the philosophy of **constructivism**, which states that reality is not an objective entity, but a reflection of observation and experience (Simon, Stierlin, & Wynne, 1985; Maturana & Varela, 1987).

At the foundation of this approach is the belief that dysfunctional people get stuck in dealing with their problems (deShazer, 1985). They use unsatisfactory methods to solve their difficulties, relying on patterns that do not work (Bubenzer & West, 1993). Solution-focused therapy is aimed at breaking such repetitive, nonproductive behavioral patterns by enabling individuals and families to take a more positive view of troublesome situations and actively participate in doing something different. "It is not necessary to know the cause of the complaint or even very much about the complaint itself in order to resolve it" (Cleveland & Lindsey, 1995, p. 145). The presenting problem is simply the problem for which a solution needs to be worked out (Kaplan, 2000). No extensive analysis is needed.

Another premise of solution-focused therapy is that individuals really want to change. To underscore this idea, deShazer (1984, 1989) considered resistance no longer a valid concept. When clients do not follow therapists' directions, they are actually cooperating by teaching therapists the best way to help them.

A related concept is that only a small amount of change is necessary. An analogy used to illustrate this point notes that a one degree error in a plane's path across the United States results in a destination that is considerably off course (deShazer, 1985). Small amounts of change can also encourage people to realize that they can make progress. Even minute change boosts confidence and optimism and creates a ripple effect (Spiegel & Linn, 1969).

Human Systems

Understanding and Mastery: Theories of human development

Critical Thinking Question: What do you think of the solution-focused idea that only a small amount of change is necessary to encourage people that they are making progress in changing?

Personal Reflection

When have you seen a small change make a difference in a person's life? Reflect on what a difference it made.

Assess your comprehension of the <u>View of Human Nature/Personality</u> by taking this quiz.

Role of the Counselor

Solution-focused therapists construct solutions in collaboration with clients (Kiser, Piercy, & Lipchik, 1993). However, one of the therapists' first roles is to determine how active clients will be in the process of change. Clients usually fall into one of three categories: visitors, complainants, or customers. **Visitors** are not involved in the problem and are not part of the solution. **Complainants** complain about situations but can be observant and describe problems even if they are not interested in solving them. **Customers** are not only able to describe a problem and their involvement in it, but are also willing to work to solve it. If therapists work with customers or can help visitors and complainants evolve into customers, appropriate intervention strategies can be developed (Fleming & Rickord, 1997).

A solution-focused therapist becomes a "facilitator of change, one who helps clients access the resources and strengths they already have but are not aware of or are not utilizing" (Cleveland & Lindsey, 1995, p. 145). In this process, practitioners work with clients to change their perspective on a problem, paying special attention to language (West, Bubenzer, Smith, & Hamm, 1997). Positive assumptions about change are constantly conveyed. For example, therapists might ask a presuppositional question, such as, "What good thing happened since our last session?" In addition, "by selecting a specific verb tense, or implying the occurrence of a particular event, … individuals are … led to believe that a solution will be achieved" (Gale, 1991, p. 43). Likewise, when an improvement occurs, therapists use positive blame and recognition of competence through such questions as, "How did you make that happen?" (Fleming & Rickord, 1997).

Solution-focused therapists believe that it is important to fit therapeutic interventions into the context of individual or family behavior. This fit has been articulated by deShazer (1985), who contends that a solution does not have to be as complex as the presenting problem. The example of locks and keys illustrates what he means. Locks may be complex, but opening them does not require a similar complexity of keys. In fact, **skeleton keys** (i.e., standardized therapeutic techniques) can be helpful in dealing with most locks, regardless of complexity.

Planning and Evaluating

Understanding and Mastery: Skills to develop goals, and design and implement a plan of action.

Critical Thinking Question: What do you think about deShazer's concept of skeleton keys and the fact that he proposes solutions do not have to be as complex as problems?

To obtain a good solution fit, deShazer (1985) used a team whenever possible to begin **mapping**, or sketching out, a course of successful intervention. However, it is up to clients to define what they wish to achieve; therapists then help them define clear, specific goals that can be conceptualized concretely (deShazer, 1985; O'Hanlon & Weiner-Davis, 1989). In this process, clients and therapists begin to identify solutions, that is, desired behaviors. "Therapy is over when the agreed upon outcome has been reached" (O'Hanlon & Wilk, 1987, p. 109).

Solution-focused therapists encourage individuals and families to make small changes—in both perception and behavior—and to do so rapidly (deShazer, 1985; O'Hanlon & Weiner-Davis, 1989). Once that small change is achieved, regardless of the method used, therapists get out of the way and let the "beneficial difference amplify itself naturally" (Fleming & Rickord, 1997, p. 289). Solution-focused therapists do not distinguish between short-term and long-term problems; some problematic behaviors endure longer than others because the right solutions have not been tried. Instead, solution-focused therapists are always challenging their clients to envision a "future that has possibilities of change" (Bubenzer & West, 1993, p. 372), a practice that "provides hope and expands the options for solutions" (Erdman, 2000, p. 100).

Goals

Solution-focused therapy encourages clients to seek solutions and tap internal resources. The belief is that all individuals and families have resources and strengths with which to resolve complaints (Cleveland & Lindsey, 1995); the task is simply to get them to use the abilities they already have. Thus, solution-focused therapy encourages, challenges, and sets up expectations for change. Therapists try to help clients unlock their set views, be creative, and generate novel approaches with broad applicability. The concept of pathology, as defined in the DSM, does not play a part in the treatment process.

Assess your comprehension of the Goals by taking this quiz.

Identifying what is a problem and what is not a problem is a key component in the solution-focused process (deShazer, 1988). It emphasizes exceptions to generally accepted ways of behaving and viewing situations (O'Hanlon & Wilk, 1987). Solution-focused therapy takes the Ericksonian position that change is inevitable and helps clients reframe their situations positively.

Personal Reflection

When have you seen an exception to a problem be the solution to the situation? For instance, people who stutter do not do so when they sing, so some individuals who stutter use singing or singing-like behavior to convey information to others.

Process and Techniques

The processes and techniques in solution-focused therapy are also geared to solutions, not problems. Focus on a detailed personal or family history of problems is believed to be unhelpful (deShazer, 1985; O'Hanlon & Weiner-Davis, 1989). To stress the idea that causal understanding is unnecessary, O'Hanlon and Wilk (1987) state that every psychotherapy office should have a couch for therapists instead of clients, because "every now and then, in the course of a session, a hypothesis might accidentally enter the therapist's head, and the best remedy for it is to lie down until it goes away" (p. 98). To increase motivation and expectation, solution-focused therapy, like strategic therapy, emphasizes short-term treatment, between 5 and 10 sessions.

One subtle but primary technique used in this therapy is to co-create a problem. Initially, an agreement is made as to which problem is to be solved. For example, both therapist and family must agree that a family's failure to discipline a child properly is the difficulty that needs to be addressed.

A second technique is to ask clients for a hypothetical solution to their situation, often using the **miracle question**. For example, "If a miracle happened tonight and you woke up tomorrow and the problem was solved, what would you do differently?" (Walter & Peller, 1993, p. 80). Such a question invites clients to suspend their present frame of reference and enter a reality that they wish to achieve.

Another novel technique in solution-focused therapy is to focus on exceptions, that is, to look for times when clients' goals may be happening (Krauth, 1995). "In a practical sense, exceptions do not exist in the real world of clients; they must be cooperatively invented or constructed by both the client and the therapist while exploring what happens when the problem does not occur" (Fleming & Rickord, 1997, p. 289). For example, a couple that is quarreling a lot might find that they are peaceful whenever they sit down to eat. By examining the dynamics of particular situations or at various times, clients may learn something about who they are and how they interact. And in the process they may become different. "Inventing exceptions to problems deconstructs the client's frame: I am this way, or it always happens that way" (Fleming & Rickord, 1997, p. 289).

> ### Interventions and Direct Services
>
> *Understanding and Mastery: Skills to facilitate appropriate direct services and interventions related to specific client or client group goals.*
>
> **Critical Thinking Question:** How does the solution-focused idea of exceptions relate to the Gestalt idea of figure/ground?

Solution-focused therapists may also use the technique of scaling, in which questions are asked using a scale of 1 (low) to 10 (high) to help clients move toward their goal. For example, a therapist might say, "On a scale of 1 to 10, how far do you think you have come in solving your problem?" If the client chooses 6, the therapist might ask what it would take to reach 7. By answering the question, the client may reach a new understanding about what immediate, realistic, and measurable steps should be taken (Fleming & Rickord, 1997).

Another technique in this approach involves **second-order** or qualitative change. The goal is to change client patterns by intervening in the order of events in clients' lives or altering the frequency and duration of a dysfunction (O'Hanlon, 1987). For example, a couple that has been having long fights at dinner might agree to finish their meal before arguing and then limit their time of disagreement to 15 minutes. This type of change in the structure and duration of events is likely to alter family dynamics.

Another intervention is to give clients compliments. For solution-focused therapists, especially deShazer (1982), a compliment is a written message designed to praise a client's strengths and build a **yes-set**, that is, a tendency to respond affirmatively. A **compliment** consists of a positive statement with which the client(s) can agree. For example, a therapist might say, "I am impressed with your hard work to bring about change and the way all of you are discussing what needs to happen next." A compliment is always planned as a lead-in to giving clients a task or assignment.

An additional technique is to provide clients with a **clue**, or an intervention that mirrors the clients' usual behavior. It is intended to alert clients to the idea that some behavior is likely to continue (deShazer, 1982). For example, a therapist's intervention might be, "Don't work too hard trying to spend time talking, because conversation is something that regularly occurs in your environment and you can do it naturally." The idea behind a clue is "to build mutual support and momentum for carrying out later interventions" (Sauber, L'Abate, & Weeks, 1985, p. 23).

One final strategy, mentioned earlier, is to use procedures that have worked before and that have a universal application. These skeleton keys help clients unlock a variety of problems (deShazer, 1985). DeShazer has refined five interventions that have been useful to him in a number of situations (deShazer & Molnar, 1984; deShazer, 1985):

1. **"Between now and next time we meet, we (I) want you to observe, so that you can tell us (me) next time, what happens in your (life, marriage, family, or relationship) that you want to continue to happen"** (deShazer & Molnar, 1984, p. 298). Such an assignment encourages clients to look at the stability, or steadiness, of the problems on which they wish to work.

2. **"Do something different"** (p. 300). This type of request encourages individuals to explore their range of possibilities, rather than to continue to do what they believe is correct. DeShazer gives an example of a woman who complained that her husband, a police detective, was staying out late every night with his friends. The deShazer team suggested that her husband might want more mysterious behavior from her. Therefore, one night she hired a babysitter, rented a motel room, and stayed out until 5:00 A.M. Her husband had come in at 2:00 A.M. Nothing was said, but her husband began staying home at night.

3. **"Pay attention to what you do when you overcome the temptation or urge to ... perform the symptom or some behavior associated with the complaint"** (p. 302). This instruction helps clients to realize that symptom behaviors are under their control.

4. **"A lot of people in your situation would have ..."** (p. 302). This type of statement again helps clients realize that they may have options other than those they are exercising. With such awareness they can begin to make needed changes.

5. **"Write, read, and burn your thoughts"** (p. 302). This experience consists of writing about past times and then reading and burning the writings the next day, in an attempt to move on. (deShazer, 1985)

Assess your comprehension of the **Process and Techniques** by taking this quiz.

Overall, solution-focused interventions help clients view their situations differently. They can also give them hope, thereby assisting them in powerful ways (Bubenzer & West, 1993). In the words of deShazer and Molnar (1984), "It now appears to us that the therapists' ability to see change and to help the clients to do so as well, constitutes a most potent clinical skill" (p. 304).

On a scale from 1 to 10 (the highest number being the most positive), how much are you enjoying learning about counseling theories? What would have to be done to get the number higher?

Multicultural Issues

Multiculturalism deals with culture, gender, disability, sexual orientation, socioeconomic disadvantage, and the world of military service. Solution-focused therapy has made strides in recent years to become more sensitive to and appropriate for different cultural groups—for example, Chinese (Yeung, 1999; Cheung, 2001), Muslims Americans (Chaudhry & Li, 2011), and African-American and Mexican-American families (Corcoran, 2000). The practice of solution-focused therapy has been extended to end-of-life and grief counseling too (Simon, 2010). Practitioners of the approach have also sought to integrate it with other cultural views of helping. For instance, Hung-Hsiu Chang and Ng (2000) compare the phenomenon of change in two different world views—I Ching and solution-focused therapy—and attempt to integrate these views for therapeutic usefulness.

Solution-focused therapy is also sensitive to gender issues. O'Hanlon and Bertolino (2002), for example, address the matter of sexual abuse and the ways in which solution-focused therapy can help victims work through their trauma. Another gender-sensitive approach to change is a "gender solution-focused genogram to help clients identify the beliefs and behaviors related to their presenting problems" (Softas-Nall, Baldo, & Tiedemann, 1999, p. 179). This special type of genogram may be particularly useful in identifying past gender-role messages that have negatively influenced present behaviors.

> ### Client-Related Values and Attitudes
>
> *Understanding and Mastery: The worth and uniqueness of individuals including ethnicity, culture, gender, sexual orientation, and other expressions of diversity*
>
> **Critical Thinking Question:** How effective do you think a gender solution-focused genogram might be in helping you as a future human services practitioner in identifying beliefs and behaviors that have negatively influenced your present behaviors?

Evaluation of the Theory

Strengths and Contributions

A strength of solution-focused therapy is that it concentrates on and is directed by a client's theory, or story. Before any attempt is made to create change, clients' experiences are accepted. Whatever clients bring to therapy is examined from a broad context, but the past is emphasized only when it calls attention to the present. O'Hanlon compares this type of approach with the Rogerian concept of first listening attentively to how people are feeling before trying to implement change (Bubenzer & West, 1993).

A second contribution of solution-focused therapy is that therapists assist clients in defining their situations with clarity, precision, and possibilities. These therapists emphasize that "the defined problem should be achievable" (Todd, 1992, p. 174). Sometimes success is measured in the elimination of a problem; at other times clients may change their perception of a situation or discover exceptions to troublesome times. Small changes in behavior are seen as the basis for larger systemic changes, and therapists encourage and reinforce any type of change. Their belief is that once change starts, it will continue. "Solution-focused brief therapy … asserts that change is inevitable" (Kok & Leskela, 1996, p. 398).

Another positive aspect of solution-focused therapy is that it does not focus on a clinical understanding of a client's situation; instead, the focus is on change. The therapist's job is to produce change by helping clients focus on their solutions to the problems they have reported. Therapists may prompt change by challenging their clients' worldviews, asking appropriate questions, and assigning tasks that help clients unlock their own potential.

A related strength of solution-focused therapy is that it is **empowering** as it assists clients in assessing and utilizing their resources. Formula tasks and awareness exercises help people help themselves. Clients "are encouraged to imagine a future without the problem(s) so that they can identify what they will be doing (solutions)" (Kok & Leskela, 1996, p. 398).

Furthermore, the flexibility of solution-focused therapy is exceptional. It can be employed in working with a variety of disorders and situations, such as children and adolescents in a family context (Berg & Steiner, 2003), problem drinkers (Berg & Miller, 1992), and eating disorders (McFarland, 1995).

Limitations and Criticisms

One drawback to solution-focused therapy is that little attention is paid to client history. Sometimes individuals need to resolve issues from their past before they can move into the present or future. However, solution-focused therapy makes no provision for such a need.

A second criticism of solution-focused therapy is that it ends when a behavioral goal is reached (O'Hanlon & Wilk, 1987). If there is no further complaint or objective, there is no further treatment. In this respect, solution-focused therapy is similar to many forms of behavioral therapy; it concentrates on resolving a concrete objective. Although behavioral accomplishments are important, some clients need additional help changing accompanying thoughts and/or feelings. And again, solution-focused therapy does not provide for such needs.

Another limitation of solution-focused therapy is that some proponents, mainly deShazer and Berg, use a **team approach** in helping clients. Even though there are generally fewer sessions in such an approach, the expense of this treatment may be great.

Assess your comprehension of the Evaluation of the Theory by taking this quiz.

Treating Linda with Solution-Focused Therapy

Conceptualization

From a solution-focused perspective, Linda is temporarily stuck in a pattern of dysfunctional behavior. She really wants to change but does not know how and, as a consequence, has suicidal thoughts. She has found some solace from the pain of her divorce in romance novels, television shows, and action movies. When she is engaged in any of these activities, she does not feel depressed. You see that these activities are exceptions. And although you do not dwell on history, you notice that Linda could have gone to a four-year college and wonder if her intelligence is one of her assets.

Treatment Process

As a solution-focused therapist you want to set up a collaborative working relationship with Linda and challenge her to envision a new future. Linda is a customer who wants to get better and is willing to work. Consequently, you convey to her that change is inevitable and set up expectations for such change, even if it is small. You also remind Linda that you have only 5 to 10 sessions in which to treat her, so it is important to get right to work.

Initially, you work with Linda to cocreate a problem, which turns out to be that she is lonely and cut off from people. When you ask Linda the miracle question, you find out that if the problem were resolved, she would have a new lover in her life and would be closer to her family and premarital friends. When you ask her to scale her handling of her problem, she puts it at a 3. For that rating to be higher, that is, more positive, Linda says she would be reading fewer books, watching less television, and seeing fewer movies.

You compliment Linda on her strength and suggest that a lesser person would have caved in to the circumstances. At the same time, you work with her to find all the exceptions to her feeling depressed, such as when she is reading. You work with her as well to find skeleton keys that she can use to overcome her situation. One such key is a telephone call to family and friends to set up times to do things together, such as share a meal. Another skeleton key is to ask friends and relatives to help her locate activities that she would enjoy and that would introduce her to new people. In both of these situations Linda is less apt to be depressed.

After Linda completes her initial homework, you ask her to scale her feelings about her life again. Her score increases to a 6. You then challenge her to envision a future that is even brighter and let her convey to you the ways that future might come about, such as her becoming more active in social outlet groups and reconnecting with her family. After this session and one more, you terminate therapy although Linda can refer herself back if necessary. You do ask her to report back to you about her progress in a couple of months, reemphasizing the fact that change is inevitable and need not be large to make a big difference in her life.

Summary and Conclusion

In the 1980s and especially in the 1990s, the work of deShazer and O'Hanlon brought national attention to solution-focused therapy. This approach concentrates on bringing change to a wider range of client problems. It is short-term, specific, and positive and concentrates on effecting small changes in the process of facilitating larger ones. Both deShazer and O'Hanlon have been greatly influenced by Milton Erickson.

Solution-focused therapy is concerned with changing present behaviors rather than examining past histories. It stresses that individuals and families have untapped resources that can and should be marshaled in helping them help themselves. This approach is creative in innovative ways that go beyond traditional forms of therapy; for example, it emphasizes that change is inevitable. Overall, solution-focused therapy represents the best of the developing therapeutic approaches.

Recall what you learned in this chapter by reviewing and completing the **Chapter Review**.

CHAPTER 16

Crisis Counseling

Iakov Filimonov/Shutterstock

Chapter Outline

"Crisis intervention skills are essential tools for clinicians working with clients who are experiencing traumatic life events or are in a state of acute crisis" (Parikh & Morris, 2011, p. 364). During the past two decades, the need for crisis intervention services has increased significantly. One reason more services are needed is the recent upsurge of large-scale violent acts occurring in the United States, as evidenced by the shootings and tragic loss of innocent lives in 2007 at Virginia Tech, in 2009 at Fort Hood, Texas; in 2012 at Sandy Hook Elementary School (Connecticut), and the Century movie theatre in Aurora, Colorado; and in 2013 at the Washington Navy Yard to name just a few of the more publicized catastrophic events. Violent acts occur "with such frequency and indiscriminateness that no one can consider him- or herself safe" (Myer, 2001, p. 3).

Other natural disasters including earthquakes, floods, fires, hurricanes, and tornadoes result in tragic losses of lives and homes. For example, Hurricane Katrina struck the southern coast of the United States in August 2005, causing devastating, long-lasting effects, as Hurricane Sandy did to the northeast coast of the United States in 2012. Likewise the wildfires in the west in the summers of 2012 and 2013, especially around Colorado Springs and Yosemite National Park, left thousands devastated and homeless. On an international level, recent tsunamis, earthquakes, and cyclones like the 2011 Tohoku earthquake have had catastrophic effects on people in Southeast Asia, Japan, Pakistan, and China. Automobile and plane accidents, injury, illness, and disease are other examples of crisis situations that can have shattering effects on victims and their families.

Before discussing crisis counseling interventions practitioners can make, it is important to clarify what is meant by the term **crisis**. Many definitions have been proposed, including the following:

- Crisis is a **perception or experiencing of an event or situation as an intolerable difficulty** that exceeds the person's current resources and coping mechanisms. Unless the person obtains relief, the crisis has the potential to cause severe affective, behavioral, and cognitive malfunctioning (James, 2008, p. 3).
- Crisis is a **personal difficulty** that immobilizes a person and prevents that individual from consciously controlling his or her life (Belkin, 1984).
- Crisis is a **state of disorganization** in which a person faces frustration of important life goals or profound disruption of his or her life cycles and methods of coping with stressors. The term *crisis* usually refers to a person's feelings of fear, shock, and distress *about* the disruption, not to the disruption itself (Brammer, 1985, p. 94).
- Crisis is a **critical phase in a person's life when his or her normal ways of dealing with the world are suddenly interrupted** (Lewis, Lewis, Daniels, & D'Andrea, 2003, p. 117).

As can be seen from the multiple concepts of crisis, there is no simple or straightforward way to define what a crisis is. However, there are three components of a crisis: **an event, a client's perception of the event**, and **the failure of the client's typical coping methods** (Miller, 2012). Although a single event may precipitate a crisis, a combination of personal traits, environmental factors, and interpersonal support systems affect the manner in which the event is perceived and managed. An event that is perceived as relatively minor by one individual, such as failing a final examination, may be perceived as a crisis by someone else. Also, the timing, intensity, and number of other stressors the person is experiencing can affect the complexity of the crisis situation.

Information Management

Understanding and Mastery: Obtain information through interviewing, active listening, consultation with others, library or other research, and the observation of clients and systems

Critical Thinking Question: What does the three-component definition of a crisis tell you about the nature of a crisis and its subjective and objective intensity?

Major Theorists: Erich Lindemann and Gerald Caplan

Erich Lindemann (1900–1974) and Gerald Caplan (1917–2008) are considered two of the most prominent pioneers in the field of crisis counseling. Lindemann (1944, 1956) helped practitioners recognize normal grief due to loss and the stages that individuals go through in resolving grief. He worked at Massachusetts General Hospital in Boston as the Chief of Psychiatry and is noted for his extensive study on the effects of traumatic events on survivors and families after the Coconut Grove Night Club fire in 1942 (Satin, 1984). Caplan (1964) expanded Lindemann's concepts to the total field of traumatic events. He viewed crisis as a state resulting from impediments to life's goals that are both situational and developmental. His life is briefly traced here.

Gerald Caplan was born in Liverpool, England, and received a bachelor's degree in anatomy and physiology and a medical degree from Victoria University of Manchester. He was trained in London at the Tavistock Clinic by John Bowlby and at the Psychoanalytic Institute by Anna Freud. As the son of a rabbi, Caplan developed a commitment to Zionism that led him to move to Israel in 1948. There he helped establish psychiatric services. A meeting with Eric Lindemann resulted in a faculty position at the Harvard School of Public Health's Community Mental Health Program.

Caplan created the Laboratory of Community Psychiatry in the Harvard Medical School, where he remained until 1977 and after which he returned to Israel to direct a department of child and adolescent psychiatry. His lifelong mission was to advance a population-oriented approach to mental health that placed prevention at its core. In advocating this view, he developed and refined crisis, mental health, and support intervention techniques that fueled the community mental health movement. He died in Jerusalem following a long struggle with Parkinson's disease.

View of Human Nature/Personality

Loss is an inevitable part of life. Developmentally and situationally, healthy people grow and move on, leaving some things behind, whether intentionally, by accident, or because of growth. In leaving, there may be **grieving**, which is a natural reaction to loss. The extent of the grief and its depth are associated with the value of what has been lost and how. In some cases, the pain may be small because the person was not attached to or invested in the object left behind, or the person had adequate time to prepare. In other cases, an individual may feel overwhelmed because of the value the person, possession, or position had in his or her life or because of the sudden and/or traumatic way the loss occurred. In such cases, a crisis occurs.

Although crises represent highly stressful and disruptive situations, they do not imply mental illness (Lewis et al., 2003). Many, but not all, crises are time-limited, usually lasting somewhere between six and eight weeks, after which the major symptoms of distress diminish. However, crises can have long-term physical and psychological outcomes, depending on how the crisis is resolved (Sandoval, Scott, & Padilla, 2009).

James (2008) emphasizes the importance of distinguishing between different types of crises. Building on the research of other crisis specialists, he described four crisis domains:

1. *Developmental crises.* Developmental crises occur during the normal flow of human growth and maturation. As people move through different developmental stages in their lives, they may experience crisis during certain changes or shifts. For example, a developmental crisis may occur for a parent when the last child leaves home or when a person retires. When the event corresponds to culturally accepted patterns and timetables, it is less likely to be experienced as a crisis than when it does not (e.g., pregnancy after marriage versus teenage pregnancy or voluntary retirement at an appropriate age versus forced early retirement) (Myer, 2001). Developmental crises are considered normal; however, individuals perceive and respond to them in different ways and with varying degrees of success. They may be especially traumatic if the timing of events is not within acceptable norms.

2. *Situational crises.* A situational crisis occurs when an unexpected, extraordinary event occurs that the person had no way of anticipating or controlling. Examples include automobile accidents, rape, job loss, sudden illness, and death of a loved one. A situational crisis is "random, sudden, shocking, intense, and often catastrophic" (James, 2008, p. 13). It is one of two categories, the other being ecosystemic, that most people consider a crisis.

When have you seen someone have a situational crisis? How did they behave? What, if any, action by the person or someone else help?

• •

3. *Existential crises.* An existential crisis includes "inner conflicts and anxieties that accompany important human issues of purpose, responsibility, independence, freedom, and commitment" (James, 2008, p. 13). At times, existential crises are precipitated by **nonevents**, such as realizing that one is never going to have children or make a significant difference in a particular field of work. For instance, an existential crisis may occur when realizing at age 50 that one has wasted one's life and cannot relive past years or a spouse/partner of 25 years questions the value of the relationship and seriously considers moving out. A major characteristic of existential crises is they are mostly mental.

4. *Ecosystemic crises.* **Ecosystemic crises** refer to natural or human-caused disasters that overtake a person or group of people who "find themselves, through no fault or action of their own, inundated in the aftermath of an event that may adversely affect virtually every member of the environment in which they live" (James, 2008, p. 14). In many ways, ecosystemic crises are situational crises that have widespread ramifications. The terrorist attacks of September 11, 2001, the breaking of the levees in New Orleans, and suicide bombings exemplify human-caused ecosystemic crises with wide-reaching effects. Examples of ecosystemic crises caused by natural phenomena include hurricanes, tornados, tsunamis, wildfires, and earthquakes.

> ### Human Systems
>
> *Understanding and Mastery: Theories of human development*
> ───────────────────────
> **Critical Thinking Question:** What do you see as the similarities between a development and an existential crisis?
> •

• **Assess your comprehension of the <u>View of Human Nature/Personality</u> by taking this quiz.**

Role of the Counselor

Practitioners who work in crises need to be mature individuals with a variety of life experiences with which they have successfully dealt. They need to also have a good command of basic helping skills, high energy, and quick mental reflexes, and yet be poised, calm, creative, and flexible in the midst of highly charged situations.

Counselors are often direct and active in crisis situations. The role is quite different from that of other forms of counseling. There are two main components of crisis counseling: **(1) first order intervention (psychological first aid)** and **(2) second order intervention (crisis therapy)**. First order intervention involves "making sure clients are safe, stress-related symptoms are reduced, clients have opportunities to rest and recover physically [when necessary], and clients are connected to resources and social supports they need to survive and recover from the crisis" (Miller, 2012, p. 3). Second order intervention involves assessing, planning, implementing, and follow-up to help the client develop new knowledge and skills.

> ### Interventions and Direct Services
>
> *Understanding and Mastery: Skills to facilitate appropriate direct services and interventions related to specific client or client group goals*
> ───────────────────────
> **Critical Thinking Question:** How do you see the two components of crisis counseling (psychological first aid and crisis therapy) relating to each other?
> •

Through second order interventions, human services practitioners strive to help those who have been in crisis create a new, productive, and mentally healthy life.

Goals

As previously noted many, but not all, crises are time-limited. Goals within crisis counseling initially revolve around getting those who are suffering immediate help in a variety of forms (e.g., psychological, financial, legal). "What occurs during the immediate aftermath of the crisis event determines whether or not the crisis will become a disease reservoir that will be transformed into a chronic and long-term state" (James, 2008, p. 5).

At first, counselors use **basic crisis theory** to help "people in crisis recognize and correct temporary affective, behavioral, and cognitive distortions brought on by traumatic events" (p. 11). This service, **psychological first aid**, is directive in nature. It focuses on the physical safety and comfort of victims while promoting social engagement and helping survivors of a trauma find missing loved ones or attend to issues associated with traumatic grief, guilt, or shame. It is different from brief counseling approaches that try to help individuals find remediation for more ongoing problems. Second, long-term adjustment and health are focused on. Individuals and even communities may require considerable follow-up on the part of crisis counselors or other helping specialists in order to rebuild and move on in their lives.

Assess your comprehension of the **Goals** by taking this quiz.

Personal Reflection

Think of when you have followed up with a project you were working on. What did you notice in follow-up that you did not observe initially? Do you think the same dynamics apply to crisis counseling? If so, how are they the same and different from your experience of task follow-up?

Process and Techniques

Techniques used in crisis counseling vary according to the type of crises mentioned earlier, and the potential for harm. However, according to James (2008), what a crisis practitioner does and when he or she does it is dependent on assessing the individuals experiencing crisis in a continuous and fluid manner.

Assessment may include what Miller (2012) defines as the **BASIC personality profile**—behavioral, affective, somatic, interpersonal, and cognitive. Strengths and weaknesses in these domains are examined. Exploring what assets clients have for moving on and healing, for example **resilience** (the ability to recover from adversity) is noted. Three essential listening activities that need to be implemented during this time are:

Interpersonal Communication

Understanding and Mastery: Establishing rapport with clients

Critical Thinking Question: Which of the three essential listening activities do you think would most put a client in crisis at ease and establish rapport?

(a) **defining continuing or major problems,** especially from the client's viewpoint;
(b) **ensuring client and other safety,** which means minimizing physical and psychological dangers; and

(c) **providing support,** which means communicating to the client genuine and unconditional caring.

After, and sometimes during, the middle of listening come **acting strategies**, or in-crisis actions, which include:

(a) **examining alternatives** (i.e., recognizing alternatives that are available and realizing some choices are better than others);
(b) **making plans,** where clients feel a sense of control and autonomy in the process so they do not become dependent; and
(c) **obtaining commitment** from the client to take actions that have been planned.

Practitioners should follow up with clients after a crisis has settled down enough for clients to have made plans they intent to complete. The emphasis in such cases is to highlight strengths in order to help clients feel they are in control (Meier & Davis, 2011). If necessary, counselors should further assess whether clients have had delayed reactions to the crisis they have experienced, such as **posttraumatic stress disorder (PTSD)**. If PTSD has occurred more intensive therapeutic interventions, possibly hospitalization, may be needed.

During and even after a crisis, helping specialists need to debrief. Two approaches to debriefing are **Critical Incident Stress Debriefing (CISD)** and **one-on-one crisis counseling** (Jordan, 2002). In CISD, a seven-stage group approach is used that helps individuals deal with their thoughts and feelings in a controlled environment using two counselors (Roberts, 2005). This approach evolves through an emphasis on introduction, facts, thoughts, reactions, symptoms, teaching, and reentry. The CISD group ranges from 1 to 3 hours and is generally provided 1 to 10 days after an acute crisis and three to four weeks after the disaster in mass disasters (Roberts, 2005). One-on-one counseling uses some of the same techniques as in CISD but the treatment lasts from 15 minutes to 2 hours and for only one to three sessions (Everly, Lating, & Mitchell, 2000).

Assess your comprehension of the <u>Process and Techniques</u> by taking this quiz.

Personal Observation

Debriefing has been compared to catharsis. How do you think it is similar to and different from catharsis? What makes you think so?

Multicultural Issues

Multiculturalism deals with culture, gender, disability, sexual orientation, socioeconomic disadvantage, and the world of military service. "The plain and simple truth is that we don't know a lot about how culture, crises, and crisis intervention interact. Very little research has been done in the area" (James, 2008, p. 25). What is known is that multicultural helping is enhanced when practitioners use methods and strategies and define goals consistent with the life experiences and cultural values of the client (Sue & Sue, 2008).

The same is true of factors related to crisis counseling and gender-sensitive issues. Counselors must tailor their approaches to helping. They must be sensitive to the gender of those they serve realizing some men who are hurting psychologically may be reluctant to talk about their pain. Likewise, some women who are suffering may cry when describing their feelings. The opposite may be true too. Adjustment on the part of the helper is what is called for in these situations and others like them.

Evaluation of the Theory

Strengths and Contributions

Dramatic and traumatic events, from earthquakes to shootings, occur in many people's lives. Crisis counseling is a two-prong approach to helping individuals deal with the physical or mental devastations associated with these happenings. This type of counseling provides psychological first aid for the immediate aftermath of such situations. Crisis counseling is also involved in helping individuals make long-term plans so that they can get on with their lives and not develop posttraumatic stress disorders.

A second strength of crisis counseling is the fact that it is direct and relatively brief. In the midst of a crisis people are often confused and need directions of what to do, when, where and how. They are not ready for reflection. They need to focus on survival skills first. Crisis counseling provides individuals with this specificity.

A third strength of crisis counseling is that it may involve physical help, for example, food and shelter, as well as psychological components, for example, finding someone to talk to. Therefore, human services practitioners along with other helping specialists can provide comfort and safety to people in need on multiple levels. This type of assistance helps individuals calm down and assess themselves and their surroundings so they can begin to see what their needs are.

Limitations and Criticisms

While crisis counseling excels in meeting the immediate needs of individuals, it does not provide for services that last for more than a few weeks. Therefore, victims of crises must follow-up with other professionals after a crisis has passed. The process of follow-up with another helper can be frustrating as well as time consuming. Sometimes those who have suffered crises feel they are being handed off from one agency or person to another and in the process they become discouraged.

A second drawback to crisis counseling is not all crises that individuals go through are amenable to crisis counseling. For instance, developmental crises, such as aging, are usually not worked with in this way. Yet these non-physical and sometimes investible types of crises are often as painful and distressing as events that are more outwardly observable.

A final criticism of crisis counseling is the fact that it lacks strong theoretical support. It could be argued that crisis counseling is built on Abraham Maslow's hierarchy of needs with the rationale that more physical needs must be satisfied before higher psychological needs can be met. However, Maslow's theory is seldom mentioned when crisis counseling is discussed and thus some individuals do not consider this approach to be little more than providing comfort and assistance for those who have suffered an injury or a loss.

Assess your comprehension of <u>Evaluation of the Theory</u> by taking this quiz

Treating Linda with Crisis Counseling

Conceptualization

Linda is facing both a developmental and an existential crisis. The developmental crisis is Linda's transition from being married seven years to suddenly being single and not used to living on her own. Even when there is abuse in a relationship, as in Linda's case, it takes time for a person to get used to being free of that behavior and being on one's own again. The matter of making likeminded friends is also developmental. At this point in her life, Linda is not connected except tangentially to her family. She is drifting and is basically alone.

The existential crisis stems from Linda seeking meaning in her life that she has not found previously. At 32, she has had seven years of a bad relationship and 12 years of mundane, dead-end jobs with what she considers sexist bosses. Linda knows she has potential because of her high school grades. Yet, out of high school she chose to do less than she was capable of because of family and society pressures. Her pattern of under-achievement has left her feeling depressed and stuck in passive behaviors such as reading romance novels, watching television, and viewing action-packed movies. None of these behaviors has proven satisfying for Linda.

Treatment Process

As a crisis counselor you realize that the two types of crises Linda is facing (developmental and existential) are interrelated and that you cannot treat one without handling the other. A first line of outreach is to work with Linda to help her understand the developmental stages in divorce and the feelings that go with them. Like other kinds of loss, there is a process that people go through when divorcing, even if it is from a bad marriage. You essentially want to help Linda learn about the nature of decoupling and reconnecting and assure her she is safe and free to do more than she is doing.

Besides gaining a different perspective through acquiring knowledge about the dynamics of divorce and the possibilities of freedom, Linda needs to make a plan about what to do with her life. This is her existential crisis. You point out options she has like returning to college for a four-year degree, moving to another city where there are more singles, becoming involved in a YWCA program of exercise, joining a local interest group such as a book club, or looking for a career that requires more of a commitment from her and rewards her better. Linda needs to know what choices she has whether she remains physically where she is now or moves. Once choices are discussed and explored, Linda then has to make an existential decision on what to do and when so she will not stay in a crisis modality.

Thus the process of helping Linda in her developmental and existential crisis is one that involves assisting her in discerning where she is now and where she wants to be as well as what she wants to become. Resolving Linda's crisis is about helping her decide how she wishes to spend her life and choosing activities she finds meaningful. This last aspect of working with Linda, that is choosing, is difficult and you may have to refer Linda to someone else who can help her with longer-term counseling. Overall, crisis counseling with Linda is of an immediate nature. It deals with matters than can be resolved quickly as well as pointing out possibilities for Linda in the future. The future goals of Linda are of a more agonizing and of an uncertain nature and may require referring Linda to a counselor who can work with her for a longer time block than you have as a crisis counselor. Once Linda gains a perspective on where she is in life, as a divorced, underachieving, hurt person she can not only plan for becoming a new person but can take concrete steps in that direction, hopefully with your help. However, your main job is to help Linda feel safe in venturing forth and reinforce her courage in trying new behaviors that are healthy and fulfilling.

Summary and Conclusion

A crisis is an event or situation that is so overwhelming that a client does not have the resources or coping abilities to deal with it. There are three components of a crisis: an event, a client's perception of the event, and the failure of the client's typical coping methods. Crisis counseling was created when professional helpers realized that there is a need to assist those who are victims of manmade or natural disasters in a way not found in other models of helping. This approach to working with others is based on the realization that those who suffer through a crisis have a need for short-term and long-term assistance in order to get back on their feet and build a new life. Thus, crisis counseling is a two-prong process that offers first- and second-degree interventions that are immediate (psychological first aid) and long term (therapy), the latter of which may need to be completed by another helping professional.

Crises take at least four different forms: developmental, situational, existential, and ecosystemic with the most noticeable and publicized of these crises being those that are situational and ecosystemic. When conducting crisis, counseling practitioners are direct and action oriented especially at the beginning of their work. This stance is because in many crisis situation, clients are confused, aimless, and in a state of shock as well as grief. Thus using acting strategies or in-crisis actions of examining alternatives, making plans, and obtaining commitment from client to take action that has been planned is essential. Because crisis counseling is so intense it is important that those who work in this area regularly debrief so they stay healthy and available to others.

Recall what you learned in this chapter by reviewing and completing the Chapter Review.

CHAPTER 17

Professional Ethics and Codes of Ethics

Pressmaster/Shutterstock

Counseling is not value-free or a neutral activity (Cottone & Tarvydas, 2007; Woodside & McClam, 2009; Welfel, 2013). Rather, it is an active profession based on **values**, which are "orienting beliefs about what is good ... and how that good should be achieved" (Bergin, 1985, p. 99). Values are at the core of relationships. All goals, "whether they are goals for symptom relief or goals to modify a lifestyle are subtended by value systems" (Bergin, 1992, p. 9). In addition, because counseling is such a complex and multifaceted profession, counselors, by necessity, must be dependent on codes of ethics (Remley & Herlihy, 2010).

Counselors who are not clear about their values and ethical responsibilities, as well as those of their clients, can cause harm despite their best intentions (Wilcoxon, Remley, & Gladding, 2012). Therefore, it is vital for them to be knowledgeable about themselves and the ethics pertaining to their professional responsibilities. The question is "How?" The answer is through knowing what ethics are, what professional ethical codes include, the limits of ethical codes, how to make ethical decisions, and how to deal with someone who acts unethical. This chapter explores these vital aspects of ethics because they are essential to the health and well-being of counselors and human services professionals.

What Are Ethics?

Ethics involve "making decisions of a moral nature about people and their interaction in society" (Kitchener, 1986, p. 306). The term is often used synonymously with morality, and in some cases the two terms overlap. Both deal with "what is good and bad or the study of human conduct and values" (Van Hoose & Kottler, 1985, p. 2). Yet each has a different meaning.

"Ethics is generally defined as a philosophical discipline that is concerned with human conduct and moral decision making" (Van Hoose & Kottler, 1985, p. 3). Ethics are normative in nature and focus on principles and standards that govern relationships between individuals. "**Professional ethics** are beliefs about behavior and conduct that guide professional practices," such as those between counselors and clients (Calley, 2009, p. 477). Morality differs. It involves judgment or evaluation of action. It is associated with such words as good, bad, right, wrong, ought, and should (Brandt, 1959; Grant, 1992). Human service professionals have morals, and the theories they employ have embedded within them moral presuppositions about human nature that explicitly and implicitly question first "What is a person?" and second, "What should a person be or become?" (Christopher, 1996, p. 18).

As a group, professional helpers are concerned with ethics and values. However, some are better informed or more attuned to these issues. Patterson (1971) has observed that one's professional identity is related to knowledge and practice of ethics. Welfel (2010) states that the effectiveness of helpers is connected to their ethical knowledge and behaviors as well. Therefore, ethics are essential.

Interpersonal Communication

Understanding and Mastery: Developing and sustaining behaviors that are congruent with the values and ethics of the profession

Critical Thinking Question: How effective can counselors be if they are knowledgeable about professional ethics but differ in their behaviors substantially?

· ·

Assess your comprehension of <u>What are Ethics?</u> by taking this quiz.

Why Are Professional Codes of Ethics Important?

To address ethical situations, helping professionals have developed codes of ethics based upon an agreed-on set of values. Professionals in all human services domains, such as social work, counseling, psychology, and rehabilitation, voluntarily abide by codes of their disciplines for many reasons. "Among its many purposes, a **code of ethical conduct** is designed to offer formal statements for ensuring protection of clients' rights while identifying expectations of practitioners" (Wilcoxon, 1987, p. 510). Three other reasons for the existence of ethical codes according to Van Hoose and Kottler (1985) are as follows:

1. **Ethical codes protect a profession from government.** They allow a profession to regulate itself and function autonomously instead of being controlled by legislation.
2. **Ethical codes help control internal disagreements and bickering,** thus promoting stability within a profession.
3. **Ethical codes protect practitioners from the public,** especially in regard to malpractice suits. If professionals behave according to ethical guidelines, the behavior is judged to be in compliance with accepted standards.

In addition, ethical codes help increase public trust in the integrity of a profession and provide clients with some protection from incompetent charlatans (Vacc, Juhnke, & Nilsen, 2001). Clients can also use codes of ethics as a guide in evaluating questionable treatment.

Developing a code of ethics is a major sign that an association has developed into a mature discipline. A code of ethics clarifies the nature of ethical responsibilities, such as the following, informs clients of the nature of helping; supports the mission of the association; establishes principles that inform best practice; assists members in constructing a course of action, such as what should I do when I do not have the necessary skills to treat a client; and serves as the basis for processing ethical complaints and inquiries (Ponton & Duba, 2009).

Most professional helping associations have several topical headings in their codes of ethics. These sections deal with the *relationships*, including professional responsibilities to clients and their welfare and ways to handle troublesome subjects such as fees, bartering, referrals, and termination. Sections covering confidentiality, privileged communication, and privacy in counseling are usually included too. They deal with exceptions to the right to privacy, records, consultation, and research as well as training and issues related to professional responsibility, such as professional competence. Public responsibility and relationships with other professionals, including colleagues, employers, and employees, are almost always included in codes of ethics.

In addition, ethical codes usually deal with evaluation, assessment, and interpretation of tests; informed consent; release of information; proper diagnosis of mental disorders; conditions of assessment administration; multicultural issues; and forensic evaluation. Research and publications, delineating research responsibilities, rights of research participants, and reporting of research results are other sections in most professional codes of ethics.

Self-Development

Understanding and Mastery: Clarification of personal and professional values

Critical Thinking Question: What are some ways human services practitioners might use codes of ethics to help them sort out their personal and professional values?

Assess your comprehension of <u>Why are Professional Codes of Ethics Important?</u> by taking this quiz.

Limitations of Ethical Codes

Kocet (2006) notes that ethical codes are general and idealistic; they seldom answer specific questions. Furthermore, he points out that these documents do not address foreseeable professional dilemmas. Rather, they provide guidelines, based on experiences and values, of how professional helpers should behave. In many ways, ethical standards represent the collected wisdom of a particular time.

A number of specific limitations exist in any code of ethics. Here are some of the limitations most frequently mentioned (Talbutt, 1981; Corey, Corey, & Callanan, 2011):

- Some issues cannot be resolved by a code of ethics.
- Enforcing ethical codes is difficult.
- Some ethical issues are not covered in codes since codes do not address every possible situation.
- Ethical codes are historical documents. Thus, what may be acceptable practice at one time may be considered unethical later.
- Sometimes **conflicts** arise between ethical and legal codes.

- There is often difficulty in bringing the interest of all parties involved in an ethical dispute together systematically.
- Ethical codes are not proactive documents for helping professionals decide what to do in new situations.

Assess your comprehension of the <u>Limitations of Ethical Codes</u> by taking this quiz.

Thus, ethical codes are useful in many ways, but they do have their limitations. Human services professionals need to be aware that they will not always find all the guidance they want when consulting these documents. Nevertheless, whenever an ethical issue arises, professional helpers should first consult ethical codes to see whether the situation is addressed.

Making Ethical Decisions

Ethical decision making is not always easy, yet it is a part of being a professional helper. It requires virtues such as character, integrity, and moral courage as well as knowledge (Welfel, 2010). Some helping professionals operate from personal ethical standards without regard to the ethical guidelines developed by professional associations. They usually function well until faced with a dilemma "for which there is no apparent good or best solution" (Swanson, 1983, p. 57). At such times, ethical issues arise and these individuals experience anxiety, doubt, hesitation, and confusion in determining their conduct. Unfortunately, when they act, their behavior may turn out to be unethical because it is not grounded in an ethical code or it is grounded in only part of a code that they have extracted to justify their behavior.

Personal Reflection

When have you seen someone try to justify his or her behavior without referencing values and ethics? What did you think about his or her actions?

It is in difficult, murky, and personally troubling situations that those in helping professions need to be aware of resources for ethical decision making such as books and articles on ethics and more experienced colleagues (Welfel, 2010). Such resources are especially important when questions arise over potentially controversial behaviors such as setting or collecting fees, conducting multiple relationships, or working with individuals whose beliefs and styles helpers do not agree with. **Ethical reasoning**, "the process of determining which ethical principles are involved and then prioritizing them based on the professional requirements and beliefs," is crucial (Lanning, 1992, p. 21).

In making ethical decisions, helping specialists should take actions "based on careful, reflective thought" about responses they think are professionally right in particular situations (Tennyson & Strom, 1986, p. 298). Six ethical principles that relate to the activities and ethical choices are:

- **Beneficence** (doing good and preventing harm),
- **Nonmaleficence** (not inflicting harm),
- **Autonomy** (respecting freedom of choice and self-determination),
- **Justice** (fairness),
- **Fidelity** (faithfulness or honoring commitments and promises), and
- **Veracity** (truthfulness) (Remley & Herlihy, 2010).

All these principles involve conscious decision making throughout the helping process. Of these principles, some experts identify nonmaleficence as the primary ethical responsibility in the field of helping relationships. Nonmaleficence involves not only the "removal of present harm" but the "prevention of future harm, and passive avoidance of harm" (Thompson, 1990, p. 105). It is the basis on which professionals respond to clients who may endanger themselves or others and why they respond to colleagues' unethical behavior (Daniluk & Haverkamp. 1993).

Personal Reflection

Think of the case of Linda that you have read about in previous chapters. What are some actions based on ethical principles that you could take in helping her?

In addition to these guidelines, Swanson (1983) lists other factors for assessing whether helpers are acting in ethically responsible ways. The first is *personal and professional honesty*. Counselors and other helping professionals need to operate openly with themselves and those with whom they work. Hidden agendas or unacknowledged feelings hinder relationships and place everyone involved in a situation on shaky ethical ground. One way to overcome personal or professional honesty problems that may get in the way of acting ethically is to receive supervision (Kitchener, 1994).

A second factor is *acting in the best interest of clients*. This ideal is easier to discuss than achieve. At times, professional helpers may impose personal values on clients and ignore what they really want (Gladding & Hood, 1974). At other times, they may fail to recognize an emergency and too readily accept the idea that clients' best interest are served by doing nothing.

A third factor is that professional helpers *act without malice or personal gain*. Some clients are difficult to like or deal with, and it is with these individuals that special care must be taken. Likewise, avoiding relationships with likable clients either on a personal or professional basis is crucial. Errors in judgment are most likely to occur when the professional helper's self-interest becomes a part of the relationship with a client (St. Germaine, 1993).

A final factor is whether a professional helper can justify an action "as the best judgment of what should be done based upon the current state of the profession" (Swanson, 1983, p. 59). To make such a decision, those who work in helping professions must keep up with current trends by reading the latest literature; attending in-service workshops and conventions; and becoming actively involved in local, state, and national activities.

In many situations, the proper behavior is not obvious (Wilcoxon et al., 2012). For example, the question of confidentiality in balancing the individual rights of a person with HIV and society's right to be protected from the spread of the disease is one with which some professional helpers struggle (Harding, Gray, & Neal, 1993). Likewise, there are multiple ethical dilemmas in counseling adult survivors of incest, including those of confidentiality and the consequences of making decisions about reporting abuse (Daniluk & Haverkamp. 1993). Therefore, when they are in doubt about what to do in a given situation, it is crucial for those involved in helping to consult and talk over situations with colleagues, in addition to using principles, guidelines, casebooks, and professional codes of ethics.

Information Management

Understanding and Mastery: Maintaining client confidentiality and appropriate use of client data

Critical Thinking Question: What do the two examples about proper behavior in the preceding paragraph tell you about the complexity of confidentiality?

Among the best ways to learn how to make ethical decisions is through taking courses and continuing education credits. Such classes can bring about significant attitudinal changes, including increased knowledge about ethical areas of self-awareness, multiple relationships, impairment, and multiculturalism (Coll, 1993). Because ethical attitudinal changes are related to ethical behavioral changes, courses in ethics on any level are extremely valuable.

Van Hoose and Paradise (1979) conceptualize the ethical behavior of counselors in terms of a five-stage developmental continuum of reasoning:

1. **Punishment orientation.** At this stage, the counseling professional believes external social standards are the basis for judging behavior. If someone violates a societal rule, he or she should be punished.
2. **Institutional orientation.** Professional helpers who operate at this stage believe in and abide by the rules of the institutions for which they work. They do not question the rules and base their decisions on them.
3. **Societal orientation.** At this stage, decisions are based on societal standards. If a question arises about whether the needs of society or an individual should come first, the needs of society are always given priority.
4. **Individual orientation.** The individual's needs receive top priority at this stage. Helpers are aware of societal needs and are concerned about the law, but they focus on what is best for the individual.
5. **Principle (conscience) orientation.** In this stage, concern for the individual is primary. Ethical decisions are based on internalized ethical standards, not external considerations.

The work of Van Hoose and Paradise is especially important because it explains directly how those in the professions of helping reason about ethical issues and indirectly how continuing education may make a difference in the way they think about ethics. It is **heuristic** (i.e., researchable or open to research) and can form the basis for empirical studies of the promotion of ethical behavior.

Overall, ethical behavior and ethical decision making is greatly influenced by the prevalent attitudes in the setting in which one works, by one's colleagues, and by the task being performed (e.g., assessing, diagnosing). Therefore, implementing ethical decisions and actions in counseling sometimes involves substantial personal and professional risk or discomfort (Faiver, Eisengart, & Colonna, 2004).

Those who go into professional helping should check thoroughly the general policies and principles of an institution before accepting employment because employment in a specific setting implies employees agree with its policies, principles, and ethics. When individuals find themselves in institutions that misuse their services and do not act in the best interests of their clients, they must act either to change the institution through educational or persuasive means or find other employment.

In making ethical decisions where there are no guidelines, it is critical for professionals to stay abreast of current issues, trends, and even legislation related to the situation they face. In the process, care must be taken not to stereotype or otherwise be insensitive to clients. Anticipation of problems and implementation of policies that produce humane and fair results are essential.

Assess your comprehension of <u>Making Ethical Decisions</u> by taking this quiz.

Unethical Behavior

Unethical behavior in helping professions can take many forms. The temptations common to people everywhere exist for those in human services. They include "physical intimacy, the titillation of gossip, or the opportunity (if the gamble pays off) to advance one's career" (Welfel & Lipsitz, 1983, p. 328). Some forms of unethical behavior are obvious and willful, whereas others are more subtle and unintentional. Regardless, the harmful outcome is the same. The following are some of the most prevalent forms of unethical behaviors in helping professions (Herlihy & Corey, 2006):

- Violation of confidentiality
- Exceeding one's level of professional competence
- Negligent practice
- Claiming expertise one does not possess
- Imposing one's values on a client
- Creating dependency in a client
- Sexual activity with a client
- Certain conflicts of interest, such as a dual or multiple relationships—where the role of the helper is combined with another relationship either personal or professional and not monitored for appropriateness of boundaries (Moleski & Kiselica, 2005).
- Questionable financial arrangements, such as charging excessive fees
- Improper advertising
- Plagiarism

Although most helping professionals act ethically, occasional situations arise in which such is not the case. In these circumstances, those who are aware of the situations must take some action. Otherwise, by condoning or ignoring these situations they risk eroding their own sense of moral selfhood and find it easier to condone future ethical breaches, a phenomenon known as the **slippery slope effect**.

Personal Reflection

When have you seen the slippery slope effect displayed in public life, such as shady financial deals? How could you see the slippery slope effect happening in professional helping relationships?

Herlihy (1996) suggests several steps to take in working through potential ethical dilemmas, especially with impaired professionals. The first is to identify the problem as objectively as possible and the helper's relationship to it. Such a process is best done on paper to clarify thinking.

The second step in the process is to apply the current associational (e.g., psychology, counseling, social work, human services) codes of ethics to the matter. In such cases, clear guidance as to a course of action may emerge. Next, a professional should consider moral principles of the helping profession discussed earlier in this chapter, such as beneficence, justice, and autonomy. Consultation with a colleague is an option, also.

If action is warranted, the colleague in question should first be approached informally. This approach involves confrontation in a caring context, which hopefully will lead to the professional in question seeking help. If it does not, the confronting helper should consider the potential consequences of all other options and then define a course of action. Such a course might include filing an ethical complaint with a national association or licensing board. A complaint may be filled by either the professional, who has queried his or her colleague, or by a client who believes he or she has been treated unethically.

In examining courses of action, there should be an evaluation of where each potential action might lead. Criteria for judgment include one's comfort surrounding

(a) **publicity** (i.e., if the actions in this matter were reported in the press),
(b) **justice** (i.e., fairness),
(c) **moral traces** (i.e., lingering feelings of doubt), and
(d) **universality** (i.e., is this a course I would recommend others take in this situation?).

Finally, a course of action is chosen and implemented. In such a case, the professional helper must realize that not everyone will agree. Therefore, he or she needs to be prepared to take criticism as well as credit for what has been done.

Summary and Conclusion

As this chapter points out, the matter of ethics in the helping professions is complex and multidimensional. To act ethically, professionals must first know what ethics are and how to distinguish them from concepts such as morality. They also need to know about codes of ethics relevant to helping situations, how to make ethical decisions, and how to deal with someone who is acting unethically as well as how to evaluate their own actions.

It is fair to say that of all the dimensions involved in helping others, those that pertain to ethics are among the hardest to understand and to implement. The reason is that ethical matters require a higher level of thinking than most other aspects of counseling or assisting others. Theories and techniques, for example, are pretty straightforward and it is not difficult to assess whether a helping professional at any level is accurately behaving in accord with the theory or technique. But ethics are a constant challenge for professionals. They are more open to interpretation and sometimes an individual must employ an ethical principle in making an ethical decision because there is no precedent. Yet ethics are vital to the health, well-being, and future of counseling and human services (Manning, 2002). It could even be said that ethics are the hub around which all other aspects of helping revolve. If that is the case, understanding ethics will always be relevant and essential, especially as the professions in human services move forward.

Recall what you learned in this chapter by reviewing and completing <u>Chapter Review</u>.

Epilogue

In the preceding chapters you have read about the importance of theories and have been able to surmise how the most popular theories of today work. You have also read about the importance of ethical issues in using theories. Counselors who are beginners and human services professionals sometimes question which theory or theories work best. They may engage in heated debates about minor issues associated with various theories. The public as well as management groups connected to mental health issues, such as health maintenance organizations, frequently has such discussions as well. The reason is that clinicians, treatment specialists, human services workers, insurance companies, and the public may become more assured and confident about outcomes and the value of treatment if a theory or theories can be proven to be effective in certain situations or with specific populations.

In recent years, there has been a tendency for research to validate cognitive, behavioral, and cognitive behavioral theories in regard to their helpfulness. This trend is not surprising, given that these approaches to counseling are probably the most objectively measured. Still, the classic question persists when a new client is seen: "What treatment, by whom, is most effective for this individual with that specific problem (or set of problems) and under which set of circumstances?" (Paul, 1967, p.111).

It is beyond the scope of this text to give a definitive answer to Paul's pondering, which would require delving into an almost inexhaustible number of variables related to a client before services begin—for example, family background and physical and psychological issues. Research has verified, though, that a number of psychologically oriented treatments are valuable with some specific disorders (Seligman, 2003; Murdock, 2013). In addition, a number of emerging theories hold significant promise (Corsini, 2001). The relationship, as well as the theoretical approach, in a clinical setting seems to be the key to individuals getting better and moving on with their lives.

Theories, Clients, and You

Regardless of the current state of research about theories, it is important to emphasize that knowing and utilizing a theory in counseling and human services practices is important both singularly and in combination. Theories ground you as a helper by making you aware of what practitioners and researchers have proposed and how their ideas and implementations have worked. However, it must be stressed that individuals respond differently to diverse theories. As stated at the beginning of this text, counselors and human services practitioners may even change theories during the course of treatment with the same person. As you have seen in the chapter vignettes, outcome in Linda's case is related to the approaches employed with her.

Yet, as crucial as the qualities and backgrounds of theories and clients are, you as the counselor and/or human service practitioner are equally important. Applying theoretical approaches to therapeutic situations is both an art and a science. It involves knowing the research behind what you do and being aware of yourself, others, and the developmental stage of helping in which you are engaged. There are no cookbooks for or shortcuts to thinking, feeling, and acting within the moments that you are engaged in assisting another human being. If you remember this fact, you will likely do well in applying the theories you have learned here and others that you may master later. Your sensitivity to the complexity of working with people will have been increased, and the helping relationships you establish will be formed by the past as well as the present.

Final Considerations

As you have seen from reading how different theories work, many reasons are given as to what various approaches emphasize and what techniques they use. These explanations are based on developmental and situational factors. Thus, the same client may be conceptualized in a number of ways, depending on who is providing services. However, even though theories are unique, they are paradoxically similar in using specialized vocabularies, terms, and procedures. Counselors and human services practitioners have their own special language that must be mastered. Backgrounds and personalities of helping specialists enter treatment, too, and appropriate ways of responding and interacting with individuals must be learned and mastered so that the personhood of helpers does not detract from theories that they know or use.

You will do well to remember that despite some drawbacks and limitations, theories provide guidance about what is occurring in the lives of people and how such issues might best be handled (Austin, 1999). Theories also influence the process of helping—that is, what will be done and how—as well as outcomes, or results. In the end, all theories deal with perception and persuasion (Frank & Frank, 1991). They seek to make life better for the individuals we are privileged to work with. But it is how theories are used that makes a difference. Like a knife, a theory may help heal or it may wound; it depends on who uses it and how.

In developing or finding your comfort level in using theoretical models, you should remember that most theories involve a number of components, such as their view of human nature, processes, techniques, multicultural issues, strengths, and limitations. No theory is perfect. Indeed, the best theories are always evolving and growing because they are being researched and practiced. You are emerging also. When all of these factors are taken into consideration, you may find working with people more complicated than you had initially imagined, but you may also find it more stimulating, rewarding, and fulfilling than you had expected. Theories can help lead the way. What could be more exciting and inviting?

References for Chapter 1

Auvenshine, D., & Noffsinger, A. L. (1984). *Counseling: An introduction for the health and human services.* Baltimore: University Park Press.

Boy, A. V., & Pine, G. J. (1983). Counseling: Fundamentals of theoretical renewal. *Counseling and Values, 27,* 248–255.

Brammer, L. M., Abrego, P. J., & Shostrom, E. L. (1993). *Therapeutic counseling and psychotherapy* (6th ed.). Upper Saddle River, NJ: Merrill/Prentice Hall.

Burger, W. R. (2011). *Human services in contemporary America* (8th ed.). Belmont, CA: Brooks/Cole.

Butcher, J., Mineka, S., & Hooley, J. (2013). *Abnormal psychology* (15th ed.). Boston: Pearson.

Carlson, J., & Engler-Carlson, M. (2011). Series preface. In R. Wubbolding (Ed.), *Reality therapy.* Washington, DC: American Psychological Association.

Cavanagh, M. E., & Levitov, J. E. (2002). *The counseling experience* (2nd ed.). Prospect Heights, IL: Waveland.

Cheston, S. E. (2000). A new paradigm for teaching counseling theory and practice. *Counselor Education and Supervision, 39,* 254–269.

English, H. B., & English, A. C. (1956). *A comprehensive dictionary of psychological and psychoanalytical terms.* New York: Longman Green.

Gladding, S. T. (1990). Let us not grow weary of theory. *Journal for Specialists in Group Work, 15,* 194.

Hansen, J. C., Stevic, R. R., & Warner, R. W. (1986). *Counseling: Theory and process* (4th ed.). Boston: Allyn & Bacon.

Harman, R. L. (1977). Beyond techniques. *Counselor Education and Supervision, 17,* 157–158.

Harper, R. A. (1959). *Psychoanalysis and psychotherapy: 36 systems.* Upper Saddle River, NJ: Prentice Hall.

Ivey, A. E., & Goncalves, O. F. (1988). Developmental therapy: Integrating developmental processes into the clinical practice. *Journal of Counseling and Development, 66,* 406–413.

Ivey, A. E., Ivey, M. B., & Zalaquett, C. P. (2010). *Intentional interviewing and counseling: Facilitating client development in a multicultural society.* Belmont, CA: Brooks/Cole.

Kelly, K. R. (1988). Defending eclecticism: The utility of informed choice. *Journal of Mental Health Counseling, 10,* 210–213.

Lazarus, A. A. (1967). In support of technical eclecticism. *Psychological Reports, 21,* 415–416.

Lazarus, A. A. (2000). Multimodal therapy. In R. J. Corsini & D. Wedding (Eds.), *Current psychotherapies* (5th ed., pp. 340–374). Itasca, IL: Peacock.

Lazarus, A. A. (2009). Multimodal behavior therapy. In W. T. O'Donohue & J. E. Fisher (Eds.), *General principles and empirically supported techniques of cognitive behavior therapy* (pp. 440–444). Hoboken, NJ: John Wiley & Sons.

Lazarus, A. A., & Beutler, L. E. (1993). On technical eclecticism. *Journal of Counseling and Development, 71,* 381–385.

Maslow, A. H. (1968). *Toward a psychology of being.* New York: John Wiley and Sons.

McBride, M. C., & Martin, G. E. (1990). A framework for eclecticism: The importance of theory to mental health counseling. *Journal of Mental Health Counseling, 12,* 495–505.

Monette, D. R., Sullivan, T. J., & DeJong, C. R. (2011). *Applied social research: A tool for the human services* (8th ed.). Belmont, CA: Brooks/Cole.

Neukrug, E. S. (2013). *Theory, practice and trends in human services* (5th ed.). Belmont, CA: Brooks/Cole.

Okun, B. F. (1990). *Seeking connections in psychotherapy.* San Francisco: Jossey-Bass.

Petrocelli, J. V. (2002). Processes and stages of change: Counseling with the transtheoretical model of change. *Journal of Counseling and Development, 80,* 22–30.

Prochaska, J. O., & DiClemente, C. C. (1992). The transtheoretical approach. In J. C. Norcross & M. R. Goldfried (Eds.), *Handbook of psychotherapy integration* (pp. 300–334). New York: Basic Books.

Prochaska, J. O., & Norcross, J. C. (2010). *Systems of psychotherapy: A transtheoretical analysis* (7th ed.). Belmont, CA: Brooks/Cole.

Sharf, R. S. (2012). *Theories of psychotherapy and counseling* (5th ed.). Belmont, CA: Brooks/Cole.

Shertzer, B., & Stone, S. C. (1974). *Fundamentals of counseling*. Boston: Houghton Mifflin.

Simon, G. M. (1989). An alternative defense of eclecticism: Responding to Kelly and Ginter. *Journal of Mental Health Counseling, 2,* 280–288.

Wilks, D. (2003). A historical review of counseling theory development in relation to definitions of free will and determinism. *Journal of Counseling and Development, 81,* 278–284.

Young, R. A. (1988). Ordinary explanations and career theories. *Journal of Counseling and Development, 66,* 336–339.

Ziff, K. K. (2012). *Asylum on the hill: History of a healing landscape*. Athens, OH: Ohio University Press.

References for Chapter 2

Bankart, C. P. (1997). *Talking cures.* Belmont, CA: Brooks/Cole.

Bule, J. (1988, November). Psychoanalysis barriers tumble. *APA Monitor, 19*(1), 15.

Capuzzi, D., & Black, D. K. (1986). The history of dream analysis and the helping relationship: A synopsis for practitioners. *Journal of Humanistic Education and Development, 24,* 82–97.

Erikson, E. H. (1963). *Childhood and society* (2nd ed.). New York: Norton.

Erikson, E. H. (1982). *The life cycle completed.* New York: Norton.

Exner, J. E., Jr. (2003). *The Rorschach: A comprehensive system* (4th ed.). New York: John Wiley and Sons.

Freud, A. (1936). *The ego and the mechanisms of defense* (J. Strachey, Trans.). New York: International Universities Press.

Freud, S. (1900/1955). *The interpretation of dreams* (J. Strachey, Trans.). London: Hogarth.

Freud, S. (1923/1933). *New introductory lectures on psychoanalysis* (W. J. H. Sprott, Trans.). New York: Norton.

Freud, S. (1923/1947). *The ego and the id* (J. Strachey, Trans.). London: Hogarth.

Freud, S. (1925/1959). An autobiographical study. In J. Strachey (Ed. & Trans.), *The standard edition of the complete psychological works of Sigmund Freud* (Vol. 20, pp. 7–74). London: Hogarth.

Glassgold, J., & Iasenza, S. (2004). *Lesbians, feminism, and psychoanalysis: The second wave.* New York: Routledge.

Hall, C. S. (1954). *A primer of Freudian psychology.* New York: New American Library.

Hall, C. S., Lindzey, L., & Campbell, J. B. (1998). *Theories of personality* (4th ed.). New York: John B. Wiley.

Hansen, J. T. (2010). Counseling and psychoanalysis: Advancing the value of diversity. *Journal of Multicultural Counseling and Development, 28,* 16–26.

Horney, K. (1967). On the genesis of the castration complex in women. In K. Horney (Ed.), *Feminine psychology* (pp. 37–53). New York: Norton.

Jones, R. M. (1979). Freudian and post-Freudian theories of dreams. In B. B. Wolman (Ed.), *Handbook of dreams: Research, theories, and applications.* New York: Litton.

Erikson, E. H. (1982). *The life cycle completed.* New York: Norton.

Kohut, H. (1971). *The analysis of the self.* New York: International Universities Press.

Kohut, H. (1984). *How does psychoanalysis cure?* Chicago: University of Chicago Press.

Levinson, D. J., Darrow, C. N., Klein, E. B., Levinson, M. H., & McKee, B. (1978). *The seasons of a man's life.* New York: Knopf.

Luborksy, E. B., O'Reilly-Landry, & Arlow, J. A. (2011). Psychoanalysis. In R. J. Corsini & D. Wedding (Eds.), *Current psychotherapies* (9th ed., pp. 15–66). Belmont, CA: Brooks/Cole.

Monte, C. F. (1991). *Beneath the mask: An introduction to theories of personality* (4th ed.). Fort Worth, TX: Holt, Rinehart, & Winston.

Nye, R. D. (2000). *Three psychologies: Perspectives from Freud, Skinner, and Rogers* (6th ed.). Pacific Grove, CA: Brooks/Cole.

Olson, M. H., & Hergenhahn, B. R. (2011). *An introduction to theories of personality* (8th ed.). Upper Saddle River, NJ: Prentice Hall.

Singer, E. (1970). *Key concepts in psychotherapy* (2nd ed.). New York: Basic Books.

Turkington, C. (1985). Analysts sued for barring non-MDs. *APA Monitor, 16*(5), 2.

Vandenbos, G. R., Cummings, N., & Deleon, P. H. (1992). A century of psychotherapy: Economic and environmental influences. In D. K. Freedheim (Ed.), *History of psychotherapy: A century of change* (pp. 65–102). Washington, DC: American Psychological Association.

Winkler, K. J. (1986). Scholars prescribe Freud's "talking cure" for problems. *Chronicle of Higher Education, 33*(8), 4–6l.

References for Chapter 3

Adler, A. (1927). *Understanding human nature*. Greenwich, CT: Fawcett.

Adler, A. (1931). *What life should mean to you*. Boston: Little, Brown.

Adler, A. (1956). *The individual psychology of Alfred Adler: A systematic presentation in selections from his writings* (H. L. Ansbacher & R. R. Ansbacher, Eds.). New York: Norton.

Adler, A. (1964). *Social interest: A challenge to mankind*. New York: Capricorn.

Adler, A. (1969). *The practice and theory of individual psychology*. Patterson, NJ: Littlefield, Adams.

Ansbacher, H. L. (1977). Individual psychology. In R. J. Corsini (Ed.), *Current personality theories*. Itasca, IL: Peacock.

Ansbacher, H. L., & Ansbacher, R. R. (Eds.). (1964). *Superiority and social interest*. Evanston, IL: Northwestern University Press.

Ansbacher, H. L., & Ansbacher, R. R. (Eds.). (1978). *Cooperation between the sexes*. New York: Anchor.

Brown, D. (1997). Implications of cultural values for cross-cultural consultation with families. *Journal of Counseling and Development, 76*, 29–35.

Carlson, J., Watts, R. E., & Maniacci, M. (2006). *Adlerian therapy: Theory and practice*. Washington, DC: American Psychological Association.

Corey, G. (2013). *Theory and practice of counseling and psychotherapy* (9th ed.). Belmont, CA: Thomson Brooks/Cole.

Corsini, R. J. (1988). Adlerian groups. In S. Long (Ed.), *Six group therapies* (pp. 1–43). New York: Plenum.

Corsini, R. J. (2000). Introduction. In R. J. Corsini & D. Wedding (Eds.), *Current psychotherapies* (6th ed., pp. 1–15). Itasca, IL: Peacock.

Datler, W., & Gstach, J. (2001, June 26). Alfred Adler and his time. *Presentation to the Wake Forest Vienna Theorists class*. University of Vienna, Vienna, Austria.

Dinkmeyer, D. (1982a). *Developing understanding of self and others* (DUSOD-1). Circle Pine, MN: American Guidance Service.

Dinkmeyer, D. (1982b). *Developing understanding of self and others* (DUSOD-2). Circle Pine, MN: American Guidance Service.

Dinkmeyer, D., & Losoncy, L. E. (1996). *The skills of encouragement*. New York: Saint Lucie Press.

Dinkmeyer, D., & Sperry, L. (2000). *Adlerian counseling and psychotherapy* (3rd ed.). Upper Saddle River, NJ: Prentice Hall.

Dinkmeyer, D., McKay, G. D., & Dinkmeyer, D., Jr. (1997). *The parent's handbook: Systematic training for effective parenting (STEP)*. Circle Pine, MN: American Guidance Service.

Dinkmeyer, D., McKay, G. D., McKay, J. L., & Dinkmeyer, D. (1998). *Parenting teenagers: Systematic training for effective parenting/Teen (STEP/Teen)*. Circle Pine, MN: American Guidance Service.

Dreikurs, R. R. (1950). *Fundamentals of Adlerian psychology*. Chicago: Alfred Adler Institute.

Dreikurs, R. R. (1967). *Psychodynamics, psychotherapy, and counseling*. Chicago: Alfred Adler Institute.

Dreikurs, R. R., & Mosak, H. H. (1966). The tasks of life. I: Adler's three tests. *Individual Psychologist, 4*, 18–22.

Dreikurs, R. R., & Soltz, V. (1964). *Children: The challenge*. New York: Hawthorne.

Eckstein, D., & Kaufman, J. A. (2012). The role of birth order in personality: An enduring intellectual legacy of Alfred Adler. *Journal of Individual Psychology, 68*, 60–61.

Gold, L. (1979). Adler's theory of dreams: An holistic approach to interpretation. In B. B. Wolman (Ed.), *Handbook of dreams: Research, theories, and applications*. New York: Van Nostrand Reinhold.

James, R. K., & Gilliland, B. E. (2003). *Theories and strategies in counseling and psychotherapy* (5th ed.). Boston: Allyn & Bacon.

Kelly, E. W., Jr., & Sweeney, T. J. (1979). Typical faulty goals of adolescents: A base for counseling. *School Counselor, 26*, 236–246.

Kern, C. W., & Watts, R. E. (1993). Adlerian counseling. *Texas Counseling Association Journal, 21*, 85–95.

Kottman, T., & Warlick, J. (1990). Adlerian play therapy. *Journal of Humanistic Education and Development*, 28, 125–132.

Lowe, R. N. (1982). Adlerian/Dreikursian family counseling. In A. M. Horne & M. M. Ohlsen (Eds.), *Family counseling and therapy* (pp. 329–359). Itasca, IL: Peacock.

Mosak, H. H., & Maniacci, M. (2000). A primer of Adlerian psychology: The analytic, behavioral, cognitive psychology of Alfred Adler. Philadelphia: Brunner/Mazel.

Mosak, H., & Maniacci, M. (2011). Adlerian psychotherapy. In R. J. Corsini & D. Wedding (Eds.), *Current psychotherapies* (9th ed., pp. 67–112). Belmont, CA: Brooks/Cole.

Nystul, M. S. (2011). *Introduction to counseling: An art and science perspective* (4th ed.). Upper Saddle River, NJ: Prentice Hall.

Purkey, W. W., & Schmidt, J. J. (1987). *The inviting relationship*. Upper Saddle River, NJ: Prentice Hall.

Seligman, L., & Reichenberg, L. W. (2010). *Theories of counseling and psychotherapy* (3rd ed.). Upper Saddle River, NJ: Pearson.

Sharf, R. S. (2012). *Theories of psychotherapy and counseling* (5th ed.). Belmont, CA: Brooks/Cole.

Slavik, S. (1991). Early memories as a guide to client movement through life. *Canadian Journal of Counselling, 25*, 331-337.

Statton, J. E., & Wilborn, B. (1991). Adlerian counseling and the early recollections of children. *Individual Psychology*, 47, 338–347.

Sweeney, T. J. (2009). *Adlerian counseling* (5th ed.). New York: Routledge.

Vaihinger, H. (1911). *The philosophy of "as if."* New York: Harcourt, Brace, & World.

Wallace, W. A. (1986). *Theories of counseling and psychotherapy*. Boston: Allyn & Bacon.

Walsh, W. M., & McGraw, A. (1996). *Essentials of family therapy*. Denver, CO: Love.

Watkins, C. E., Jr. (1985). Early recollections as a projective technique in counseling: An Adlerian view. *AMHCA Journal*, 7, 32–40.

Watts, R. E. (1996). Social interest and the core conditions: Could it be that Adler influenced Rogers? *Journal of Humanistic Education and Development*, 34, 165–170.

References for Chapter 4

Austin, L. (1999). *The counseling primer*. Philadelphia: Accelerated Development.

Baldwin, C. (1989). Peaceful alternatives: Inner peace. *Journal of Humanistic Education and Development, 28,* 86–92.

Bretherton, R., & Orner, R. (2003). Positive psychotherapy in disguise. *Psychologist, 16,* 136–137.

Buber, M. (1970). *I and thou.* New York: Charles Scribner's Sons

Buhler, C., & Allen, M. (1972). *Introduction to humanistic psychology.* Pacific Grove, CA: Brooks/Cole.

Chandler, C. K., Holden, J. M., & Kolander, C. A. (1992). Counseling for spiritual wellness: Theory and practice. *Journal of Counseling & Development, 71,* 168–176.

Corey, G. (2013). *Theory and practice of counseling and psychotherapy* (9th ed.). Belmont, CA: Brooks/Cole.

Cunningham, L. M., & Peters, H. J. (1973). *Counseling theories.* Upper Saddle River, NJ: Prentice Hall.

Das, A. K. (1998). Frankl and the realm of meaning. *Journal of Humanistic Education and Development, 36,* 199–211.

Dollarhide, C. T. (1997). Counseling for meaning in work and life: An integrated approach. *Journal of Humanistic Education and Development, 35,* 178–187.

Epp, L. R. (1998). The courage to be an existential counselor: An interview with Clemmont E. Vontress. *Journal of Mental Health Counseling, 20,* 1–12.

Frankl, V. (1962). *Man's search for meaning: An introduction to logotherapy.* New York: Washington Square Press.

Frankl, V. (1967). *Psychotherapy and existentialism: Selected papers on logotherapy.* New York: Washington Square Press.

Frankl, V. (1959). The spiritual dimension in existential analysis and logotherapy. *Journal of Individual Psychology, 15,* 157–165.

Frankl, V. (1969). *The will to meaning: Foundations and applications of logotherapy.* New York: New American Library.

Hoffman, E. (1990). Abraham Maslow's legacy for counseling. *Journal of Humanistic Education and Development, 29,* 2–9.

Ivey, A. E., D'Andrea, M., & Ivey, M. B. (2012). *Theories of counseling and psychotherapy* (7th ed.). Thousand Oaks, CA: Sage.

Jackson, M. L. (1987). Cross-cultural counseling at the crossroads: A dialogue with Clemmont E. Vontress. *Journal of Counseling and Development, 66,* 20–23.

Kemp, C. G. (1976). Existential counseling. In G. S. Belkin (Ed.), *Counseling directions in theory and practice.* Dubuque, IA: Kendall/Hunt.

Maglio, A. S. T., Butterfield, L. D., & Borgen, W. A. (2005). Existential considerations for contemporary career counseling. *Journal of Employment Counseling, 42,* 75–92.

May, R. (1939). *The art of counseling.* New York: Abingdon-Cokesbury.

May, R. (Ed.). (1961). *Existential psychology.* New York: Random House.

May, R. (1967). Part three: Psychotherapy. In *Psychology and the human dilemma* (pp. 87–160). Princeton, NJ: Van Nostrand.

May, R. (1975). *The courage to create.* New York: Bantam.

May, R. (1977). *The meaning of anxiety* (Rev. ed.). New York: Norton.

May, R. (1985). *My quest for beauty.* New York: Norton.

May, R., Angel, E., & Ellenberger, H. (Eds.). (1958). *Existence.* New York: Simon & Schuster.

McIllroy, J. H. (1979). Career as life-style: An existential view. *Personnel and Guidance Journal, 57,* 351–354.

Miars, R. D. (2002). Existential authenticity: A foundational value for counseling. *Counseling and Values, 46,* 218–226.

Moodley, R., & Walcott, R. (Eds.). (2010). *Counseling across and beyond cultures: Exploring the work of Clemmont E. Vontress in clinical settings.* Toronto: University of Toronto Press.

Partenheimer, D. (1990). Teaching literature toward a humanistic society. *Journal of Humanistic Education and Development, 29,* 40–44.

Rabinowitz, F. E., Good, G., & Cozad, L. (1989). Rollo May: A man of meaning and myth. *Journal of Counseling and Development, 67,* 436–441.

Reeves, C. (1977). *The psychology of Rollo May.* San Francisco: Jossey-Bass.

Schultze, G., & Miller, C. (2004). The search for meaning and career development. *The Career Development International, 9,* 142–152.

Stevens, M. J., Pfost, K. S., & Wessels, A. B. (1987). The relationship of purpose in life to coping strategies and time since the death of a significant other. *Journal of Counseling and Development, 65,* 424–426.

Vontress, C. (1979). Cross-cultural counseling: An existential approach. *Personnel and Guidance Journal, 58,* 117–122.

Vontress, C. E., Johnson, J. A., & Epp, L. R. (1999). *Cross-cultural counseling: A case book.* Alexandria, VA: American Counseling Association.

Wallace, W. A. (1986). *Theories of counseling and psychotherapy.* Boston: Allyn & Bacon.

Wilbur, M. P., Roberts-Wilbur, J., & Morris, J. R. (1990). A humanistic alternative for counseling alcoholics. *Journal of Humanistic Education and Development, 28,* 146–165.

Yalom, I. D. (1980). *Existential psychotherapy.* New York: Basic Books.

Yalom, I. D., & Josselson, R. (2011). Existential psychotherapy. In R. J. Corsini & D. Wedding (Eds.), *Current psychotherapies* (9th ed., pp. 310–341). Belmont, CA: Brooks/Cole.

References for Chapter 5

Bankart, C. P. (1997). *Talking cures*. Belmont, CA: Brooks/Cole.

Benjamin, P., & Looby, J. (1998). Defining the nature of spirituality in the context of Maslow's and Rogers's theories. *Counseling and Values, 42*, 92–100.

Boy, A. V., & Pine, G. J. (1982). *Client-centered counseling: A renewal*. Boston: Allyn & Bacon.

Braaten, L. J. (1986). Thirty years with Rogers's necessary and sufficient conditions of therapeutic personality change. *Person-Centered Review, 1*, 37–49.

Brammer, L. M., Abrego, P. J., & Shostrom, E. L. (1993). *Therapeutic counseling and psychotherapy* (6th ed.). Upper Saddle River, NJ: Merrill/Prentice Hall.

Carkhuff, R. R. (1969a). *Helping and human relations* (Vol. 1). New York: Holt, Rinehart, & Winston.

Carkhuff, R. R. (1969b). *Helping and human relations* (Vol. 2). New York: Holt, Rinehart, & Winston.

Cooper, M., & Mcleod, J. (2011). Person-centered therapy: A pluralistic perspective. *Person-Centered and Experiential Psychotherapies, 10*, 210–223.

Cormier, W. H., & Cormier, L. S. (1998). *Interviewing strategies for helpers: A guide to assessment, treatment, and evaluation* (4th ed.). Pacific Grove, CA: Brooks/Cole.

Gazda, G. M. (1973). *Human relations development: A manual for education*. Boston: Allyn & Bacon.

Gelso, C. J., & Carter, J. A. (1985). The relationship in counseling and psychotherapy: Components, consequences, and theoretical antecedents. *Counseling Psychologist, 13*, 155–243.

Glauser, A. S., & Bozarth, J. D. (2001). Person-centered counseling: The culture within. *Journal of Counseling and Development, 79*, 142–147.

Goodyear, R. K. (1987). In memory of Carl Ransom Rogers. *Journal of Counseling and Development, 65*, 523–524.

Grummon, D. L. (1972). Client-centered therapy. In B. Stefflre & W. H. Grant (Eds.), *Theories of counseling* (2nd ed.). New York: McGraw-Hill.

Hart, J. (1970). The development of client-centered therapy. In J. T. Hart & T. M. Tomlinson (Eds.), *New directions in client centered therapy*. Boston: Houghton Mifflin.

Henderson, D. A., & Thompson, C. (2011). *Counseling children* (8th ed.). Pacific Grove, CA: Brooks/Cole.

Heppner, P. P., Rogers, M. E., & Lee, L. A. (1990). Carl Rogers: Reflections on his life. In P. P. Heppner (Ed.), *Pioneers in counseling and development: Personal and professional perspectives* (pp. 54–59). Alexandria, VA: American Association for Counseling and Development.

Hergenhahn, B. R. & Olson, M. H. (2007). *An introduction to theories of personality* (7th ed.). Upper Saddle River, NJ: Pearson.

Kirschenbaum, H. (2004). Carl Rogers's life and work: An assessment on the 100th anniversary of his birth. *Journal of Counseling and Development, 82*, 116–124.

Kirschenbaum, H. (2007). *The life and work of Carl Rogers*. Alexandria, VA: American Counseling Association.

Kirschenbaum, H. (2012). What is "person-centered"? A posthumous conversation with Carl Rogers on the development of the person-centered approach. *Person-Centered and Experiential Psychotherapies, 11*, 14–30.

Miller, M. J. (1996). Client-centered reflections on career decision making. *Journal of Employment Counseling, 33*, 43–46.

Neukrug, E. S. (2011). *Counseling theory and practice*. Belmont, CA: Brooks/Cole.

Nye, R. D. (2000). *Three psychologies: Perspectives from Freud, Skinner, and Rogers* (6th ed.). Pacific Grove, CA: Brooks/Cole.

Olson, M. H., & Hergenhahn, B. R. (2011). *An introduction to theories of personality* (8th ed.). Upper Saddle River, NJ: Prentice Hall.

Poppen, W. A., & Thompson, C. L. (1974). *School counseling: Theories and concepts*. Lincoln, NE: Professional Educators Publications.

Raskin, N. J., Rogers, C. R., & Witty, M. (2011). Person-centered therapy. In R. J. Corsini & D. Wedding (Eds.), *Current psychotherapies* (9th ed., pp. 148–195). Belmont, CA: Brooks/Cole.

Rogers, C. R. (1951). *Client-centered therapy*. Boston: Houghton Mifflin.

Rogers, C. R. (1955). Persons or science? A philosophical question. *American Psychologist, 10,* 267–278.

Rogers, C. R. (1957). The necessary and sufficient conditions of therapeutic personality change. *Journal of Consulting Psychology, 21,* 95–103.

Rogers, C. R. (1959). A theory of therapy, personality, and inter- personal relationships, as developed in the client-centered framework. In S. Koch (Ed.), *Psychology: A study of science* (Vol. 3, pp. 184–256). New York: McGraw-Hill.

Rogers, C. R. (1961). *On becoming a person*. Boston: Houghton Mifflin.

Rogers, C. R. (1965). Client-centered therapy: Part I. In E. Shostrom (Producer), *Three approaches to psychotherapy* [film]. Santa Anna, CA: Psychological Films.

Rogers, C. R. (1967a). Autobiography. In E. G. Boring & G. Lindzey (Eds.), *A history of psychology in autobiography* (Vol. 5, pp. 341–384). New York: Appleton.

Rogers, C. R. (1967). The conditions of change from a client- centered viewpoint. In B. Berenson & R. Carkhuff (Eds.), *Sources of gain in counseling and psychotherapy* (pp. 71–86). New York: Holt, Rinehart, & Winston.

Rogers, C. R. (1974). In retrospect: Forty-six years. *American Psychologist, 29,* 115–123.

Rogers, C. R. (1975). Empathic: An unappreciated way of being. *Counseling Psychologist, 5,* 2–10.

Rogers, C. R. (1977). *Carl Rogers on personal power: Inner strength and its revolutionary impact*. New York: Delacorte.

Rogers, C. R. (1980). *A way of being*. Boston: Houghton Mifflin.

Rogers, C. R. (1986). Rogers, Kohut, and Erickson: A personal perspective on some similarities and differences. *Person-Centered Review, 1,* 125–140.

Rogers, C. R. (1987). The underlying theory: Drawn from experience with individuals and groups. *Counseling and Values, 32,* 38–46.

Rogers, N., Tudor, K., Tudor, L. E., & Keemar, K. (2012). Person-centered expressive arts therapy: A theoretical encounter. *Person-Centered and Experiential Psychotherapies, 11,* 31–47.

Seligman, L., & Reichenberg, L. W. (2010). *Theories of counseling and psychotherapy* (3rd ed.). Upper Saddle River, NJ: Pearson.

Sharf, R. S. (2012). *Theories of psychotherapy and counseling* (5th ed.). Belmont, CA: Brooks/Cole.

Spangenberg, J. J. (2003). The cross-cultural relevance of person-centered counseling in postapartheid South Africa. *Journal of Counseling and Development, 81,* 48–54.

Watts, R. E. (1996). Social interest and the core conditions: Could it be that Adler influenced Rogers? *Journal of Humanistic Education and Development, 34,* 165–170.

Whiteley, J. M. (1987). The person-centered approach to peace. *Counseling and Values, 32,* 5–8.

References for Chapter 6

Assagioli, R. (1965). *Psychosynthesis*. New York: Hobbs, Dorman.

Bankart, C. P. (1997). *Talking cures*. Belmont, CA: Brooks/Cole.

Bernard, J. M. (1986). Laura Perls: From ground to figure. *Journal of Counseling and Development, 64,* 367–373.

Corey, G. (2013). *Theory and practice of counseling and psychotherapy* (9th ed.). Belmont, CA: Brooks/Cole.

Covin, A. B. (1977). Using Gestalt psychodrama experiments in rehabilitation counseling. *Personnel and Guidance Journal, 56,* 143–147.

Fagan, J. (1970). The task of the therapist. In J. Fagan & I. L. Shepherd (Eds.), *Gestalt therapy now* (pp. 88–106). Palo Alto, CA: Science and Behavior Books.

Gelso, C. J., & Carter, J. A. (1985). The relationship in counseling and psychotherapy: Components, consequences, and theoretical antecedents. *Counseling Psychologist, 13,* 155–243.

Gilliland, B. E., & James, R. K. (2003). *Theories and strategies in counseling and psychotherapy* (5th ed.). Boston: Allyn & Bacon.

Glinnwater, J. T. (2000). Gestalt therapy: Treatment of the affective self. *Gestalt Journal, 23,* 81–97.

Harman, R. L. (1975). A Gestalt point of view on facilitating growth in counseling. *Personnel and Guidance Journal, 53,* 363–366.

Harman, R. L. (1997). *Gestalt therapy techniques: Working with groups, couples, and sexually dysfunctional men.* Northvale, NJ: Aronson.

Hatcher, C., & Himelsteint, P. (Eds.). (1997). *The handbook of Gestalt therapy*. Northvale, NJ: Aronson.

Henderson, D. A., & Thompson, C. (2011). *Counseling children* (8th ed.). Pacific Grove, CA: Brooks/Cole.

Ivey, A. E., D'Andrea, M., & Ivey, M. B. (2012). *Theories of counseling and psychotherapy* (7th ed.). Thousand Oaks, CA: Sage.

Kempler, W. (1973). Gestalt therapy. In R. Corsini (Ed.), *Current psychotherapies* (pp. 251–286). Itasca, IL: Peacock.

Levine, T. B. Y. (Eds.). (2012). *Gestalt therapy: Advances in theory and practice*. New York: Routledge.

Levitsky, A., & Perls, F. S. (1970). The rules and games of Gestalt therapy. In J. Fagan & I. L. Shepherd (Eds.), *Gestalt therapy now* (pp. 140–149). Palo Alto, CA: Science and Behavior Books.

Mackay, B. (2002). Effects of Gestalt therapy two-chair dialogue on divorce decision making. *Gestalt Review, 6,* 220–235.

Mann, D. (2010). *Gestalt therapy: 100 key points and techniques*. New York: Routledge.

Masquelie, G. (2006). *Gestalt therapy: Living creatively today*. Cambridge, MA: Gestalt Press Books.

Melnick, J. (2003). Making the learning last. *Gestalt Review, 7,* 1–4.

Passons, W. R. (1975). *Gestalt approaches to counseling*. New York: Holt, Rinehart, & Winston.

Perls, F. (1969). *Gestalt therapy verbatim*. Lafayette, CA: Real People Press.

Perls, F. (1970). Four lectures. In J. Fagan & I. L. Shepherd (Eds.), *Gestalt therapy now* (pp. 14–38). Palo Alto, CA: Science and Behavior Books.

Perls, F. (1976). *The Gestalt approaches and eye witnesses to therapy*. New York: Bantam.

Perls, F., Hefferline, R. F., & Goodman, P. (1951). *Gestalt therapy*. New York: Dell.

Polster, E., & Polster, M. (1973). *Gestalt therapy integrated: Contours of theory and practice*. New York: Brunner/Mazel.

Sharf, R. S. (2012). *Theories of psychotherapy and counseling* (5th ed.). Belmont, CA: Brooks/Cole.

Simkin, J. S. (1975). An introduction to Gestalt therapy. In F. D. Stephenson (Ed.), *Gestalt therapy primer* (pp. 3–12). Springfield, IL: Thomas.

Viking.Miller, M. V. (2008). What lies beyond the field? *International Gestalt Journal, 31,* 133–144.

Yontef, G., & Jacobs, L. (2011). Gestalt therapy. In R. J. Corsini & D. Wedding (Eds.), *Current psychotherapies* (9th ed., pp. 342–382). Belmont, CA: Brooks/Cole.

Zerbetto, R., & Tantam, D. (2001). The Survey of European Psychotherapy Training 3: What psychotherapy is available in Europe? *European Journal of Psychotherapy, Counselling and Health, 4,* 396–406.

Zinker, J. (1978). *Creative process in Gestalt therapy*. New York: Random House.

References for Chapter 7

Evans, D. (1982). What are you doing? An interview with William Glasser. *Personnel and Guidance Journal, 60,* 460–464.

Gilliland, B. E., & James, R. K. (2003). *Theories and strategies in counseling and psychotherapy* (5th ed.). Boston: Allyn & Bacon.

Glasser, W. (1965). *Reality therapy: A new approach to psychiatry.* New York: Harper & Row.

Glasser, W. (1969). *Schools without failure.* New York: Harper & Row.

Glasser, W. (1972). *The identity society.* New York: Harper & Row.

Glasser, W. (1976). *Positive addiction.* New York: Harper & Row

Glasser, W. (1988). Reality therapy. Workshop presented at the Alabama Association for Counseling and Development, Fall Conference, November, Birmingham.

Glasser, W. (1986). *Control theory in the classroom.* New York: Harper & Row.

Glasser, W. (1961). *Mental health or mental illness.* New York: Harper & Row.

Glasser, W. (1980). Reality therapy: An explanation of the steps of reality therapy. In W. Glasser (Ed.), *What are you doing? How people are helped through reality therapy.* New York: Harper & Row.

Glasser, W. (1981). *Stations of the mind.* New York: Harper & Row.

Glasser, W. (1984). *Control theory: A new explanation of how we control our lives.* New York: Harper & Row.

Glasser, W. (1998). *Choice theory.* New York: HarperCollins.

Glasser, W. (2000). *Counseling with choice theory.* New York: HarperCollins.

Glasser, W., & Wubbolding, R. (1995). Reality therapy. In R. Corsini & D. Wedding (Eds.), *Current psychotherapies* (5th ed., pp. 293–321). Itasca, IL: Peacock.

Ivey, A. E., D'Andrea, M., & Ivey, M. B. (2012). *Theories of counseling and psychotherapy* (7th ed.). Thousand Oaks, CA: Sage.

James, R. K., & Gilliland, B. E. (2003). *Theories and strategies in counseling and psychotherapy* (5th ed.). Boston: Allyn & Bacon.

Seligman, L. (1997). *Diagnosis and treatment planning in counseling* (2nd ed.). New York: Plenum.

Sharf, R. S. (2012). *Theories of psychotherapy and counseling* (5th ed.). Belmont, CA: Brooks/Cole.

Wallace, W. A. (1986). *Theories of counseling and psychotherapy.* Boston: Allyn & Bacon.

Wubbolding, R. E. (1975). Practicing reality therapy. *Personnel and Guidance Journal, 53,* 164–165.

Wubbolding, R. E. (1988). *Using reality therapy.* New York: HarperCollins.

Wubbolding, R. E. (1991). *Understanding reality therapy.* New York: Perennial HarperCollins.

Wubbolding, R. E. (1994). The early years of control theory: Forerunners Marcus Aurelius & Norbert Wiener. *Journal of Reality Therapy, 13,* 51–54.

Wubbolding, R. E. (1998). *Cycle of managing, supervising, counseling, and coaching using reality therapy.* Cincinnati: Center for Reality Therapy.

Wubbolding, R. E. (2000). *Reality therapy for the 21st century.* Philadelphia: Brunner-Routledge.

Wubbolding, R. E. (2007). Reality therapy theory. In D. Capuzzi & D. Gross (Eds.), *Counseling and psychotherapy: Theories and interventions* (4th ed., pp. 289–312). NJ: Upper Saddle River.

Wubbolding, R. E. (2011). *Reality therapy.* Washington, DC: American Psychological Association.

References for Chapter 8

Alberti, R. E., & Emmons, M. L. (2008). *Your perfect right: A guide to assertive behavior* (9th ed.). Atascadero, CA: Impact.

Azrin, N. H., Stuart, R. B., Risely, T. R., & Stolz, S. (1977). Ethical issues for human services. *AABT Newsletter, 4,* 11.

Bandura, A. (1969). *Principles of behavior modification.* New York: Holt, Rinehart & Winston.

Bandura, A. (1986). *Social foundations of thought and action: A social cognitive theory.* Upper Saddle River, NJ: Prentice Hall.

Bandura, A., & Walters, R. H. (1963). *Social learning and personality development.* New York: Holt, Rinehart & Winston.

Bellack, A. S., & Hersen, M. (1998). *Behavioral assessment: A practical handbook.* Boston: Allyn & Bacon.

Blackham, G. J., & Silberman, A. (1979). *Modification of child and adolescent behavior.* Belmont, CA: Wadsworth.

Bussey, K., & Bandura, A. (1999). Social cognitive career theory of gender development and differentiation. *Psychological Review, 106,* 676–713.

Cautela, J. R. (1976). The present status of covert modeling. *Journal of Behavior Therapy and Experimental Psychiatry, 6,* 323–326.

Christopher, J. C. (1996). Counseling's inescapable moral vision. *Journal of Counseling & Development, 75,* 17–25.

Eysenck, H. J. (1960). *Behavior therapy and the neuroses.* New York: Pergamon.

Elms, A. C. (1981). Skinner's dark year and Walden Two. *American Psychologist, 36,* 470–479.

Fowler, R. D. (1990, October). B. F. Skinner: Farewell, with admiration and affection. *APA Monitor, 21*(10), 2.

Goldiamond, I. (1976). Self-reinforcement. *Journal of Applied Behavior Analysis, 9,* 509–514.

Goldstein, A. (1973). Behavior therapy. In R. Corsini (Ed.), *Current psychotherapies* (pp. 207–249). Itasca, IL: Peacock.

Hackney, H., & Cormier, L. S. (2012). *The professional counselor: A process guide to helping* (8th ed.). Upper Saddle River, NJ: Pearson.

Hosford, R. E. (1980). The Cubberley conference and the evolution of observational learning strategies. *Personnel and Guidance Journal, 58,* 467–472.

James, R. K., & Gilliland, B. E. (2003). *Theories and strategies in counseling and psychotherapy* (5th ed.). Boston: Allyn & Bacon.

Jones, M. C. (1924). The elimination of children's fears. *Journal of Experimental Psychology, 7,* 383–390.

Kipper, D. A. (1986). *Psychotherapy through clinical role playing.* New York: Brunner/Mazel.

Krasner, L., & Ullmann, L. P. (1973). *Behavior influence and personality: The social matrix of human action.* New York: Holt, Rinehart & Winston.

Krumboltz, J. D. (1966). Behavioral goals of counseling. *Journal of Counseling Psychology, 13,* 153–159.

Krumboltz, J. D., & Thoresen, C. E. (1976). *Counseling methods.* New York: Holt, Rinehart & Winston.

Lazarus, A. A. (1985). Behavior rehearsal. In A. S. Bellack & M. Hersen (Eds.), *Dictionary of behavior therapy techniques* (p. 22). New York: Pergamon.

Olson, M. H., & Hergenhahn, B. R. (2011). *An introduction to theories of personality* (8th ed.). Upper Saddle River, NJ: Prentice Hall.

Perry, M. A., & Furukawa, M. J. (1980). Modeling methods. In F. H. Kanfer & A. P. Goldstein (Eds.), *Helping people change* (pp. 131–171). New York: Pergamon.

Rescorla, R. A. (1988). Pavlovian conditioning: It's not what you think it is. *American Psychologist, 43,* 151–160.

Rose, S. D. (1983). Behavior therapy in groups. In H. I. Kaplan & B. J. Sadock (Eds.), *Comprehensive group psychotherapy* (2nd ed.). Baltimore: Williams & Wilkins.

Rimm, D. C., & Cunningham, H. M. (1985). Behavior therapies. In S. J. Lynn & J. P. Garske (Eds.), *Contemporary psychotherapies: Models and methods* (pp. 221–259). Upper Saddle River, NJ: Prentice Hall.

Seligman, L. (1997). *Diagnosis and treatment planning in counseling* (2nd ed.). New York: Plenum.

Sharf, R. S. (2012). *Theories of psychotherapy and counseling* (5th ed.). Belmont, CA: Brooks/Cole.

Skinner, B. F. (1953). *Science and human behavior*. New York: Macmillan.

Skinner, B. F., & Vaughan, M. E. (1983). *Enjoy old age*. New York: Norton.

Skinner, B. F. (1976). *Particulars of my life*. New York: McGraw-Hill.

Skinner, B. F. (1974). *About behaviorism*. New York: Knopf.

Skinner, B. F. (1967). Autobiography. In E. G. Boring & G. Lindzey (Eds.), *A history of psychology in autobiography* (Vol. 5, pp. 387–413). New York: Appleton-Century-Croft

Sprinthall, N. A. (1971). A program for psychological education: Some preliminary issues. *Journal of School Psychology, 9,* 373–382.

Thoresen, C. E. (1969). The counselor as an applied behavioral scientist. *Personnel and Guidance Journal, 47,* 841–848.

Thoresen, C. E., & Coates, T. J. (1980). What does it mean to be a behavior therapist? In C. E. Thoresen (Ed.), *The behavior therapist* (pp. 1–41). Pacific Grove, CA: Brooks/Cole.

Thoresen, C. E., & Mahoney, M. J. (1974). *Behavioral self-control*. New York: Holt, Rinehart, & Winston.

Watson, J. B., & Raynor, R. (1920). Conditioned emotional reactions. *Journal of Experimental Psychology, 3,* 1–14.

Wilson, G. T. (2011). Behavior therapy. In R. J. Corsini & D. Wedding (Eds.), *Current psychotherapies* (9th ed., pp. 235–275). Belmont, CA: Brooks/Cole.

Wolpe, J. (1958). *Psychotherapy by reciprocal inhibition building*. Stanford, CA: Stanford University Press.

Watson, J. B. (1913). Psychology as a behaviorist views it. *Psychological Review, 20,* 158–177.

Watson, J. B. (1925). *Behaviorism*. New York: Norton.

Yates, A. J. (1970). *Behavior therapy*. New York: Wiley.

Zimbardo, P. G., & Leippe, M. R. (1991). *The psychology of attitude change and social influence*. Philadelphia: Temple University Press.

References for Chapter 9

Arnkoff, D. B., & Glass, C. R. (1992). Cognitive therapy and psychotherapy integration. In D. K. Freedheim (Ed.), *History of psychotherapy: A century of change* (pp. 657–694). Washington, DC: American Psychological Association.

Bankart, C. P. (1997). *Talking cures*. Belmont, CA: Brooks/Cole.

Barkley, R. A. (1987). *Defiant children: A clinician's manual for parent training*. New York: Guilford.

Barkley, R. A. (1991). *Attention-deficit hyperactivity disorder*. New York: Guilford.

Beck, A. T. (1976). *Cognitive therapy and emotional disorders*. New York: International Universities Press.

Beck, A. T. (1991). Cognitive therapy: A 30-year retrospective. *American Psychologist, 46,* 368–375.

Beck, A. T., & Alford, B. A. (2009). *Depression: Causes and treatments* (2nd ed.). Baltimore, MD: University of Pennsylvania Press.

Beck, J. S. (2011). *Cognitive behavior therapy: Basics and beyond*. New York: Guilford.

Beck, A. T., Rush, A. J., Shaw, B. F., & Emery, G. (1979). *Cognitive therapy of depression*. New York: Guilford.

Beck, A. T., & Weishaar, M. (2008). Cognitive therapy. In R. J. Corsini & D. Wedding (Eds.), *Current psychotherapies* (8th ed., pp. 263–294). Belmont, CA: Thomson Brooks/Cole.

Bhar, S. S., & Beck, A. T. (2009). Treatment integrity of studies that compare short-term psychodynamic psychotherapy with cognitive-behavior therapy. *Clinical psychology: Science and practice, 16,* 370–378.

Burns, D. D. (1980). *Feeling good: The new mood therapy*. New York: Signet.

Burns, D. D. (1989). *The feeling good handbook: Using the new mood therapy in everyday life*. New York: Morrow.

Clark, D. A., & Beck, A. T. (2010). *Cognitive therapy of anxiety disorders: Science and practice*. New York: Guilford.

Clark, D. A., & Beck, A. T. (2012). *The anxiety and worry workbook: The cognitive behavioral solution*. New York: Guilford.

Corey, G. (2013). *Theory and practice of counseling and psychotherapy* (9th ed.). Belmont, CA: Brooks/Cole.

Cormier, W. H., & Cormier, L. S. (1998). *Interviewing strategies for helpers: A guide to assessment, treatment, and evaluation* (4th ed.). Pacific Grove, CA: Brooks/Cole.

Craighead, L. W., Craighead, W. E., Kazdin, A. E., & Mahoney, M. J. (1994). *Cognitive and behavioral interventions: An empirical approach to mental health problems*. Boston: Allyn & Bacon.

Creed, T. A., Reisweber, J., & Beck, A. T. (2011). *Cognitive therapy for adolescents in school settings*. New York: Guilford.

Dattilio, F. M., & Padesky, C. A. (1990). *Cognitive therapy with couples*. Sarasota, FL: Professional Resource Exchange.

DeRubeis, R. J., Webb, C. A., Tang, T. Z., & Beck, A. T. (2010). Cognitive therapy. In K. S. Dobson (Ed.), *Handbook of cognitive-behavioral therapies* (3rd ed., pp. 277–316). New York: Guilford.

Dobson, K. S. (Ed.). (2010). *Handbook of cognitive-behavioral therapies* (3rd ed.). New York: Guilford.

Dodson, K. S., Beck, J. S., & Beck, A. T. (2005). The Academy of Cognitive Therapy: Purpose, history, and future prospects. *Cognitive and Behavioral Practice, 12,* 263–266.

Ellis, A. (1962). *Reason and emotion in psychotherapy*. New York: Stuart.

Fursland, A., Byrne, S., Watson, H., La Puma, M., Allen, K., & Byrne, S. (2012). Enhanced cognitive behavior therapy: A single treatment for all eating disorders. *Journal of Counseling and Development, 90,* 319–329.

Holden, 1993a Holden, J. (1993a). *Behavioral consequences on behavior*. Unpublished manuscript, University of North Texas, Denton.

Holden, 1993a Holden, J. (1993a). Cognitive counseling [Videotape]. Greensboro, NC: ACES/Chi Sigma Iota.

Holden, 1993b Holden, J. A. (1993b). *Learning module: Cognitive counseling*. Denton, TX: Author.

Holden, J. (1993b). *Respondent learning*. Unpublished manuscript

James, R. K., & Gilliland, B. E. (2003). *Theories and strategies in counseling and psychotherapy* (5th ed.). Boston: Allyn & Bacon.

Kalodner, C. R. (1995). Cognitive-behavioral theories. In D. Capuzzi & D. R. Gross (Eds.), *Counseling & psychotherapy* (pp. 353–384). Upper Saddle River, NJ: Merrill/Prentice Hall.

Kendall, P. C. (2007). *Cognitive-behavioral therapy for impulsive children: Therapist manual* (3rd ed.). Ardmore, PA: Workbook Publishing.

Mahoney, M. J. (1995). *Cognitive and constructive psychotherapies: Theory, research, and practice.* New York: Springer.

Meichenbaum, D. (1977). *Cognitive-behavior modification: An integrated approach.* New York: Plenum.

Meichenbaum, D. (1985). *Stress inoculation training.* New York: Pergamon.

Meichenbaum, D. (1986). Cognitive behavior modification. In F. H. Kanfer & A. P. Goldstein (Eds.), *Helping people change: A textbook of methods* (pp. 346–380). New York: Pergamon.

Meichenbaum, D. (1995). Cognitive-behavioral therapy in historical perspective. In B. M. Bongar & L. E. Beutler (Eds.), *Comprehensive textbook of psychotherapy: Theory and practice* (Vol. 1, pp. 140–158). London: Oxford University Press.

Meichenbaum, D. (1997). The evolution of a cognitive-behavior therapist. In J. K. Zeig (Ed.), *The evolution of psychotherapy: The third conference* (pp. 95–104). Philadelphia: Brunner/Mazel.

Newman, C. F., & Beck, A. T. (2009). Cognitive therapy. In H. I. Kaplan & B. J. Sadock (Eds.), *Comprehensive textbook of psychiatry* (9th ed., Vol. II, pp. 2857–2872). Philadelphia: Lippincott Williams & Wilkins.

Pennebaker, J. W. (1990). *Opening up: The healing power of confiding in others.* New York: Avon.

Schuyler, D. (1991). *A practical guide to cognitive therapy.* New York: Norton.

Sharf, R. S. (2012). *Theories of psychotherapy and counseling* (5th ed.). Belmont, CA: Brooks/Cole.

Weinrach, S. G. (1988). Cognitive therapist: A dialogue with Aaron Beck. *Journal of Counseling and Development, 67,* 159–164

References for Chapter 10

Backx, W. (2011). Views on REBT, past, present, and future: Albert Ellis' contribution to the field. *Journal of Rational Emotive and Cognitive-Behavior Therapy, 29,* 263–271.

Banks, T. (2011). Helping students manage emotions. *Education Psychology in Practice, 27,* 383–394.

Cohen, E. D. (1987). The use of syllogism in rational-emotive therapy. *Journal of Counseling and Development, 66,* 37–39.

Dryden, W. (1989). Albert Ellis: An efficient and passionate life. *Journal of Counseling and Development, 67,* 539–546.

Dryden, W. (1994). Reason and emotion in psychotherapy: Thirty years on. *Journal of Rational Emotive and Cognitive Behavior Therapy, 12,* 83–89.

Dryden, W. (2010). Elegance in REBT: Reflections on Ellis' and Dryden's sessions with Jane. *Journal of Rational-Emotive & Cognitive Behavior Therapy, 28,* 157–163.

Ellis, A. (1962). *Reason and emotion in psychotherapy.* New York: Stuart.

Ellis, A. (1977). The basic clinical theory of rational-emotive therapy. In A. Ellis & R. Grieger (Eds.), *Handbook of rational-emotive therapy* (pp. 3–34). New York: Springer.

Ellis, A. (1980). Foreword. In S. R. Walen, R. DiGiuseppe, & R. L. Wessler (Eds.), *A practitioner's guide to rational-emotive therapy* (pp. vii–xii). New York: Oxford University Press.

Ellis, A. (1984). Rational-emotive therapy (RET) and pastoral counseling: A reply to Richard Wessler. *Personnel and Guidance Journal, 62,* 266–267.

Ellis, A. (1986). An emotional control card for inappropriate and appropriate emotions in using rational-emotive imagery. *Journal of Counseling and Development, 65,* 205–206.

Ellis, A. (1995). Changing rational-emotive therapy (RET) to Rational Emotive Behavioral Therapy (REBT). *Journal of Rational Emotive and Cognitive Behavioral Therapy, 13,* 85–89.

Ellis, A. (1996a). *Better, deeper, and more enduring brief therapy: The rational emotive behavior therapy approach.* New York: Brunner/Mazel.

Ellis, A. (1996b). The humanism of rational emotive behavior therapy and other cognitive behavior therapies.*Journal of Humanistic Education and Development, 35,* 69–88.

Ellis, A. (2002). *Overcoming resistance: A rational emotive behavior therapy integrated approach* (2nd ed.). New York: Springer.

Ellis, A. (2011). Rational-emotive behavior therapy. In R. Corsini & D. Wedding (Eds.), *Current psychotherapies* (9th ed., pp. 196–234). Belmont, CA: Brooks/Cole.

Ellis, A., & Ellis, D. J. (2011). *Rational emotive behavior therapy.* Washington, DC: American Psychological Association.

Ellis, A., & Harper, R. A. (1975). *A new guide to rational living.* North Hollywood, CA: Wilshire.

James, R. K., & Gilliland, B. E. (2003). *Theories and strategies in counseling and psychotherapy* (5th ed.). Boston: Allyn & Bacon.

Johnson, N. (1980). Must the RET therapist be like Albert Ellis? *Personnel and Guidance Journal, 59,* 49–51.

Krumboltz, J. D. (1992). Challenging troublesome career beliefs. *CAPS Digest,* EDO-CG-92-4.

Maultsby, M. C., Jr. (1984). *Rational behavior therapy.* Upper Saddle River, NJ: Prentice Hall.

Morris, K. T., & Kanitz, M. (1975). *Rational-emotive therapy.* Boston: Houghton Mifflin.

Newhorn, P. (1978). Albert Ellis. *Human Behavior, 7,* 30–35.

Powell, J. (1976). *Fully human, fully alive.* Niles, IL: Argos.

Roush, D. W. (1984). Rational-emotive therapy and youth: Some new techniques for counselors. *Personnel and Guidance Journal, 62,* 414–417.

Seligman, L. (2001). *Systems, strategies, and skills of counseling and psychotherapy.* Upper Saddle River, NJ: Prentice Hall.

Sharf, R. S. (2012). *Theories of psychotherapy and counseling* (5th ed.). Belmont, CA: Brooks/Cole.

Sklare, G., Taylor, J., & Hyland, S. (1985). An emotional control card for rational-emotive imagery. *Journal of Counseling and Development, 64,* 145–146.

Vernon, A. (1996). Counseling children and adolescents: Rational emotive behavior therapy and humanism. *Journal of Humanistic Education and Development, 35,* 120–127.

Walen, S. R., DiGiuseppe, R., & Dryden, W. (1992). *A practitioner's guide to Rational-emotive therapy.* New York: Oxford University Press.

Watts, R. E. (1996). Social interest and the core conditions: Could it be that Adler influenced Rogers? *Journal of Humanistic Education and Development, 34,* 165–170.

Weinrach, S. G. (1980). Unconventional therapist: Albert Ellis. *Personnel and Guidance Journal, 59,* 152–160.

Wilde, J. (1996). The efficacy of short-term rational-emotive education with fourth-grade students. *Elementary School Guidance & Counseling, 31,* 131–138.

References for Chapter 11

Barnes, G. (1977). Introduction. In G. Barnes (Ed.), *Transactional analysis after Eric Berne: Teachings and practices of three TA schools* (pp. 3–31). New York: Harper & Row.

Barrow, G. (2007). Wonderful world, beautiful people: Reframing transactional analysis as positive psychology. *Transactional Analysis Journal, 37,* 206–209.

Berne, E. (1964). *Games people play.* New York: Grove.

Berne, E. (1966). *Principles of group treatment.* New York: Oxford University Press.

Dusay, J. M. (1977). The evolution of transactional analysis. In G. Barnes (Ed.), *Transactional analysis after Eric Berne: Teachings and practices of three TA schools* (pp. 32–52). New York: Harper & Row.

Dusay, J. M., & Dusay, K. M. (1989). Transactional analysis. In R. J. Corsini & D. Wedding (Eds.), *Current psychotherapies* (4th ed., pp. 405–453). Itasca, IL: Peacock.

Eisenberg, M. (1992). Compassionate math. *Journal of Humanistic Education and Development, 30,* 157–166.

Erskine, R. G. (2009). The culture of transactional analysis: Theory, methods, and evolving patterns. *Transactional Analysis Journal, 39,* 14–21.

Goulding, M., & Goulding, R. (1997). *Changing lives through redecision therapy* (Rev ed.). New York: Grove/Atlantic.

Harris, T. (1967). *I'm ok; You're ok.* New York: Harper & Row.

Henderson, D. A., & Thompson, C. (2011). *Counseling children* (8th ed.). Pacific Grove, CA: Brooks/Cole.

James, M., & Jongeward, D. (1971). *Born to win: Transactional analysis with Gestalt experiments.* Reading, MA: Addison-Wesley.

James, R. K., & Gilliland, B. E. (2003). *Theories and strategies in counseling and psychotherapy* (5th ed.). Boston: Allyn & Bacon.

Karpman, S. (1968). Script drama analysis. *Transactional Analysis Bulletin, 26,* 16–22.

Miller, C., & Capuzzi, D. (1984). A review of transactional analysis outcome studies. *AMHCA Journal, 6,* 30–41. Penfield, W. (1952).

Penfield, W. (1952). Memory mechanisms. *Archives of Neurology and Psychiatry, 67,* 178–198. Penfield, W., & Jasper, H. (1954).

Penfield, W., & Jasper, H. (1954). *Epilepsy and the functional anatomy of the human brain.* Boston: Little, Brown.

Steward, I., & Joines, V. S. (2011). TA tomorrow. *Transactional Analysis Journal, 41,* 221–229.

Tyrangiel, H. (2011). On Skype with Eric Berne: What did he say after he said hello? *Transactional Analysis Journal, 41,* 16–22.

Widdowson, M. (2010). *Transactional analysis: 100 key points and techniques.* New York: Routledge.

References for Chapter 12

Austin, L. (1999). *The counseling primer*. Philadelphia: Accelerated Development.

Ballou, M., Hill, M., & West, C. (2008). *Feminist theory therapy and practice: A contemporary perspective*. New York: Springer.

Brown, L. S. (2008). Feminist therapy. In J. S. Lebow (Ed.), *Twenty-first century psychotherapies: Contemporary approaches to theory and practice* (pp. 277–306). Hoboken, NJ: John Wiley and Sons.

Brown, L. S. (2010). *Feminist therapy—Not for women only*. Washington, DC: American Psychological Association.

Corey, G. (2013). *Theory and practice of counseling and psychotherapy* (9th ed.). Belmont, CA: Brooks/Cole.

Crawford, M. (2012). *Transformations: Women, gender, and psychology* (2nd ed.). New York: McGraw-Hill.

Enns, C. Z. (1997). *Feminist theories and feminist psychotherapies: Origins, themes, and variations*. New York: Haworth.

Enns, C. Z., & Hackett, G. (1993). A comparison of feminist and nonfeminist women's and men's reactions to nonsexist and feminist counseling: A replication and extension. *Journal of Counseling and Development, 71*, 499–509.

Gilligan, C. (1982). *In a different voice: Psychological theory and women's development*. Cambridge, MA: Harvard University Press.

Herlihy, B., & McCollum, V. J. C. (2011). Feminist theory. In D. Capuzzi & D. Gross (Eds.), *Counseling and psychotherapy* (5th ed., pp. 313–333). Alexandria, VA: American Counseling Association.

Jordan, J. V. (2000). A relational-cultural model: Healing through mutual empathy. *Bulletin of the Menninger Clinic, 65,* 92–103.

Levant, R. E. (2001). Men and masculinity. In J. Worrell (Ed.), *Encyclopedia of women and gender* (Vol. 2, pp. 717–728). San Diego: Academic Press.

Miller, J. B. (1986). *Toward a new psychology of women*. Boston: Beacon.

Miller, J. B. (1991). The development of women's sense of self. In J. V. Jordan, A. G. Kaplan, J. B. Miller, I. P. Stiver, & J. L. Surrey (Eds.), *Women's growth in connection* (pp. 11–26). New York: Guilford.

Nwachuka, U., & Ivey, A. (1991). Culture-specific counseling: An alternative model. *Journal of Counseling & Development, 70,* 106–111.

Okun, B. F. (1990). *Seeking connections in psychotherapy*. San Francisco: Jossey-Bass.

Okun, B. F., & Kantrowitz, R. E. (2008). *Effective helping* (7th ed.). Belmont, CA: Brooks/Cole.

Prochaska, J. O., & Norcross, J. C. (2010). *Systems of psychotherapy: A transtheoretical analysis* (7th ed.). Belmont, CA: Brooks/Cole.

Remer, P. (2008). Empowerment feminist therapy. In K. Jordan (Ed.), *The quick theory reference guide: A resource for expert and novice mental health professionals* (pp. 167–181). Hauppauge, NY: Nova Science Publishers.

Sharf, R. S. (2012). *Theories of psychotherapy and counseling* (5th ed.). Belmont, CA: Brooks/Cole.

Worrell, J., & Remer, P. (2003). *Feminist perspectives in therapy* (2nd ed.). New York: Wiley.

References for Chapter 13

Anonymous. (1972). Differentiation of self in one's family. In J. L. Framo (Ed.), *Family interaction*. New York: Springer.

Bowen, M. (1960). A family concept of schizophrenia. In D. Jackson (Ed.), *The etiology of schizophrenia*. New York: Basic Books.

Bowen, M. (1961). Family psychotherapy. *American Journal of Orthopsychiatry, 31*, 40–60.

Bowen, M. (1965). Family psychotherapy with schizophrenia in the hospital and in private practice. In I. Boszormenyi-Nagy & J. T. Framo (Eds.), *Intensive family therapy* (pp. 213–243). Hagerstown, MD: Harper & Row.

Bowen, M. (1972). Toward the differentiation of self in one's family of origin. In F. D. Andres & J. P. Lorio (Eds.), *Georgetown Family Symposia* (pp. 70–86). Washington, DC: Georgetown University.

Bowen, M. (1975). Family therapy after twenty years. In S. Arieti, D. X. Freedman, & J. E. Dyrud (Eds.), *American handbook of psychiatry, V. Treatment* (2nd ed.). New York: Basic Books.

Bowen, M. (1976). Theory in the practice of psychotherapy. In P. J. Guerin (Ed.), *Family therapy: Theory and practice* (pp. 42–90). New York: Gardner Press.

Bowen, M. (1978). *Family therapy in clinical practice*. New York: Jason Aronson.

David, J. R. (1979). The theology of Murray Bowen or the marital triangle. *Journal of Psychology and Theology, 7*, 259–262.

Dunn, A. B., & Levitt, M. M. (2000). The genogram: From diagnostics to mutual collaboration. *The Family Journal: Counseling and Therapy for Couples and Families, 8*, 236–244.

Frame, M. W. (2000). Constructing religious/spiritual genograms. In R. E. Watts (Ed.), *Techniques in marriage and family counseling* (pp. 69–74). Alexandria, VA: American Counseling Association.

Friedman, E. H. (1985). *Generation to generation: Family process in church and synagogue*. New York: Guilford.

Friedman, E. H. (1991). Bowen theory and therapy. In A. S. Gurman & D. P. Kniskern (Eds.), *Handbook of family therapy* (Vol. II, pp. 134–170). New York: Brunner/Mazel.

Gibson, J. M., & Donigian, J. (1993). Use of Bowen theory. *Journal of Addictions and Offender Counseling, 14*, 25–35.

Gilbert, R. M. (2006). *The eight concepts of Bowen theory*. Falls Church, VA: Leading Systems Press.

Greene, G. J., Hamilton, N., & Rolling, M. (1986). Differentiation of self and psychiatric diagnosis: An empirical study. *Family Therapy, 8*, 187–194.

Guerin, P. J. (1976). Family therapy: The first twenty-five years. In P. J. Guerin (Ed.), *Family therapy: Theory and practice* (pp. 2–22). New York: Gardner.

Hertlein, K. M., & Killmer, J. M. (2004). Toward differentiated decision-making: Family systems theory with the homeless clinical population. *American Journal of Family Therapy, 32*, 255–270.

Hooper, L. M., & Doehler, K. (2011). The mediating and moderating effects of differentiation of self on body mass index and depressive symptomatology among an American college sample. *Counselling Psychology Quarterly, 24*, 71–82.

Kaplan, D. M. (2000). Who are our giants? *The Family Digest, 12*(4), 1, 6.

Kerr, M. (1981). Family systems theory and therapy. In A. S. Gurman & D. P. Kniskern (Eds.), *Handbook of family therapy*. New York: Brunner/Mazel.

Kerr, M. E. (1988). Chronic anxiety and defining a self. *The Atlantic Monthly, 262*, 35–37, 40–44, 46–58.

Kerr, M. E. (2003, August 9). *Process of differentiation*. Paper presented at the 111th Annual Convention of the American Psychological Association, Toronto, Canada.

Kerr, M. E., & Bowen, M. (1988). *Family evaluation: An approach based on Bowen theory*. New York: Norton.

Kilpatrick, A. C. (1980). The Bowen family intervention theory: An analysis for social workers. *Family Therapy, 7*, 167–178.

Knudson-Martin, C. (2002). Expanding Bowen's legacy to family therapy: A response to Horne and Hicks. *Journal of Marital and Family Therapy, 28*, 115–118.

Learner, S. (1983). *Constructing the multigenerational family genogram: Exploring a problem in context* [Videotape]. Topeka, KS: Menninger Video Productions.

Levy, P. A., & Hadley, B. J. (1998). Family-of-origin relationships and self-differentiation among university students with bulimic-type behavior. *The Family Journal: Counseling and Therapy for Couples and Families, 6,* 19–23.

McGoldrick, M. (2011). *The genogram journey: Reconnecting with your family.* New York: Norton.

Papero, D. V. (1991). The Bowen theory. In A. M. Horne & J. L. Passmore (Eds.), *Family counseling and theory* (2nd ed., pp. 47–76). Itasca, IL: Peacock.

Peleg-Popko, O. (2004). Differentiation and test anxiety in adolescents. *Journal of Adolescence, 27,* 645–662.

Piercy, F. P., & Sprenkle, D. H. (1986). *Family therapy source-book.* New York: Guilford.

Sauber, S. R., L'Abate, L., & Weeks, G. R. (1985). *Family therapy: Basic concepts and terms.* Rockville, MD: Aspen.

Sherman, R. (1993). The intimacy genogram. *The Family Journal: Counseling and Therapy for Couples and Families, 1,* 91–93.

Skowron, E. A. (2000). The role of differentiation of self in marital adjustment. *Journal of Counseling Psychology, 47,* 229–237.

Skowron, E. A., & Platt, L. F. (2005). Differentiation of self and child abuse potential in young adulthood. *The Family Journal: Counseling and Therapy for Couples and Families, 13,* 281–290.

Smith, R. L. (1991). Marriage and family therapy: Direction, theory, and practice. In J. Carlson & J. Lewis (Eds.), *Family counseling* (pp. 13–34). Denver, CO: Love.

Thomas, A. J. (1998). Understanding culture and worldview in family systems: Use of the multicultural genogram. *The Family Journal: Counseling and Therapy for Couples and Families, 6,* 24–32.

Toman, W. (1961). *Family constellation: Its effects on personality and social behavior.* New York: Springer.

Tuason, M. T., & Friedlander, M. L. (2000). Do parents' differentiation levels predict those of their adult children? And other tests of Bowen theory in a Philippine sample. *Journal of Counseling Psychology, 47,* 27–35.

White, H. (1978). Exercises in understanding your family. In *Your family is good for you.* New York: Random House.

Wylie, M. S. (1991, March/April). Family therapy's neglected prophet. *Family Therapy Networker, 15,* 24–37, 77.

References for Chapter 14

Alexander, J., & Parsons, B. (1982). *Functional family therapy*. Pacific Grove, CA: Brooks/Cole.

Fish, J. M. (1988, July/August). Reconciling the irreconcilable. *Family Therapy Networker, 12,* 15.

Friesen, J. D. (1985). *Structural-strategic marriage and family therapy*. New York: Gardner.

Gardner, B. C., Burr, B. K., & Wiedower, S. E. (2006). Reconceptualizing strategic family therapy: Insights from a dynamic systems perspective. *Contemporary Family Therapy: An International Journal, 28,* 339–352.

Haley, J. (1963). *Strategies of psychotherapy*. New York: Grune & Stratton.

Haley, J. (1973). *Uncommon therapy*. New York: Norton.

Haley, J. (1976). *Problem-solving therapy*. San Francisco: Jossey-Bass.

Haley, J. (1980). *Leaving home: The therapy of disturbed young people*. New York: McGraw-Hill.

Haley, J. (1984). *Ordeal therapy*. San Francisco: Jossey-Bass.

Haley, J. (1990). Interminable therapy. In J. Zeig & S. Gilligan (Eds.), *Brief therapy: Myths, methods, and metaphors*. New York: Brunner/Mazel.

Keim, J. (2000). Strategic family therapy. In A. Horne (Ed.), *Family counseling and therapy* (3rd ed., pp. 170–207). Itasca, IL: Peacock.

Madanes, C. (1981). *Strategic family therapy*. San Francisco: Jossey-Bass.

Madanes, C. (1984). *Behind the one-way mirror: Advances in the practice of strategic therapy*. San Francisco: Jossey-Bass.

Madanes, C. (1990). *Sex, love, and violence*. New York: Norton.

Madanes, C. (1991). Strategic family therapy. In A. S. Gurman & D. P. Kniskern (Eds.), *Handbook of family therapy* (Vol. 2, pp. 396–416). New York: Brunner/Mazel.

Papp, P. (1984, September/October). The creative leap. *Family Therapy Networker, 8,* 20–29.

Piercy, F. P., & Sprenkle, D. H. (1986). *Family therapy source-book*. New York: Guilford.

Priebe, S., & Pommerien, W. (1992). The therapeutic system as viewed by depressive inpatients and outcome: An expanded study. *Family Process, 31,* 433–439.

Ray, W. A. (2007). Jay Haley—A memorial. *Journal of Marital and Family Therapy, 33,* 291–292.

Richeport-Haley, M. (1998). Ethnicity in family therapy: A comparison of brief strategic therapy and culture-focused therapy. *American Journal of Family Therapy, 26,* 77–90.

Santisteban, D. A., Coatsworth, J. D., Perez-Vidal, A., Kurtines, W. M., Schwartz, S. J., LaPerriere, A., & Szapocznik, J. (2003). Efficacy of brief strategic family therapy in modifying Hispanic adolescent behavior problems and substance use. *Journal of Family Psychology, 17,* 121–133.

Sexton, T. L., & Montgomery, D. (1994). Ethical and therapeutic acceptability: A study of paradoxical techniques. *The Family Journal: Counseling and Therapy for Couples and Families, 2,* 215–228.

Simon, R. (1982, September/October). Behind the one-way mirror: An interview with Jay Haley. *Family Therapy Networker, 6,* 18–25, 28–29, 58–59.

Simon, R. (1984, November/December). Stranger in a strange land: An interview with Salvador Minuchin. *Family Therapy Networker, 8,* 20–31.

Snider, M. (1992). *Process family therapy*. Boston: Allyn & Bacon.

Soo-Hoo, T. (1999). Brief strategic family therapy with Chinese Americans. *American Journal of Family Therapy, 27,* 163–179.

Stanton, D., Todd, T., & Associates. (1982). *The family therapy of drug abuse and addiction*. New York: Guilford.

Steinberg, E. B., Sayger, T. V., & Szykula, S. A. (1997). The effects of strategic and behavioral family therapies on child behavior and depression. *Contemporary Family Therapy, 19,* 537–551.

Watzlawick, P. (1978). *The language of change*. New York: Basic Books.

Watzlawick, P. (1983). *The situation is hopeless but not serious*. New York: Norton.

Wylie, M. S. (1990, March/April). Brief therapy on the couch. *Family Therapy Networker, 14,* 26–35, 66.

Wylie, M. S. (1992, January/February). The evolution of a revolution. *Family Therapy Networker, 16,* 17–29, 98–99.

References for Chapter 15

Berg, I. K., & Miller, S. (1992). *Working with the problem drinker: A solution-focused approach*. New York: Norton.

Berg, I. K., & Steiner, T. (2003). *Children's solution work*. New York: Norton.

Bubenzer, D. L., & West, J. D. (1993). William Hudson O'Hanlon: On seeking possibilities and solutions in therapy. *The Family Journal, 1,* 365–379.

Chaudhry, S., & Li, C. (2011). Is solution-focused brief therapy culturally appropriate for Muslim American counselees? *Journal of Contemporary Psychotherapy, 41,* 109–113.

Cheung, S. (2001). Problem-solving and solution-focused therapy for Chinese: Recent developments. *Asian Journal of Counselling, 8,* 111–128.

Cleveland, P. H., & Lindsey, E. W. (1995). Solution-focused family interventions. In A. C. Kilpatrick & T. P. Holland (Eds.), *Working with families* (pp. 145–160). Boston: Allyn & Bacon.

Corcoran, J. (2000). Solution-focused family therapy with ethnic minority clients. *Crisis Intervention and Time Limited Treatment, 6,* 5–12.

deShazer, S. (1982). *Patterns of brief family therapy*. New York: Guilford.

deShazer, S. (1984). The death of resistance. *Family Process, 23,* 11–21.

deShazer, S. (1985). *Keys to solution in brief therapy*. New York: Norton.

deShazer, S. (1988). *Clues: Investigating solutions in brief therapy*. New York: Norton.

deShazer, S. (1989). Resistance revisited. *Contemporary Family Therapy, 11,* 227–233.

deShazer, S. (1991). *Putting differences to work*. New York: Norton.

deShazer, S., & Molnar, A. (1984). Four useful interventions in brief family therapy. *Journal of Marital and Family Therapy, 10,* 297–304.

Erdman, P. (2000). Bringing a symbol: An experiential exercise for systematic change. In R. E. Watts (Ed.), *Techniques in marriage and family counseling* (pp. 99–102). Alexandria, VA: American Counseling Association.

Fleming, J. S., & Rickord, B. (1997). Solution-focused brief therapy: One answer to managed mental health care. *The Family Journal, 5,* 286–294.

Gale, J. E. (1991). *Conversion analysis of therapeutic discourse: The pursuit of a therapeutic agenda*. Norwood, NJ: Ablex.

Hudson, P. O., & O'Hanlon, W. H. (1991). *Rewriting love stories: Brief marital therapy*. New York: Norton.

Hung-Hsiu-Chang, T., & Ng, K. S. (2000). I Ching, solution-focused therapy and change: A clinical integrative framework. *Family Therapy, 27,* 47–57.

Kaplan, D. M. (2000). Who are our giants? *The Family Digest, 12*(4), 1, 6.

Kiser, D. J., Piercy, F. P., & Lipchik, E. (1993). The integration of emotion in solution-focused therapy. *Journal of Marital and Family Therapy, 19,* 233–242.

Kok, C. J., & Leskela, J. (1996). Solution-focused therapy in a psychiatric hospital. *Journal of Marital and Family Therapy, 22,* 397–406.

Krauth, L. D. (1995, December). Strength-based therapies. *Family Therapy News, 26,* 24.

Maturana, H., & Varela, F. (1987). *The tree of knowledge*. Boston: New Science Library.

McFarland, B. (1995). *Brief therapy and eating disorders: A practical guide to solution-focused work with clients*. San Francisco: Jossey-Bass.

O'Hanlon, B., & Bertolino, B. (2002). *Even from a broken web: Brief, respectful solution-oriented therapy for sexual abuse and trauma*. New York: Norton.

O'Hanlon, W. H. (1987). *Taproots: Underlying principles of Milton Erickson's therapy and hypnosis*. New York: Norton.

O'Hanlon, W. H., & Weiner-Davis, M. (1989). *In search of solutions: A new direction in psychotherapy*. New York: Norton.

O'Hanlon, W. H., & Wilk, J. (1987). *Shifting contexts: The generation of effective psychotherapy*. New York: Guilford Press.

Sauber, S. R., L'Abate, L., & Weeks, G. R. (1985). *Family therapy: Basic concepts and terms*. Rockville, MD: Aspen.

Sharry, J., Madden, B., & Darmody, M. (2012). *Becoming a solution detective: A strengths-based guide to brief therapy* (2nd ed.). New York: Routledge.

Simon, F., Stierlin, H., & Wynne, L. (1985). *The language of family therapy*. New York: Family Process Press.

Simon, J. K. (2010). *Solution focused practice in end-of-life and grief counseling*. New York: Springer.

Softas-Nall, B. C., Baldo, T. D., & Tiedemann, T. R. (1999). A gender-based, solution-focused genogram case: He and she across the generations. *The Family Journal, 7,* 177–180.

Spiegel, H., & Linn, L. (1969). The "ripple effect" following adjunct hypnosis in analytic psychotherapy. *American Journal of Psychiatry, 126,* 53–58.

Todd, T. (1992). Brief family therapy. In R. L. Smith & P. Stevens-Smith (Eds.), *Family counseling and therapy* (pp. 162–175). Ann Arbor, MI: ERIC/CAPS.

Walter, J., & Peller, J. (1993). Solution-focused brief therapy. *The Family Journal, 1,* 80–81.

West, J. D., Bubenzer, D. L., Smith, J. M., & Hamm, T. L. (1997). Insoo Kim Berg and solution-focused therapy. *The Family Journal, 5,* 346–354.

Yeung, F. K. C. (1999). The adaptation of solution-focused therapy in Chinese culture: A linguistic perspective. *Transcultural-Psychiatry, 36,* 477–489.

References for Chapter 16

Belkin, G. S. (1984). *Introduction to counseling* (2nd ed.). Dubuque, IA: William C. Brown.

Brammer, L. M. (1985). *The helping relationship: Process and skills* (3rd ed.). Upper Saddle River, NJ: Prentice Hall

Caplan, G. (1964). *Principles of preventive psychiatry*. New York: Basic Books.

Everly, G. S., Lating, J. M., & Mitchell, J. T. (2000). Innovations in group interventions: Critical Incident Stress Debriefing (CISD) and Critical Incident Stress Management (CISM). In R. Roberts (Eds.), *Crisis intervention handbook: Assessment, treatment, and research*. New York: Oxford Press.

James, R. K. (2008). *Crisis Intervention Strategies* (6th ed.). Belmont, CA: Brooks Cole.

Jordan, K. (2002). Providing crisis counselling to New Yorkers after the terrorist attack on the World Trade Center. *The Family Journal: Counseling and Therapy for Couples and Families, 10*, 139–144.

Lewis, M. D., Daniels, J. A., & D'Andrea, M. J. (2003). *Community counselling: Empowering strategies for a diverse society* (3rd ed.). Pacific Grove, CA: Brooks/Cole.

Lindemann, E. (1944). Symptomatology and management of acute grief. *American Journal of Psychiatry, 101*, 141–148.

Lindemann, E. (1956). The meaning of crisis in individual and family. *Teachers College Record, 57*, 310.

Meier, S. T., & Davis, S. R. (2011). *The elements of counseling* (7th ed.). Belmont, CA: Brooks/Cole.

Miller, G. (2012). *Fundamentals of crisis counseling*. Hoboken, NJ: John Wiley & Sons.

Myer, R. (2001). *Assessment for crisis intervention: A triage assessment model*. Belmont, CA: Brooks/Cole.

Parikh, S. J. T., & Morris, C. A. W. (2011). Integrating crisis theory and individual psychology: An application and case study. *Journal of Individual Psychology, 67*, 364–379.

Roberts, A. R. (2005). *Crisis intervention handbook: Assessment, treatment, and research* (3rd ed.). New York: Oxford Press.

Sandoval, J., Scott, A. N., & Padilla, I. (2009). Crisis counseling: An overview. *Psychology in the Schools, 46*, 246–256.

Satin, D. G. (1984). Erich Lindemann as humanist, scientist, and change agent. *American Journal of Community Psychology, 12*(5), 519–527.

Sue, D. W., & Sue, D. (2008). *Counseling the culturally diverse: Theory and practice* (5th ed.). Hoboken, NJ: John Wiley and Sons.

References for Chapter 17

Bergin, A. E. (1985). Proposed values for guiding and evaluating counseling and psychotherapy. *Counseling and Values, 29,* 99–115.

Bergin, A. E. (1992). Three contributions of a spiritual perspective to counseling, psychotherapy, and behavior change. In M. T. Burke & J. G. Miranti (Eds.), *Ethical and spiritual values incounseling* (pp. 5–15). Alexandria, VA: American Counseling Association.

Brandt, R. (1959). *Ethical theory.* Upper Saddle River, NJ: Prentice Hall.

Calley, N. G. (2009). Promoting a contextual perspective in the application of the ACA Code of Ethics: The ethics into action map. *Journal of Counseling & Development, 87,* 476–482.

Christopher, J. C. (1996). Counseling's inescapable moral vision. *Journal of Counseling & Development, 75,* 17–25.

Coll, K. (1993). Student attitudinal changes in a counseling ethics course. *Counseling and Values, 27,* 165–170.

Corey, G., Corey, M. S., & Callanan, P. (2011). *Issues in ethics in the helping profession* (8th ed.). Belmont, CA: Brooks/Cole.

Cottone, R. R., & Tarvydas, V. M. (2007). *Ethical and professional issues in counseling* (3rd ed.). Upper Saddle River, NJ: Merrill/Prentice Hall.

Daniluk, J. C., & Haverkamp, B. E. (1993). Ethical issues in counseling adult survivors of incest. *Journal of Counseling & Development, 72,* 16–22.

Gladding, S. T., & Hood, W. D. (1974). Five cents, please. *School Counselor, 21,* 40–43.

Grant, B. (1992). The moral nature of psychotherapy. In M. T. Burke & J. G. Miranti (Eds.), *Ethical and spiritual values in counseling* (pp. 27–35). Alexandria, VA: American Counseling Association.

Harding, A. K., Gray, L. A., & Neal, M. (1993). Confidentiality limits with clients who have HIV: A review of ethical and legal guidelines and professional policies. *Journal of Counseling & Development, 71,* 297–304.

Herlihy, B., & Corey, G. (2006). *ACA Ethical Standards Casebook* (6th ed.). Washington, DC: American Counseling Association.

Kitchener, K. S. (1986). Teaching applied ethics in counselor education: An integration of psychological processes and philosophical analysis. *Journal of Counseling & Development, 64,* 306–310.

Kitchener, K. S. (1994). Doing good well: The wisdom behind ethical supervision. *Counseling and Human Development,* 1–8.

Kocet, M. M. (2006). Ethical challenges in a complex world: Highlights of the 2005 ACA Code of Ethics. *Journal of Counseling & Development, 84,* 228–234.

Lanning, W. (1992, December). Ethical codes and responsible decision-making. *ACA Guidepost, 35,* 21.

Moleski, S. M., & Kiselica, M. S. (2005). Dual relationships: A continuum ranging from the destructive to the therapeutic. *Journal of Counseling & Development, 83,* 3–11.

Patterson, C. H. (1971). Are ethics different in different settings? *Personnel and Guidance Journal, 50,* 254–259.

Ponton, R. F., & Duba, J. D. (2009). The ACA Code of Ethics: Articulating counseling's professional covenant. *Journal of Counseling & Development, 87,* 117–121.

Remley, T. P., Jr., & Herlihy, B. (2010). *Ethical, legal, and professional issues in counseling* (3rd ed.). Upper Saddle River, NJ: Prentice Hall.

St. Germaine, J. (1993). Dual relationships: What's wrong with them? *American Counselor, 2,* 25–30.

Swanson, C. D. (1983). Ethics and the counselor. In J. A. Brown & R. H. Pate, Jr. (Eds.), *Being a counselor* (pp. 47–65). Pacific Grove, CA: Brooks/Cole.

Talbutt, L. C. (1981). Ethical standards: Assets and limitations. *Personnel and Guidance Journal, 60,* 110–112.

Tennyson, W. W., & Strom, S. M. (1986). Beyond professional standards: Developing responsibleness. *Journal of Counseling and Development, 64,* 298–302.

Thompson, A. (1990). *Guide to ethical practice in psychotherapy.* New York: Wiley.

Vacc, N. A., Juhnke, G. A., & Nilsen, K. A. (2001). Community mental health service providers' code of ethics and the Standards for Educational and Psychological Testing. *Journal of Counseling and Development, 79,* 217–224.

Van Hoose, W. H., & Kottler, J. (1985). *Ethical and legal issues in counseling and psychotherapy* (2nd ed.). San Francisco: Jossey-Bass.

Welfel, E. R. (2013). *Ethics in counseling and psychotherapy* (5th ed.). Belmont, CA: Brooks/Cole.

Wilcoxon, S. A. (1987). Ethical standards: A study of application and utility. *Journal of Counseling and Development, 65,* 510–511.

Wilcoxon, S. A., Remley, T. P., Jr., & Gladding, S. T. (2012). *Ethical, legal and professional issues in the practice of marriage and family therapy* (5th ed.). Upper Saddle River, NJ: Merrill/Prentice Hall.

Woodside, M. R., & McClam, T. (2009). *An introduction to human services* (6th ed.). Belmont, CA: Brooks/Cole.

Index